MW01029393

Philosophy, Ideology and Social Science

Philosophy, Ideology and Social Science

Essays in Negation and Affirmation

István Mészáros

Professor of Philosophy
University of Sussex

St. Martin's Press New York

First published in the United States of America in 1986

Printed in Great Britain

ISBN 0-312-00230-0
ISBN 0-312-00231-9 (pbk.)

Library of Congress Cataloging-in-Publication Data

Mészáros, István, 1930-
Philosophy, ideology, and social science.

Bibliography: p.
Includes index.
1. Political sociology. 2. Marxian school of Sociology. 3. Marx, Karl, 1818-1883. I. Title.
JA76.M485 1986 306'.2 86-21996
ISBN 0-312-00230-0
ISBN 0-312-00231-9 (pbk.)

Contents

Introduction

Ever since Menenius Agrippa addressed the people of Rome who went on strike and occupied the Sacred Mount in sixth Century B.C., the 'organic' conception of the social order has been advocated on numerous occasions. According to this much revered Roman Consul—who, in the characteristic words of *The Encyclopaedia Britannica,* 'was known to be *a man of moderate views'*—every social rank has its 'proper place' in the great organism. The lower ranks should derive their satisfaction from the 'reflected glory' that, no matter how lowly, they are 'equally important' for the functioning of the body to which they belong.

This was, of course, a most powerful exercise in ideology. Legend has it that the protesting people were so moved by the Consul's 'moderate views' that they immediately abandoned their stand of collective defiance and returned to the place assigned to them.

Be that as it may, at least one historical fact is beyond dispute. Namely, that they remained tied to their 'proper place' in society in all those two-and-a-half-thousand years that elapsed since the delivery of Agrippa's paradigmatic State Sermon on the Sacred Mount, 'participating' in the reproduction of the established order through all its necessary adjustments to the changing conditions of domination.

What directly concerns us here is the specific role which ideology plays in this process of structural adjustments. For the successful reproduction of the conditions of domination could not take place without the most active intervention of powerful ideological factors on the side of maintaining the order in existence.

Naturally, the ruling ideology has a vested interest in the preservation of the *status quo* in which even the most glaring inequalities are already *structurally* entrenched and safeguarded. Hence it can afford to be 'consensual', 'organic', 'participatory', and the like, claiming thereby also the self-evident reasonableness of (ruling) 'moderation', 'objectivity' and 'ideological neutrality'.

Yet, the fact of the matter is that we are talking about *class societies* which are, of necessity, torn by internal contradictions and antagonisms, no matter how successful the reproduction of the hierarchical structural framework of super- and sub-ordination and the *semblance* of 'communality' across the ages. And since the exploitative class parameters of society remain *untouchable,* the various theories of 'organic social life', 'consensus', 'participation', etc., are either impotent *moral postulates* (even with great radical thinkers like Rousseau), or apologetic rationalizations and legitimations of the unjustifiable, from Menenius Agrippa to his distant cousins in our own days.

It must be stressed, the power of the dominant ideology is as great as undoubtedly it is, not simply because of the overwhelming material might and commensurate political/cultural arsenal at the diposal of the ruling classes. For such ideological power itself can only prevail thanks to the positional advantage of *mystification* through which the people at the receiving end can be induced to endorse, 'consensually', the values and practical policies which are in fact quite inimical to their vital interests.

In this respect the situation of the contending ideologies is decidedly *non-symmetrical.* The critical ideologies which attempt to negate the established order cannot possibly mystify their adversaries for the simple reason that they have nothing to offer—not even bribes and rewards for accommodation—to those who are already well established in their positions of command, conscious of their tangible immediate interests. Accordingly, the power of mystification over the adversary is a privilege of the ruling ideology only.

This circumstance, already on its own, shows how self-defeating it would be to try to explain ideology simply under the heading of 'false consciousness'. For what defines ideology as ideology is not its alleged defiance of 'reason', nor its departure from the preconceived rules of an imaginary 'scientific discourse', but its very real situation in a determinate type of society. The complex functions of ideology arise precisely from such a situation, and they are not in the least intelligible in terms of abstract rationalistic and scientistic criteria counterposed to them, which merely beg the question.

What calls for an explanation is the ubiquitous presence and immense practical impact of ideology in a multiplicity of very different societies, from Ancient times (as we have seen with reference to Agrippa's discourse) to the present. At the same time, it is equally necessary to focus attention on the historical dimension of ideology. For failure to do so would make it impossible to avoid the (no matter how positivistically updated) circularity of the 'Enlightenment illusion' which castigates non-conformity to its proclaimed rules as some kind of 'aberration of the mind', to be overcome by the prescribed 'theoretical insight'.

It is a necessary precondition to understanding the nature of ideology that we:

(1) acknowledge its persistence in diverse social formations that succeed one another and demonstrate the paradoxical continuity of ideological reproduction over thousands of years, with no end in sight as yet;

(2) put into relief the concrete socioeconomic parameters in terms of which one can conceptualize the historical emergence and continued functioning—as well as the potential supersession—of ideology;

(3) bear constantly in mind the practical mode of operation of ideological discourse and the institutional/instrumental forms required to make its impact feasible; and

(4) identify the type of rationality at work in ideology, so as to be able, on the one hand, to dispose of the question-begging 'rationality versus irrationality' and 'science versus ideology' dichotomies and, on the other, to explain both the potentialities and the limitations of the ideological forms of social consciousness.

The *trans*-historical—but in no way *supra*- historical—characteristics of ideology, as a form of consciousness *sui generis,* can only be understood in the context of the *continued reproduction* of some vital structural determinations of the *type* of society from whose soil they arise. In other words, the *socioeconomically* embedded and inherently *historical/transhistorical* character of ideology as a distinctive type of consciousness must be in the forefront of our attention when we try to explain—through the dialectic of continuity in change, and *vice versa*—the stubborn recurrence of its salient features across the long trajectory of historical transformations known to us.

Ideology, as a specific form of social consciousness, is inseparable from *class societies.* It is constituted as the *inescapable practical consciousness* of such societies, concerned with the articulation of rival sets of values and strategies aimed at controlling the social metabolism under all its major aspects. The historically unfolding and *conflictually intertwined* social interests find their manifestations at the plane of social consciousness in the great diversity of relatively *autonomous* (but, of course, by no means *independent*) ideological discourse, with its powerful impact even on the most tangible material processes of the social metabolism.

Since the societies in question are themselves internally divided, the principal ideologies—in contrast to the minor or 'hybrid' ones which tend to accommodate themselves, by more or less extensive assimilation and adaptation, to the general framework of the representative world views—must define their respective positions both as *'totalizing'* in their explanatory claims, and as meaningful strategic *alternatives* to one another. Thus, the contending ideologies of any given historical period constitute the necessary practical consciousness in terms of which the major classes of society relate to, and indeed more or less openly confront, each other and articulate their vision of the right and proper social order as a comprehensive whole.

Understandably, the most fundamental conflict in the social arena concerns the social structure itself which provides the regulatory framework of any particular society's productive and distributive practices. And precisely because that conflict is so fundamental, it cannot be simply left to the blind mechanism of unaffordably wasteful and potentially lethal collisions. The less so, in fact, the higher the risk of actualizing the calamities implicit in the growing power of destruction at the disposal of the antagonists.

Nor can such conflict be resolved within the legislative domain of 'theoretical reason' alone, no matter how fashionable a name one may confer upon the latter. This is why the structurally most important conflict—whose object is to sustain, or, on the contrary, to negate the prevailing mode of control over the social metabolism within the confines of the established relations of production—finds its *necessary* manifestations in the *practice-orientated* 'ideological forms in which men become *conscious* of this conflict and *fight it out*'—to quote from Marx's Preface to *A Contribution to the Critique of Political Economy.*

In this sense, what determines the nature of ideology more than anything else is the imperative to become *practically conscious* of the fundamental social conflict—from the mutually exclusive standpoints of the hegemonic alternatives that face one another in the given social order—for the purpose of *fighting it out.* To put it in another way, the various ideological forms of social consciousness carry far-reaching (even if to varying degrees direct or indirect) practical implications in all their varieties, in art and literature no less than in philosophy and social theory, irrespective of their sociopolitical anchorage to progressive or conservative positions.

It is this practical orientation that defines also the type of rationality appropriate to ideological discourse. For the concerns of the latter must be articulated not as abstract theoretical propositions (from which nothing except some more of the same kind of abstract theoretical propositions follow), but as well grounded practical pointers and effective mobilizing inducements towards the socially viable actions of real collective subjects (in contrast to artificially constructed 'ideal types'). Moreover, under the conditions of class society the social interests depicted and conceptualized by the rival ideologies are not only conflictually enmeshed (which undoubtedly they are), but done so in such a way that the *partial* issues are deeply affected by their location within the *overall* dynamic of the ongoing hegemonic conflict. Consequently, what might appear to be rational (or otherwise) on the very limited scale of a given partial issue, may very well turn out to be the exact opposite when inserted into its appropriate broader context, in accordance with the historically changing margin of action of the principal social agencies.

Thus, the question of ideological rationality is inseparable from recognizing the objective constraints within which the alternative strategies are formulated in favour of, or against, the continued reproduction of the given social order. This is not a matter of conformity or non-conformity to some predetermined set of logical rules on account of which the particular thinkers should be praised or blamed, as the case might be. Rather, it is a question of understanding how the fundamental structural characteristics of a determinate social order assert themselves on the relevant scale and circumscribe the alternative modes of conceptualization of all the major practical issues. For the structural determinations in question offer significantly different vantage points to the rival social subjects according to their respective positions with regard to the available levers of social control, which in turn themselves are subject to the question of how enduring or transient their socioeconomic and cultural/political viability will turn out to be in terms of the irrepressible dynamics of the overall historical development. It is the combination of the two—the adopted vantage point in its affirmative/supportive or critical/negating posture vis-à-vis the established levers of social control, and the historically changing effectiveness and legitimacy of those levers themselves—that defines the practice-oriented rationality of ideologies in relation to their age and, within it, in relation to the ascending or declining phases of development of the social forces whose interests they assert.

As a result of such inherently practical determinations (which can be clearly identified on a comprehensive temporal and social scale), the major ideologies bear the all-important mark of the *social formation* whose dominant productive practices (e.g. the value-orienting horizon of capitalistic private enterprise) they adopt as their ultimate frame of reference. The question of 'false consciousness' is a *subordinate moment* of this epochally-circumscribed practical consciousness, and as such it is subject to a multiplicity of qualifying conditions which must be concretely assessed in their proper setting.

Ideologies are epochally circumscribed in a twofold sense. *First,* in that the *conflictual* orientation of the various forms of practical social consciousness remains their prominent feature for as long as society is divided into classes. In other words, the practical social consciousness of all such societies cannot help being ideological—i.e. synonymous with ideology—because of the insuperably antagonistic character of their social structures. (The fact of such—structurally determined—conflictual orientation of ideology is in no way contradicted by the pacificatory discourse of the ruling ideology which we shall consider in a moment.) And *second,* that the *specific character* of the fundamental social conflict which leaves its indelible mark on the contending ideologies in different historical periods arises from the epochally—and not on a short-term basis—changing character of society's productive and distributive practices and from the corresponding need to question their continued imposition as they become increasingly undermined in the course of historical development. Accordingly, the limits of such questioning are set *epochally,* bringing to the fore new forms of ideological challenge in close conjuction with the emergence of more advanced ways of satisfying the fundamental requirements of the social metabolism.

Without recognizing the epochal determination of ideologies as the practical social consciousness of class societies, their internal structure remains thoroughly unintelligible. We must differentiate, however, between three fundamentally different ideological positions, with serious implications for the kinds of knowledge compatible with each. The first, in the spirit of Menenius Agrippa, supports the given order with uncritical attitude, adopting and glorifying the immediacy of the dominant system—no matter how problematical and full of contradictions—as the *absolute horizon* of social life itself. The second, exemplified by radical thinkers like Rousseau, succeeds to a significant extent, in exposing the irrationalities of the *specific form* of, rather anachronistic, class society which it rejects from a new vantage point, but its critique is vitiated by the contradictions of its own—equally class-determined, even if historically more advanced—social position. And the third, in contrast to the previous two, radically questions the continued historical viability of the class horizon itself, anticipating as the objective of its conscious practical intervention the supersession of all forms of class antagonism.

Naturally, in the history of thought all the way down to the present even the most positive varieties of becoming conscious of the fundamental social conflict could not help being affected by the structural limitations of class confrontation. Only the third type of ideology can even attempt—without any aprioristic guarantee of success—to overcome the constraints associated with the production of practical knowledge within the horizon of divided social consciousness under the conditions of divided class society.

In this respect, the Marxian insight that at the present juncture of historical development the question of 'transcendence' must be raised as the necessity to go *beyond class society as such,* and not merely beyond one *particular type* of class society in favour of yet another, does not mean at all that one can escape, on the strength of that insight alone, the need to articulate social consciousness—oriented towards the strategic objective of reshaping society in accordance with the repressed productive potentialities of an identifiable collective agency—as a coherent and forceful ideology. For the relevant practical issue remains as before, namely, how to 'fight out' the fundamental conflict over the structural stake of control over the social metabolism as a whole. Hence, to imagine that socialist theory could afford to be 'ideology free', and to stipulate that it should aim at defining its position in such—nowhere beyond the self-enclosed terrain of vacuous 'theoretical discourse' viable—terms, is in fact a self-disarming strategy. One which can only play into the hands of the adversary who has a very sound interest indeed in misrepresenting its own position as genuinely 'consensual', 'objective', scientific', and thoroughly 'free from ideological bias'. The point is not to oppose science to ideology in a positivistic dichotomy but to establish their practically viable unity from the new historical vantage point of the socialist project.

The myth of 'organic unity' dominated ideological discourse ever since social intercourse had to conform to the material imperatives of securing the continuity of production within the potentially explosive framework of the hierarchical social division of labour that repeatedly changed its forms in the course of history but not its exploitative substance.

This correlation between pacificatory ideology and hierarchical social structure is perfectly understandable. For no matter how deeply divided and antagonistically torn all class societies are in their basic structural relationships, they must, nevertheless, be able to function under normal circumstances as *integrated wholes* (and in that sense 'organic systems'), with the exception, that is, of those periods of *explosion* which tend to draw the historical line of demarcation between one social formation and another.

The plausibility and spontaneous influence of the dominant ideological discourse well beyond the ranks of its true beneficiaries resides precisely in its soothing appeal to 'unity' and associated concerns, from 'observing the rules of objectivity' to finding the right 'balance' in the necessary—but, of course, because of the normally prevailing unequal relation of forces quite iniquitous—'reciprocal adjustments' of the conflicting social forces. The necessary cementing function of the ruling ideology becomes all the more evident (and significant) if we recall that even its more agressive variants—from chauvinism to Nazism and to the most recent ideologies of the 'Radical Right'—must claim to represent the overwhelming majority of the population, against the outside 'enemy', the 'racially inferior' minorities, the so-called 'mere handful of trouble-makers' who are supposed to be the cause of strikes and social unrest, and the like.

From the standpoint of the ruling ideology, the ongoing hegemonic conflict can never be allowed to be depicted as one between potential equals. For that would *ipso facto* throw wide open the question of legitimacy and confer historical rationality on their adversary. It is therefore a matter of insuperable structural determination that the ruling ideololgy—in view of its aprioristic legitimatory aspirations—cannot function at all without misrepresenting its self-interest, no matter how narrow, as the 'general interest' of society. But precisely for the same reason, the ideological discourse of the ruling order must maintain its cult of 'unity' and 'proper balance', even if—particularly at times of major crises—this amounts to no more than empty rhetorics when set against the real operative principle of *divide et impera;* another highly prized rule of social control formulated by the Romans thousands of years ago.

Naturally, very different constraints apply to critical ideologies. For all those who try to articulate the interests of the subordinate classes have to assume—again as a matter of insuperable structural determination—a negating posture not only with regard to the pretended 'organicity' (the ideological Potyemkin 'village' or façade) of the established order but also in relation to its objective determinations and institutions of socioeconomic and political/cultural control. It is therefore by no means accidental that all of Marx's major works have for their subtitle 'A Critique of Political Economy': that is, the critique of a body of doctrines in which the *strongest* points of the capitalist system are coherently conceptualized. And while no one would wish to deny today this correlation, it is nevertheless conveniently obscured by the dominant ideological discourse that the same sort of determination prevails in all critical ideologies, in all historical periods. For the original conceptions of the liberal creed—today heavily involved in the defence of the *status quo*—in their day were radically negating the 'dark ages' and their social survivals in the name of 'Reason'.

However, it must be also recognized that the story cannot end at the point of sheer negativity. For no social force can put forward its claims as a *hegemonic alternative* without also indicating, at least in its broad outlines, the positive/affirmative dimension of its radical negation. Again, this is true of thousands of years of history, not only of the last few centuries. Ideologies which exhaust themselves in pure negation as a rule fizzle out within a very short time and thus fail to assert any real claim to constitute a viable alternative. Moreover, somewhat paradoxically, it is a characteristic feature of none but the ruling ideologies that once the declining phase in the development of the social forces whose interests they express is reached, they are unable to offer other than a thoroughly negative conceptual framework, notwithstanding their 'positive' identification with the status quo. For their affirmative dimension is really quite *mechanical/determinist*—as well exemplified in the frequently repeated dictum: *'there is no alternative',* which self-contradictorily claims to be the defence of 'freedom', 'liberty', 'individual sovereignty', etc.—and all their *active* concern is directed at dismissing their adversary with an *aprioristic negativity,* remaining thus entirely dependent (i.e. intellectually parasitic) on the arguments which they reject from the ground of their mechanical 'no alternative' preconception.

The ideological/theoretical debates of the postwar era clearly demonstrate these connections. For a while they evolved around the wishful rejection of the socialist project as *'The Opium of the Intellectuals'* (Aron), soon to be followed by the even more wishful celebration of the success of such approach as *'The End of Ideology'* (Bell). This in its turn was succeeded by theorizations which wanted to remove even the possibility of the hegemonic conflict, talking about *'The Industrial System'* (Aron again) and *'The New Industrial State'* (Galbraith), postulating wishful 'convergences' that never materialized. The next phase, therefore, had to try to get out of the difficulties by talking about the *post-industrial society* which promised to transcend the remaining contradictions of contemporary capitalism. And now that the expectations of the latter have been proved totally illusory, since the weighty problems at the roots of ideology stubbornly refuse to go away, we are presented with the ideologies of 'modernity', or 'modernity and its discontents', and—in the very latest efforts—with the gratuitous postulate of 'post-modernity'. Thus, while the contradictions of the social world become stronger than ever and manifest themselves more and more in a way that approaches an all-engulfing global scale, they are repeatedly declared to be already 'left behind'—or just about to be 'superseded'—in an unending succession of ideological constructs that verbally metamorphose, under a new desocialized 'post-'

label, the same soothing rationalization as soon as its previous version loses its credibility.

However, we cannot adequately explain these developments simply with reference to the postwar conjuncture of social conflict. For their intellectual roots reach back a great deal further; with regard to their favourite themes and categories to the first two decades of the century (particularly Weber), and in their deeper theoretical foundations to the 'heroic phase' of the bourgeois world-view (i.e. the eighteenth and early nineteenth centuries) with which the accounts are now skeptically settled.

These and related issues constitute the main concern of the present volume. They are explored critically, in their appropriate historical context, and affirmatively, whenever there is scope for positive affirmation. Hence the subtitle of the volume.

The interested reader can find a complementary discussion of some other important aspects of ideology in my book on *The Power of Ideology* (Harvester Press, 1987).

I Ideology and Social Science*

This essay is closely related to a study which deals with the fundamental structural features of the various forms of ideology—from moral and religious discourse to politics and to art—taken individually as well as in their manifold interconnections; with the material and social conditions and mechanisms that determine the emergence and subtle transformations of particular ideologies; with the complex instruments and institutions required to secure the more or less enduring impact of ideological systems; and, last but not least, with the intricate relationship between ideology and social science considered both as specific modes of discourse and as determinate social complexes which fulfil a multiplicity of vital functions in the global framework of social practice.

Since several aspects of the problems we are concerned with are discussed elsewhere, the present essay[1] concentrates on a brief survey and critique of some characteristic approaches to our subject matter, attempting at the same time the formulation of a few—very tentative—criteria for the assessment of ideology and social science. With this in mind, let us now turn to an area of debate whose complexities and importance no one is likely to deny—at least not today.

1. THE IDEOLOGY OF 'THE END OF IDEOLOGY'

The astonishing thing is that so many people did deny these in the by no means distant past. Thus, generations of students—particularly in

* First published in *The Socialist Register,* Merlin Press 1972, pp. 35-81.

the post-war period—were led to believe by a considerable number of Foundation-sponsored social scientists that ideology had been done away with altogether and that it had been replaced, for good, by the sound and sober systems of strictly factual social science.

That such boasts themselves were disguised manifestations of a peculiar kind of ideological 'false consciousness'—one which arbitrarily labels its adversary as an 'ideologist' so as to be able to claim to itself, *by definition,* full immunity from all ideology; i.e. one which 'proved' both vice and virtue by *begging the question*—escaped the attention not only of the theoretically and politically naive but often even of those who should have known better. This is how as serious and critical a scholar as Robert L. Heilbroner hailed in *The Reporter* Daniel Bell's notorious book, *The End of Ideology,* at the time of its publication:

> A book of unusual interest . . . we find here more than a commentary on 'the exhaustion of political ideas in the fifties'; we also have *revealed to us the appearance of social reality once the ideological glasses of the past have been removed.*

A sad submission to sheer mystification!

Economy of space requires that we confine ourselves to quoting one single example in order to test the claims of this ideology-free, solidly factual and unprejudiced 'social science'. As we shall see, however, even this single example is abundantly revealing about the approach which was supposed to have 'revealed to us the appearance of social reality' in its purity, thanks to the removal of the 'ideological glasses of the past'. The example I have in mind comes from page 385 of *The End of Ideology:*

> The NEP was an extraordinary step for Lenin. For he had to admit that there was nothing in the 'old books' to prepare the party for such a radical step as the partial restoration of capitalism. In an essay written just before his death—an essay which demonstrates the doctrinal cast which had ruled Lenin's mind—he declared ruefully: 'It did not even occur to Marx to write about the subject; and he died without leaving a single precise quotation or irrefutable instruction on it. That is why we must get out of the difficulty entirely by our own efforts.'

Now the unpalatable truth is that Daniel Bell's great non-ideological 'revelations' are nothing but grave violations of the most elementary conditions of scientific research and analysis—but of course violations committed in the name of 'genuine social science' as radically opposed to 'outmoded ideology'.

If we take the time-consuming trouble of checking the alleged facts—as, unfortunately, not enough people do, thus often allowing the diffusion of even the most tendentious distortions as incontrovertible evidence[2]—we find not only that there is absolutely nothing to support Bell's contentious judgements but also that the Lenin quote in question (that is, Lenin's own text and not Bell's distorted version of it) demonstrates the *exact opposite* of what we are given to believe in a 'truly scientific' fashion. For this is how Lenin's actual text goes:

> On the question of state capitalism, I think that generally our press and our Party make the mistake of dropping into intellectualism, into liberalism; we philosophise about how state capitalism is to be interpreted, and look into old books. But in those old books you will not find what we are discussing; they deal with the state capitalism that exists under capitalism. Not a single book has been written about state capitalism under communism. It did not occur even to Marx to write a word on this subject; and he died without leaving a single precise statement or definite instruction on it. That is why we must overcome the difficulty entirely by ourselves. And if we make a general mental survey of our press and see what has been written about state capitalism, as I tried to do when I was preparing this report, we shall be convinced that it is missing the target, that it is looking in an entirely wrong direction.

As we can see then, Bell's version not only lifts Lenin's words out of their context—if he did not do so no one could take seriously for a moment his claims and accusations—but also it assumes the form of a translation which turns the original passage into the doctrinal 'single precise *quotation* or *irrefutable instruction*' (whatever on earth an 'irrefutable instruction' might mean).

There is no trace whatsoever, in the original quotation, of a *'rueful'* behaviour on Lenin's part. Nor indeed of *'admitting'* under the constraint of quite unique circumstances that this time the 'old books' cannot help. In point of fact he often took—from his early youth onwards—'extraordinary steps' of adapting his theoretical position to the changing socio-historical conditions. (As is well known, he has been accused more than once of being merely a 'clever realist' by critics who thought that he ought to be censured for *lack* of doctrinal purity).[3] On the contrary, he most emphatically insists that 'intellectualism' and 'philosophizing' about the problems at stake with references to old books is totally mistaken: the press that follows such procedure *'is missing the target, is looking in an entirely wrong direction'.* Also, in his closing speech to the debate he reproaches Preobrazhensky for arguing in terms of *'pure scholasticism'* in that he bases his analysis on old books and past events while 'this is the first time in human history that we see anything like it' and therefore *'we must not look to the past'.*[4]

And all this is supposed to be proof of *'the doctrinal cast which had ruled Lenin's mind'*—proof, that is, in the eyes of the supremely objective 'social scientist' who has succeeded in definitively freeing himself from the 'ideological glasses of the past' to such an extent that he can not only announce *'The End of Ideology'* but also see things in Lenin's text which are simply not there for us ideologically bespectacled lesser mortals.

But irony apart, Daniel Bell's allegedly scientific text is scandalously misleading even in its minor details. It states that the quote comes from an 'essay' written by Lenin *'just before his death'.* As a matter of fact, it comes from a speech delivered at the eleventh party congress and published on the basis of a stenographic record. More important in case one wants to trace the debated quotation: it was not written by Lenin 'just before his death' but almost *two years prior to his death:* the opening speech was delivered on 27 March 1922, and his reply to Preobrazhensky one day later, to be precise. As to the source, we are told that the quotation can be found on page 338 of Lenin's *'Selected Works,* vol. XIV, cited in Theodore Draper, *The Roots of American Communism'.* But even this secondhand reference is ludicrously misleading. For Draper gives volume *IX*—not *XIV*—as his reference.[5] (The interested reader can find Lenin's text in vol. XXXIII of his *Collected Works.*)

Such is then the actual performance of this non-ideological, objective, factual and rigorously scholarly social science. And since this 'science' can conjure up its ideological adversary in the shape and form it pleases, it can also dispose of problems of extreme complexity with the greatest ease. Ideology? That is the *other* side. And even on the other side it represents only the *past,* since we now all live in a delightful 'post-capitalist' and purely 'industrial' society. Consequently, the problems of ideology simply do not exist any longer. Conflict and complexity are *readily replaced* by simple and sound 'social engineering' and we can now all live happily ever after.

Most annoyingly, however, social reality refuses to take any notice of the revolutionary solutions of this 'social science' and insists on the actuality of conflicts and crises which escape the streamlined simplicity of wishfully prefabricated models and schemas. Thus our former champions of the 'post-capitalist industrial society' are forced to make a spectacular turn-about. Daniel Bell, for instance, is now engaged in theorizing about the so-called *'post-industrial* society'. Indeed, he now goes as far as talking about the *'dismal record'* of recent social science (not of his own, of course), adding that:

> In the areas of education, welfare, social planning, there has been little knowledge that one can draw upon for policy purposes. *Social scientists have reluctantly begun to admit that the problems are more 'complex' than they thought.*'[6]

Yet, the reluctant admission of dismal failure is far from amounting to an identification of the ideological roots of such failure. On the contrary: since the original assumptions of the 'ideology-free' posture remain unquestioned, the fundamental construction stays as it used to be. Only the façade gets a topical veneer which is meant to emphasize the building's adequacy to the more turbulent present-day circumstances. That an elementary condition of improving that 'dismal record' would be a radical re-examination of the ideological preconceptions of 'value-free' social science, this must, of course, systematically escape the attention of those who have a major vested interest in maintaining their not so long ago almost completely uncontested ideological stranglehold over social science.

2. MAX WEBER AND 'VALUE-FREE SOCIAL SCIENCE'

It goes without saying, that the roots of these problems reach much deeper than might be suggested by the ideological debates of the recent past. We have to go a great deal further back into the past if we want to get to grips with some major difficulties of the relationship between ideology and social science.

Let us turn first of all to a classic with whom many of the more recent theories have originated: Max Weber. Let us examine in the first place Weber's claims on the nature and validity of his 'ideal types'. He writes in a famous text:

> the elementary duty of scientific self-control and the only way to avoid serious and foolish blunders requires a sharp, precise distinction between the *logically comparative analysis of reality by ideal types in the logical sense* and the *value judgement of reality on the basis of ideals.* An 'ideal type' in our sense... has *no connection at all* with value-judgments, and it has nothing to do with any type of perfection other than a purely logical one.[7]

Since we are going to encounter much greater difficulties in a moment, we may disregard the question whether or not Weber's talk about 'the elementary duty of scientific self-control' constitutes an intrusion of value-judgement into his general scheme. Also, for the reason just stated, we should now simply bypass the issue of whether it is legitimate to confine social science to the sphere of 'purely logical perfection'. Our primary concern, at this stage, is whether or not it is possible for Weber himself to live up to the standards he has laid down for the evaluation of social science in general.

To cut a long answer short, clearly it is not possible, even though Weber and his followers refuse to give up their illusions in this matter.

To examine Weber's claims more closely, take his definition of capitalism which is supposed to be such a 'neutral' ideal type. He defines capitalism as a *'culture'*:

> in which *the governing principle is the investment of private capital.*[8]

The choice of such defining characteristics is, however, far from being 'value-free', although on the surface it seems to express a self-evident truth: namely that capitalism and the investment of private capital are linked together. But this is, of course, merely a tautological truth, and by no means a very accurate one at that. What goes in Weber's definition beyond sheer tautology is either blatantly ideological and 'value-bound', or false—or indeed both ideologically biased and false.

Weber's definition is formulated from a definite standpoint: not that of 'pure logic' but one which very conveniently blocks out the possibility of rival definitions without establishing itself on other than purely *assumptional* grounds. The adoption of this ideal type as the principle of selection of all available data necessarily carries with it that 'scientifically self-controlled' research is confined to data which easily fit into the ideological framework of Weber's definitional assumptions.

Let us see, briefly, how the Weberian definition of capitalism fulfils its ideological functions under the appearance of a 'non-ideological' and 'descriptive' formulation:

The *first* thing we have to notice is the choice of the term '*culture*' (in place of available alternatives, such as 'social formation', or 'mode of production', etc.): a term which anticipates a determinate type of interpretation as to the development of the capitalistic social formation. (See in this respect his approach to *The Protestant Ethic and the Spirit of Capitalism.*)

Secondly, Weber's capitalism is characterized by the assumption of a *'governing principle'*, without any attempt at explaining the grounds—if any—of this strange metaphysical entity. The methodological consequences of this assumption are extremely serious, for its adoption nullifies the possibility of a comprehensive historical enquiry into the actual grounds of the development of capitalism. In its place, we find an ahistorical projection of the developed form backwards into the past, since the 'governing principle' must be exhibited at all stages. (This is why in the last analysis it must be identified with the somewhat mysterious 'spirit of capitalism'). And Weber's qualifications concerning the relationship between the 'ideal type' and empirical reality are, in this respect, nothing more than an ideological *escape clause* to provide blanket coverage against possible objections to his general model.

Thirdly, the definitional assumption of the *'investment of private capital'* as the governing principle of capitalism conveniently blocks out the absolutely crucial question of structural interrelationship between capital and *labour*. The term which is conspicuously absent from the Weberian type of discourse is, of course, 'labour'. And since no 'spirit'—not even 'the spirit of capitalism'—can explain the *actual* constitution of capital (the 'mechanism' of its constitution, so to speak), such questions must be either disregarded or relegated to the intellectually secondary realm of describing a determinate stage of empiria. It is, thus, ideologically highly significant that 'labour' does not appear in the general model. Why bother with the thorny issues of '*the extraction of surplus-value*' if you have the 'investment of private capital' conveniently at your disposal in a ready-made form as the 'governing principle' of capitalism?

Fourth, while 'labour' is conspicuously absent from Weber's social equation, the definition of the governing principle of capitalism as the '*investment* of private capital' conveniently supplies the necessary justification for and legitimation of the continued existence of the capitalist mode of production against the counter-claims of appropriated labour. That private capital is invested only when it anticipates *profit*—i.e., that the underlying 'governing principle' is *profit* and not *investment* as such—this vital fact is quietly and significantly hidden from sight by Weber's definitional assumption.

Fifth, it is by no means true that capitalism is characterized by the '*investment* of private capital'. As is well known, capitalism is, equally, characterized by the *failure to invest* overproduced capital and, thus, by periodic *crises* and social upheavals. By taking the 'investment of private capital' for granted as the 'governing principle' of capitalism, Weber successfully blocks out a fundamental area of enquiry: namely a critical questioning of the extremely *problematic* character of the capitalistic type of investment insofar as it is *necessarily* associated with crises and upheavals.

Sixth, it is quite inaccurate to describe capitalism in general as characterized by the 'investment of *private* capital'. Such a characterization is valid—with the qualifications made above—only of a determinate historical phase of capitalistic development, and by no means as an 'ideal type' in its Weberian sense. By stressing the investment of *private* capital Weber uncritically champions the subjective standpoint of the individual capitalist, disregarding at the same time one of the most important objective trends of development of the capitalist mode of production: namely the ever-increasing involvement of *state-capital* in the continued reproduction of the capitalist system. In principle the outer limit of this development is nothing less than the transformation of the prevailing form of capitalism into an all-comprehensive system of *state-capitalism,* which theoretically implies the complete abolition of the specific phase of capitalism idealized by Weber. But precisely because of such implications, this crucial trend of development must be excluded from the ideological framework of Weber's 'ideal type'.

And last but not least, the definition taken as a whole constitutes a completely *static* model. Unfortunately there is no space here to go into the details of this issue. Let me merely indicate that the elimination of the fundamental structural interrelationship between capital and labour and its replacement by the frozen metaphysical entity, 'governing principle', excludes all dynamism from the picture. Thus, not only can there be no room for a dynamic account of the actual genesis and development of the capitalist social formation, as we have already seen; equally—and this is the point at which the ideological function of the static model becomes obvious—there can be no question of a possible dissolution and ultimate replacement of capitalism by a new type of social formation. There are no traces of dynamic contradictions in the model; consequently it can only comprehend the stable features of continuity—completely disregarding the dialectic of discontinuity—of a prevailing *status quo.* Such continuity is simply assumed, in the form of an already prevailing 'principle', and once it exists it cannot be altered in terms of the Weberian static model. (We shall see in a moment the same static approach to the strategically important question of the administrative system of capitalist society.)

These are then, roughly, the ideological features we can detect in *one single line* of Weber's voluminous writings, provided that we do not simply accept his claims at their face value. As we have seen, notwithstanding his theoretical awareness of the 'elementary duty of scientific self-control', Weber ended up defining capitalism as 'a culture in which the governing principle is the investment of private capital'. To this definition we may oppose the following: *'capitalism is a mode of production characterized by the extraction of surplus-value for the sake of the production and reproduction of capital on an ever-enlarging scale.'* It may be left to the reader to decide which of the two definitions is more 'ideological'. What must be clear, however, is that they are not *complementary* but *diametrically opposed* to one another: which just could not be the case if Weber's claim to the 'purely logical' and 'value-free' character of his 'ideal types' were valid.

3. THE IDEOLOGICAL CHARACTER OF THE 'IDEAL TYPES'

Let me quote another passage which exemplifies perhaps even more sharply, the ideological character of Weber's 'ideal types'. The passage in question comes from his treatment of 'bureaucracy' in *Wirtschaft und Gesellschaft.* It goes as follows:

> The ruled, for their part, *cannot* dispense with or replace the bureaucratic apparatus of authority once it exists. For this bureaucracy rests upon *expert* training, a *functional specialization* of work, and an *attitude* set for habitual and *virtuoso-like mastery* of single yet methodically integrated functions. If the official stops working, or if his work is forcefully interrupted, *chaos results*, and it is *difficult to improvise* replacements from among the governed who are *fit to master such chaos.* This holds for public administration as well as for private economic management. More and more the material fate of the *masses* depends upon the steady and correct functioning of the *increasingly bureaucratic* organizations of *private capitalism. The idea of eliminating these organizations becomes more and more utopian.*[9]

It is astonishing to see Max Weber—who can be so rigorous, subtle and precise in ideologically less sensitive contexts—producing such a sequence of assertions dense with inconsistencies, mythical exaggerations and arbitrary declarations. A closer inspection of this passage will reveal that Weber's 'evidence'—and I can only use the term 'evidence' in inverted commas—is sandwiched between two *categorical* and thoroughly *arbitrary* assertions, namely that:

(1) 'the ruled *cannot* dispense with or replace the bureaucratic apparatus once it exists'; and that

(2) 'the idea of eliminating these organizations becomes more and more utopian'.

Now if we try to discover what substantiates Weber's peremptory conclusion, we find one single point that might possibly qualify: i.e., the statement according to which the organizations of private capitalism are becoming *'increasingly bureaucratic'*. But even this statement is wrapped up in a fateful postulate which stipulates as a categorical imperative the *'steady* and *correct functioning'* of such organizations (strictly in the interest of the 'masses', of course). The rest is mythology coupled with inconsistency.

Take, for instance, the categorical assertion that the ruled *cannot* replace the bureaucratic apparatus of authority once it exists. Nothing warrants such an assertion apart from the mythological postulate of inevitable *chaos* in the event that 'the official's work is forcefully interrupted', followed by the pronouncement according to which 'it is *difficult to improvise* replacements from among the governed who are fit to master such chaos'. But clearly, what might be 'difficult' is by no means 'impossible', which is suggested by 'cannot'. Thus, Weber's categorical assertion does not stand up even to his own attempt at a justification. Furthermore, if it is difficult to dispense with or replace the bureaucratic apparatus of authority by *'improvisation',* perhaps it might be somewhat easier to accomplish this by sustained effort at devising and preparing an alternative system of control within the contradictory framework of the established system of society. (We may here refer to the idea of 'dual power' and to the—however embryonic—societal facts corresponding to it.) But, of course, if there is no room for objective contradictions within the general model, there can be no room for the manifestation of such contradictions either.

Here, again, we can see the thoroughly *static* character of Weber's ideal types. His idea which asserts the necessary permanence of the bureaucratic apparatus of authority is conceived on the basis of the implicit assumption that the *prevailing* separation (or alienation) of *'expertise'* from the 'masses' is destined to remain a *permanent* feature of social life. Consequently even the tendencies within the capitalist framework of development which point in the opposite direction—tendencies noticed by Marx some sixty years before Weber's reflections (i.e. no one can accuse us of reproaching Weber with ignoring something visible only from the vantage point of our own days)—must be left completely outside the compass of the Weberian model.

The only point at which we might be under the impression of facing a genuinely historical element is where Weber refers to 'the increasingly bureaucratic organization of private capitalism'. However, a closer look reveals that the function of this reference is entirely *anti-historical* and ideological in that it serves merely the *uncritical legitimation* of the bureaucratic apparatus of authority. For even if for the sake of argument we grant that the increasing bureaucratization is the necessary consequence of increasing complexity and specialization, it is by no means self-evident that bureaucracy will be able to meet indefinitely the challenge of such complexity. Yet for Weber this must be so; complexity advances only so far as is required to provide the necessary legitimation for the absolute permanence of the bureaucratic structure; at which point the historical challenge of increasing complexity is conveniently ruled out of court through the arbitrary assumption according to which bureaucracy is *a priori* capable of meeting this challenge. In a passage that just precedes the one quoted above we read:

> The more complicated and specialized modern culture becomes the more its external supporting apparatus *demands* the personally detached and *strictly 'objective' expert*... Bureaucracy offers the *attitudes* demanded by the external apparatus of modern culture in the most favourable combination[10]

As we can see, the *objective demand* inherent in the alleged functional complexity is turned, in a most mystifying way, into a demand for a *subjective attitude* which is supposed to be supplied by bureaucracy. (The latter is characterized—*by definition*—as fully supplying the demand demanded of it.) The question whether or not the objective demand is successfully met—i.e. whether bureaucracy is actually *capable* of supplying what is *objectively,* and not merely in terms of a *definitional tautology,* demanded of it—is systematically evaded by means of the bewildering subjectivization of the issue of demand. In other words, the problem is 'solved' by means of a mystifying *ambiguity.*

Moreover, in our original quotation—which comes from the section significantly dedicated to arguing 'the *permanent* character of the bureaucratic machine'—Weber is compelled to go even further in mythologizing: he postulates the bureaucrat as the *'virtuoso-like master of chaos'*. He has to inflate the prosaic bureaucrat into a demi-god in order *a priori* to exclude the possibility of an alternative system of social control. At the same time, the fundamental question concerning the objective demand inherent in the given complexity remains evaded as before. For—as contemporary virtuosos can testify—the 'complexity' of some modern music can assume such proportions that even the most accomplished virtuosos find themselves at a loss.

And the final point to make, very briefly, is that the claimed '*functional* specialization' is in fact basically a *structural* 'specialization': that is, the *structural separation of the function of control* from those who are controlled by it. Consequently, if we treat this question merely as that of a 'functional specialization', we are trapped by premises which anticipate the claimed *a priori* irreplaceability of the *system within which* the given 'functional specialization' necessarily occurs. If we merely challenge a particular set of functional specializations without putting into question at the same time the underlying system which gives rise to such 'specializations', we are condemned to futility. As Weber writes elsewhere:

> Today, it is primarily the capitalist market economy which demands that the official business of the administration be discharged precisely unambiguously continuously and with as much speed as possible. Normally, the very large, modern capitalist enterprises are themselves unequalled models of strict bureaucratic organization.[11]

Indeed. All this, however, does not warrant in the least Weber's own conclusions which postulate nothing less than the permanence of the bureaucratic exercise of authority. What it warrants, however, is simply the conclusion that the critique of 'functional specialization' is inseparable from a radical questioning of the system of 'capitalist market economy' as a whole. Since, however, Weber could not entertain the latter idea, he had to dismiss all efforts directed at replacing the bureaucratic exercise of authority not even as just 'utopian' but—betraying an all too obvious eagerness to champion the 'neutral' position of the *status quo*—as *'more and more utopian'*.

4. THEORY AND META-THEORY

Naturally I do not wish to deny Weber's achievements. The preceding few pages were not meant to be what is called a 'balanced view' of his work as a whole, but a brief critical examination of the claims to validity of one of Weber's most influential and fundamental methodological principles in the context of our topic.

As we have seen, Weber sets out to construct a *neutral instrument of analysis* and ends up producing an *ideological weapon* which—far from being 'neutral'—enables him to dispose of the ideological adversary without even giving him a hearing, and on a terrain of Weber's own choice. The question remains though: is this the result of personal failure, or is it inherent in the method itself? In other words: is the programme itself valid, irrespective of its ideologically biassed realization by Weber himself?

The answer seems to me to be in the negative for the fundamental reason that the instruments and methods of social analysis can never be radically neutral with regard to their object.

The level of 'meta-theory' cannot be separated *in principle* from the theory itself; it is only as a *moment* of analysis that it can by this be separated, but it must then be reintegrated again in the *overall synthesis.* That is to say: meta-theory is an *integral dimension* of all theory, and not a privileged department governed by radically different principles. There can be no coherent social theory without its own, specific meta-theoretical dimension and vice-versa, there can be no meta-theory—not even that of the claimed 'ideal types'—which is not deeply rooted in a set of theoretical propositions inseparably linked to determinate social *values.*

The models and principles of meta-theory are constituted on the basis of a given set of already structured—i.e. specifically evaluated—data, and in turn they act as general principles of all further selection and articulation of the available data. The refusal to consider the ideological implications of 'societal' model-making brings with it the unintended transformation of a tool of analysis into a self-supporting ideology. (It is by no means accidental that the century which produced some of the most self-complacent forms of ideology in the guise of the final supersession of all ideology should pride itself as being 'The Age of Analysis'.)

Does this mean then that we are advocating a *relativistic* position in this matter?

Quite the contrary. For it is precisely the radical separation of 'meta-theory' from theory, of the 'ideal type' from the categories of empirical reality which necessarily leads to relativism, in that neither of the two qualitatively opposed theoretical 'realms' can provide criteria of evaluation for the adequacy of the other. If, however, we conceive their relationship in terms of a *dialectical reciprocity,* and both levels as inherently linked to the various manifestations of social practice itself, in that case the question of 'objectivity' need not be put in an uneasy Weberian fashion in inverted commas and confined to the realm of the 'purely logical' ideal type. In other words, there will be no need to attempt the impossible: namely the solution of basically ontological problems within the confines of purely epistemological criteria.

Thus we are envisaging a system of constant readjustments—one of reciprocal 'feedback'—between the meta-theoretical level of 'ideal types' and the specific propositions of societal evaluation related to it. The comprehensive model or 'ideal type' is modified whenever the confrontation of the various sets of societal evaluation with the complex phenomena of social reality indicates the need for an overall readjustment; for the specific theoretical propositions can only go as far as the general framework of theory allows them to go. This is why the general framework cannot set itself up as a privileged final arbiter over everything else, but is itself in need of a constant critical reassessment on the basis of its results as compared with the immensely complex and dynamic manifestation of the social totality.

This means that the concepts and principles which constitute the general framework of social theory are subject to the same criteria of objectivity and relevance as all the other elements. In other words, given the dialectical interrelatedness of the various levels of enquiry, the question concerning the ontological status of the meta-theoretical level cannot be evaded without serious consequences for the enterprise as a whole. For, granted that the concepts and principles described as 'ideal types' express a higher level of generality than those which indicate, for instance, the pattern of decision-making in a particular gypsy community, it does not follow in the least that the former ought to be assigned to a radically different sphere to which only considerations of 'pure logical perfection' would apply. If the latter were the case there could be no guarantee whatsoever of the applicability and relevance of the 'ideal type' to the multiplicity of 'empirical data'. (And indeed, the precise relationship between the two spheres remains largely a matter of mystery in the Weberian framework of analysis.)

We have to claim, then, the same objectivity for concepts like 'classes and class-relations'—described by many as 'ideal types'—as for concepts denoting some particular social fact or relation. There is, however, a significant difference in that the former comprehend the fundamental *structural* features of the object of enquiry—be it 'capitalism' or 'bureaucracy'— and thus circumscribe the general framework of investigation, whereas the latter articulate themselves (on the basis of the often inexplicit comprehensive structural concepts) in the form of more or less direct references to the immediately given specific social phenomena. All the same, the point is that the general structural aspects of social phenomena are by no means less objective than the direct phenomenal manifestations of social interchange but, if anything, only more so: in the sense that they comprehend the areas and modalities of dynamic change and transition on a much larger scale than the immediate conceptualizations of phenomenal data and therefore they can capture the most fundamental and far-reaching trends of development already in the making.

This is why, in the end, the question of objectivity cannot be separated from that of the dynamic or static character of societal models and 'ideal types'. Social phenomena are inherently dynamic in that they are constitutive parts of an overall social structure which necessitates an enlarged form of reproduction for its continued existence. (We may think of the dialectic of expanding human needs and of the conditions of gratification of the ever-expanding range of needs.) Thus, the construction of static models and 'ideal types'—in place of inherently dynamic frameworks of social explanation—can only result in more or less sophisticated ideological pictures of objectively conservative intent.

5. HOMANS' METHODOLOGICAL INDIVIDUALISM

Now let us turn our attention for a moment to a rather different type of approach. It is well exemplified by Professor George Homans' little book on *The Nature of Social Science.* The author is a strict determinist of the behaviourist type, and he sees the difficulties facing social science primarily in terms of the sheer complexity of averaging out the *resultants* of manifold individual actions. This is how he describes the issues in his conclusions:

In many situations, and not only in economics, we can make much progress in explaining the behaviour of men by *taking as simply given,* for the time being, the institutional structures within which they operate, even if their behaviour *within* the structures will *eventually* change the structures. In explaining institutions and the relations between them, our task is often made easier by the presence of powerful *convergent* processes. And in the most difficult problem of synthesis, the problem of explaining the *possibly divergent* resultants of complex interactions between individuals and groups over time, the *high speed computer* has just arrived to help us. It will not do everything for us; it won't ask the right questions—that remains our job—but *the answers, so far as they depend on the mechanics of calculation,* the computer will get for us with a speed no man can match.[12]

Which all boils down to the singularly illuminating proposition that the high speed computer can compute at a high speed.

But what exactly the computer is asked to provide, remains, unfortunately, a mystery all the way through. The central problem of the social sciences is defined as the demonstration of 'how the behaviour of individuals creates the characteristics of groups'—a very doubtful proposition indeed—and then it is further specified as the task of producing *'psychological* propositions' on the basis of directly observable *'small-group research'.* The key terms are 'conformity' and 'convergence':

In the *small* group we can *really observe* and explain how *conformity* occurs, how *power* is exercised, and how *status systems* arise. These are surely among the most *convergent* of social phenomena, and ones we must begin by understanding intimately if we are ever to grasp the nature of larger societies.'[13]

It is, significantly, postulated that the large-scale structures will exhibit essentially the same characteristics as conformity-producing small groups, and all in perfect agreement, of course, with a 'human nature' identified by behavioural psychology:

the general propositions of all the social sciences are propositions of behavioural psychology.'[14]

In the meantime—and this is an equally significant ideological feature—we are expected to take the institutional structures *within* which the individuals operate *'as simply given,* for the time being': though, of course, 'for the time being' becomes *for good* in virtue of the systematic avoidance of the question of when and how we are going to examine the institutional structures as *not* 'simply given'. The reference to economics—allegedly 'the most advanced of the social sciences'[15] because it was 'lucky in being able to take institutions pretty much for granted'[16]—proves nothing more than the ideological prejudices of the author. For insofar as economics takes the institutions of capitalist economy for granted it is not the 'model' of social science but merely unashamed apologetics. And the moment of truth arrives when the prescriptions of manipulative pseudo-science miserably fail to work: at times when the overall institutional structure of capitalist society cannot be taken for granted any longer as 'simply given' but calls for major transformations. At such times, watching the performance of established economic wisdom vis-à-vis the problems of rising inflation *coupled with* rising unemployment (while in its 'scientific' books the two factors were supposed to be of necessity in an inverse ratio to one another), and vis-à-vis other, similarly bewildering, manifestations of 'economic disturbances', we get some measure of the 'scientific' value of Professor Homans' model of social science.

But there is another passsage worth quoting from the same book at some length. It goes as follows:

In the social sciences our only general propositions are propositions about individual behaviour. Many of our aggregative propositions are only statistically true and hold good only within particular historical circumstances.... If these conditions make trouble for us as social scientists, remember that they are a great advantage to humanity, by

> leaving men the illusion of choice. I speak of the illusion because I myself believe that what each of us does is absolutely determined. . . .
>
> The illusion of free will is going to be saved by cost considerations, but it is a vital illusion. If there were—as there are not—a few macroscopic laws about society, rather than laws about individuals, that hold good across the board, mankind would lose the conviction, which some part of it, thank God, preserves, that it can by taking thought change its condition in ways it considers better—even if by its own standards not all the changes would turn out to be so. The most amusing case is that of the Marxists, who theoretically believe in macroscopic laws inevitably converging on a certain result, but who will not let the laws alone to produce the result, and insist on helping them along.[17]

Never mind that the Marxian position is given a rather caricatural presentation. The important point is that the idea of genuine human choice is declared to be a mere *illusion*—one to be maintained out of 'cost-considerations'. Thus, the whole enterprise displays its pseudo-scientific character by wanting to integrate the openly advertised ideology of 'cost-effective illusion' with the claims of rigorous scientificity. This approach—which rejected the idea of comprehensive social laws in favour of the position of so-called 'methodological individualism'—ends up by advocating the *double standard* of ideological self-deceit for 'humanity' and 'mankind' and the sobriety of absolute determinism for the 'social scientist'. And notice the propositional *non-sequiturs* in which this idea is carefully wrapped up:

> If there were—as there are not—a few macroscopic laws about society, rather than laws about individuals, that hold good across the board, mankind would lose the conviction, which some part of it, thank God, preserves, that it can by taking thought change its condition in ways it considers better—even if by its own standards not all the changes would turn out to be so.

Now why should 'mankind'—suddenly we are dealing with 'mankind' and not with individuals, though we are supposed to be rigorous 'methodological individualists'—why should this 'mankind' keep its illusory 'conviction' of freely changing its 'condition' if there are laws which manifest themselves *indirectly,* through complex social intermediaries, rather than *directly,* in the form of an 'absolute determinism' that dominates every single individual? And why should the existence of social laws by itself inevitably lead to the loss of such illusions? After all, illusions can be maintained whether such laws exist or not.

Furthermore, if the above-named 'conviction' amounts to nothing more than mere illusion, why should its loss be so fatal? If, on the other hand, this 'conviction-illusion' is an effective instrument of change, it cannot be just an illusion.

Moreover, if the claimed 'absolute determinations' are really at work, it would require a great deal more than simply 'taking thought' to achieve the postulated change of mankind's 'condition'. And in the final line the idea of 'changes for the better' is taken back again in a half-hearted way, coupled with two watering-down clauses: namely that 'not *all* the changes would turn out to be better' and that not 'by *its own* standards'.

Which all put together must presumably mean that, thank God, we live in the best of all possible worlds, though of course best 'not by our own standards'.

Need I say more about the ideological character of this 'scientific' approach?

Theoretically its main defect is the total neglect of all those *complex mediations* which link the individual to his society as a whole. It goes without saying that the dynamic system of such mediations cannot be reduced to 'a few macroscopic laws' which operate with a timeless 'absolute determinism across the board'. It cannot be grasped through mechanical models and averages, but only through understanding the dialectical interrelationship between subjective and objective, partial and totalizing, end-positing and instrumental, individual and institutional factors.

The paradoxical thing about our social environment is that we are both its 'authors' and—as a result of alienation and reification—its unceremoniously dominated subjects. Thus, the question of human choice is inseparable from a critical examination of the conditions under which men turn themselves into mere instruments to the realization of reified social ends. Consequently, so long as the fundamental premise of 'social science' remains the assumption of the prevailing system of social institutions *'as simply given'*, so long the issue of human choice itself—and not just its ideologically biassed formulation—must appear nothing but a *'permanent illusion'*.

6. COSER'S VIEW OF THE FUNCTIONS OF SOCIAL CONFLICT

An adequate discussion of the problems we are confronted with is quite impossible without a precise identification of the ideological determinants of various social theories. Failure in this respect inevitably confines analysis to the level of vague and evasive generality; so much so, in fact, that the claimed 'supersession' of the criticized trend becomes so marginal as to be almost completely insignificant. An instructive case in point is Lewis Coser's book on *The Functions of Social Conflict.*

While Coser undoubtedly *intends* his book as a critique of and an alternative to the 'conservatism' of Parsonian-type social analysis, his own solution of the problems turns out to be thoroughly compatible with the criticized approach. And this is by no means accidental. For from the very beginning—given his total failure to identify the social determinants of Parsonian ideology—he waters down his terms of criticism to such an extent that his conclusions cannot be other than *complementary* to Parsons' 'conservatism'. For a start, he quotes with reverent approval Charles H. Cooley's following words:

> Conflict, of *some sort,* is the *life of society,* and progress emerges from a struggle in which *individual, class or institution* seeks to realize *its own idea of good.*[18]

Now, if someone wants to have a brief illustration of 'conflict analysis' in terms completely devoid of scientific content, this is it. Yet, Coser closes his eyes to the obvious unscientific qualities of Cooley's quote because this enables him to idealize what he calls 'the earlier generation' as against 'the contemporary generation'. (Two exceedingly scientific categories indeed.)

Similarly, Coser reproaches Parsons with ignoring Weber's teaching that '"Peace" is nothing more than a change in the form of conflict, or in the antagonists or in the objects of the conflict, or finally in the chances of selection.'[19] He stresses a little further on that the indexes of Parsons' *Essays in Sociological Theory* 'contain sixteen entries under "strain" and twenty entries under "tension"; however, there are only nine entries under "social conflict", although there are additional entries under value conflict and emotional conflict'.[20] (Since Coser makes so much depend on this point, we should complete his strangely selective picture by adding the entries he omitted: namely, 'class conflict', 'ideological conflict', 'conflict of interests' and 'legal conflict'. Of course, this whole business of the entries matters very little in itself either way. What matters, however, is that since the investigation of the fundamental social determinants of the criticized ideology is systematically avoided, the author is confined to thoroughly secondary or marginal issues which he then desperately tries to inflate into substantial ones with the help of revealing distortions.)

Having thus attained the level of mathematical certainty, Coser is now in a position to conclude that:

> While, by and large, the men of the earlier generation were concerned with *progressive change in the social order* Parsons is primarily interested in the *conservation of existing structures.*[21]

This is, of course, nothing but *word-fetish.* For even if we could find ninety-nine entries on 'social conflict' in the index of Parsons' *Essays,* instead of nine, this would not change in the least the substantive issues. It is the whole network of closely interlinked *concepts* which indicates the general orientation of a specific sociological approach, and not merely the choice of allegedly 'progressive' *words* (or terms). And one single treatment of 'social conflict' can be just as characteristically class-biassed as any number of it. (Besides: index entries are meant to indicate the problems discussed, and not the solutions given to them—and even that, more often than not, is compiled by someone other than the author.)

It is just not true that 'the men of the earlier generation' were concerned with 'progressive change in the social order'. For even if, for the sake of argument, we ignore the fact that generalities of this kind are next to meaningless, Coser's own examples of 'the men of the earlier generation'—Cooley and Weber—are far from substantiating the big claim that they were concerned with 'progressive change in the social order'. Change yes, but not in the *social order.* On the contrary, they were concerned with *'adaptive change'* which would not affect the fundamental structural characteristics of the established social order. As to Weber's definition of 'peace'—put by Weber himself in inverted commas—as 'nothing more than a change in the *form* of conflict' (which is a pendant of Clausewitz's paradoxical definition of *war* as 'a mere continuation of politics by *other means'),* it could not be further removed from a genuine concern with 'progressive change in the social order'. Already Hobbes knew that the capitalist social order is characterized by the 'war of all against all' and the Clausewitz-Weber-like variation on the same theme merely asserts the naturalness of this social order. As we have seen above, Weber not only did not advocate any 'progressive change in the social order' but, on the contrary, he contemptuously dismissed the advocacy of such a change with the label 'more and more utopian'.

If Talcott Parsons appears to be more conservative than 'the men of the earlier generation', this is certainly not because of the inherent 'progressiveness' of that generation. It is true to say, however, that significant changes have taken place in the 'existing structures' since the days of Cooley and Weber; changes that have been given due recognition in Parsons' writings. To put it in a nutshell, while Parsons' acknowledged master, Max Weber, theorized on the whole from the standpoint of the *individual capitalist,* in accordance with the given stage of development of capitalistic structures, Parsons to a large extent consciously adopted the standpoint of the *big corporations* and—at a far more advanced stage of the 'modern industrial society' than Weber could even dream about—he continued to idealize the structures of *corporate capitalism.* (His bible was, from the very beginning, A.A. Berle's and G. Means' book published in 1932: *The Modern Corporation and Private Property.*[22] We shall return to Parsons' theories in a moment.) Thus, although in different ways and under substantially different conditions, both Weber and Parsons were concerned with the 'conservation of existing structures'—and definitely not with 'progressive change in the social order'. That—given the ever-increasing dominance of the monopolistic structures of big corporations in capitalist society as a whole—there had to be a characteristic shift of emphasis as regards the status of 'conflict' in the theoretical scheme of Parsons vis-à-vis that of Weber, is obvious. The fact of such shift, however, should not be turned into a retrospective idealization of the 'men of the earlier generation' as champions of a 'progressive change in the social order'.

The main function of this idealization is the legitimation—with the help of respectable authorities of the past—of Coser's rather timid plea for 'institutionalized conflict' at the dying stages of the cold war. Since, however, the anachronistic appeal to the authority of 'the men of the earlier generation' ignores precisely those objective changes in the social body which constitute the foundations of Parsonian ideology, such an appeal can amount to no more than a rather Quixotic idealization of a mythical 'open society'. And since the latter, in its turn, is unashamedly identified with the existing structures of US capitalism, Coser's book becomes the romanticized counterpart of the more realistic Parsonian picture of society which our author naîvely believes he has criticized. The accent is now on a 'responsible integration' of conflict in an 'open society'. Needless to say, nothing could be more complementary to Parsons' theories than such a conception of 'The Functions of Social Conflict'. And the 'men of the earlier generation' in question are well suited to this exercise precisely because they never questioned the fundamentals of the established social order.

A further peculiarity of Coser's conception is that insofar as he takes notice of the changes that have occurred in American capitalist society since the days of Cooley and Weber, he does this in terms of Berle-Means-Parsons type mystifications like this:

> one reason for the apparently decreased combativeness of American management in labour struggles today, as compared with fifty years ago, can perhaps be found in a decreased belief in the absolute righteousness of maximizing profits both in the society at large and in the business community itself.[23]

Similarly, he accepts the Berle-Means-Parsons type of characterization of the big corporations ('the large business enterprises') in which, allegedly, 'profit-making becomes the sole obligation of a role *on behalf of the collectivity*'[24]. And these are by no means isolated examples. Thus, given the rather confused adoption of Parsons' general conceptual framework, it would be quite surprising if Coser's half-hearted critical intentions could bring to the fore some fundamental divergences in their respective approaches.

The key concepts of Coser's analysis all remain vaguely undefined. We are never told what would qualify as 'progressive change in the social order', nor indeed are we given any criteria for its alleged opposite, namely the 'conservation of existing structures'. (The adjective 'progressive' is meant to do the job in the first case, and 'conservation' in the second. At the same time, we learn nothing about the real nature of 'social order' and 'existing structures' about which Coser's claims are made.) Instead of sociological categories identified on the basis of a coherent account of the prevailing (capitalist) social structures, we are presented with mythical 'generations'. Ideological trends, equally, remain merely hinted at in terms of vague generalities, instead of being characterized with reference to their tangible socio-economic functions and setting—except, of course, when criticism is directed against Marxian theory. (See for instance the chapter on 'Ideology and Conflict' in which the specific examples given by the author all revolve around an anti-Marxist axis, and the whole analysis culminates in the assertion according to which 'The modern Marxian labour movement exemplifies the radicalizing effects of objectification of conflict. Strict ideological alignments are more likely to occur in rigid than in flexible adjustive structures.')[25]

The term 'capitalism' is conspicuous by its absence, and in place of an adequate socio-economical identification of special formations we get apologetic vagaries like this:

> The *rigidity of Europe's class structure* called forth the intensity of the class struggle and the *lack of such rigidity in America* favoured the pragmatism of the American labour movement.[26]

No wonder, therefore, that the whole analysis reaches its climax in the quasi-tautologies of the book's concluding lines which are worth quoting in their entirety:

> Our discussion of the distinction between types of conflict, and between types of social structures, leads us to conclude that conflict tends to be *dysfunctional* for a social structure in which there is no or insufficient toleration and *institutionalization of conflict.* The intensity of a conflict which threatens to 'tear apart', which attacks the *consensual basis* of a social system, is related to the *rigidity of the structure.* What threatens the *equilibrium* of such structure is not *conflict as such,* but the rigidity itself which permits hostilities to accumulate and to be channelled along one *major line of cleavage* once they break out in conflict.[27]

Thus, conflict is *'dysfunctional'* if it cannot be *'institutionalized'* (an exceedingly profound truth). And the conflict that cannot be institutionalized is not 'conflict as such' (if it were it would undermine the power of Coser's quasi-tautology) but 'cleavage': i.e. the degeneration of institutionalizable conflict, due to the 'rigidity' of non-flexible 'adjustive structures'. In other words, 'conflict', 'institutionalization' and 'consensus' all belong together as of necessity (i.e. as of tautological—not empirical—necessity), and they constitute the happily functional and tolerantly flexible world of American 'open society' while, on the other side, non-institutionalizable cleavage and lack of consensus are characteristic of the sadly 'dysfunctional' predicament of the rigid European (and now presumably also Asian, African, Latin American and possibly even Canadian) societies. (Not to mention the fact that in recent years 'major cleavages' also appeared in the paradigm-land of 'flexible adjustive structures'—namely in the United States of America itself.)

Thanks to this kind of approach, then, everything can be solved *by definition;* and if the first definition is not enough, some additional definition or redefinition can always help out (like 'not conflict as such' but 'one major line of cleavage'—which is nothing but a characteristically ideological way of describing 'class conflict' and 'class antagonism'). Coser's failure to identify in concrete terms the socio-economic determinants of Parsonian ideology—a failure inseparable from his adoption of the basic values inherent in that ideology with regard to the capitalist social order—carries with it categories entirely devoid of critical power. Thus, whatever his original intentions, Coser remains a captive in Parsons' universe of discourse. Ironically, he praises the 'positive functions' of social conflict and describes them as a *'stabilizing* and *integrative* function in *open societies* and loosely structured groups', as a *'check* against the breakdown of *consensus'.* as a *'readjustment* of norms and *power relations within groups',* as a 'help to *revitalize existent norms',* as a 'mechanism for the *maintenance* or continual *readjustment of the balance of power',* as a mechanism for producing a *'new equilibrium'* and for *'redressing conditions of disequilibrium',* as *'preventing* alliances along *one major line of cleavage',*[28] etc., etc. And all this in the name of an allegedly 'radical critique' of *Parsons'* conservatism.

7. THE PRACTICAL EMBEDDEDNESS OF SOCIAL THEORIES

This takes us to a methodologically vital question: the relationship between a proper identification of the *ideological determinants* of a particular conception, and an adequate *theoretical solution* of a complex of problems in whose formulation and articulation a specific ideology is directly or indirectly involved. This relationship is basically that of *reciprocity:* that is to say, on the one hand, the prevailing ideological determinants set marked limits to the required theoretical solutions which simply cannot be obtained without pushing back at the same time, to some extent at least, the original ideological boundaries; and on the other hand, genuine theoretical achievements significantly contribute to further overcoming the negative ideological limits of the whole complex. (It must be stressed, though, that we are not talking about a straightforward, linear development, since a number of additional factors must also be taken into account. We shall return to this problem a little later on.)

Let us now illustrate this point with a passage from Marx's *Capital.* In the chapter on 'Commodities', Marx praises Aristotle as 'the first to analyse so many forms, whether of thought, society, or nature, and amongst them also the form of value'. This is how he stresses Aristotle's great achievements and socio-historical limitations:

> In the first place, he clearly enunciates that the money-form of commodities is only the further development of the simple form of value—i.e., of the expression of the value of one commodity in some other commodity taken at random; for he says—
>
> 5 beds = 1 house
> is not to be distinguished from
> 5 beds = so much money.
>
> He further sees that the value-relation which gives rise to this expression makes it necessary that the house would quantitively be made the equal of the bed, and that, without such equalisation, these two clearly different things could not be compared with each other as commensurable quantities. 'Exchange', he says, 'cannot take place without equality, and equality not without commensurability.' Here, however, he comes to a stop, and gives up the further analysis of the form of value. 'It is, however, in reality impossible, that such unlike things can be commensurable'—i.e., qualitatively equal. Such an

> equalisation can only be something *foreign to their real nature,* consequently only *'a makeshift for practical purposes'.*
>
> Aristotle therefore, himself, tells us what barred the way to his further analysis; it was the *absence of any concept of value.* What is that equal something, that common substance, which admits of the value of the beds being expressed by a house? Such a thing, in truth, cannot exist, says Aristotle. And why not? Compared with the beds, the house does represent something equal to them, in so far as it represents what is really equal, both in the beds and the house. And that is—human labour.
>
> There was, however, an important fact which *prevented Aristotle from seeing* that, to attribute value to commodities, is merely a mode of expressing all labour as equal human labour, and consequently as labour of equal quality. Greek society was founded upon slavery, and had, therefore, for its natural basis, the *inequality of men and of their labour-powers.* The secret of the expression of value, namely, that all kinds of labour are equal and equivalent, because, and so far as they are human labour in general, cannot be deciphered, until the notion of *human equality* has already acquired the fixity of a popular prejudice. This, however, is possible only in a society in which the *great mass* of the produce of labour takes the form of commodities, in which, consequently, the *dominant relation* between man and man, is that of *owners of commodities.* The brilliancy of Aristotle's genius is shown by this alone, that he discovered, in the expression of the value of commodities, a *relation of equality.* The peculiar conditions of the society in which he lived, alone prevented him from discovering what, 'in truth', was at the bottom of this equality.[29]

Thus, the *practical* embeddedness of Aristotle's theory—its relationship to a socio-economic formation founded on slavery—'prevents Aristotle from seeing' the objective conditions of exchange and the crucial role of labour in this whole complex. This failure, however, is not merely an absence. Rather, the absence of an adequate concept of value leaves an enormous gap in the whole theoretical framework which must be filled *somehow.* And indeed it is filled by a mere *postulate:* the concept of a *'makeshift for practical purposes'* which claims to be a *solution* while in fact it is nothing but an *evasion of the problem* itself. For the question that remains unanswered—namely: 'how is it possible for a mere makeshift to function with dependable regularity?' or, in other words, what are the objective foundations of the practical transactions of exchange?—is not just avoided but, worse, it is hidden from sight through the pseudo-answer: 'makeshift' which declares the problem to be non-existent. As a result of the introduction of this pseudo-solution, the whole theoretical enquiry is 'derailed' and turned into a self-supporting ideology whose principal function is not the *solution* but the *concealment* (or 'dissolution') of those problems which cannot be reconciled with the practical functions of the Aristotelian conception as a whole.

Of course, this is not an isolated element in Aristotle's general outlook but an integral part of a closely interwoven network of concepts. There is no space here to attempt a detailed demonstration. The only point we can touch upon concerns the revealing role Aristotle assigns to the concept of 'nature' (and 'natural') in his social theory. With respect to commodity-exchange he declares that the equalization involved in such transactions is 'foreign to the *real nature*' of the goods exchanged; and also, that the use of a commodity (e.g. a sandal) in exchange is a use which cannot be described as a use 'in its *natural way*': that is, a way corresponding to the 'real nature' of the thing in question. Aristotle's fundamental criterion for the adequacy of social intercourse at all levels—and both in terms of institutions and modes of rule or government—is 'naturalness'. Thus, the family is 'the association established *by nature*'; the village community is 'the most *natural* form' of organization; the state is 'a creation of *nature*'. etc. Similarly, 'man is *by nature* a political animal', and 'a social instinct is implanted in all men *by nature*'. As to existing social hierarchies, they are described in terms of two inherently interconnected concepts: 'slavery *by nature*' and 'freedom *by nature*'. And, of course, radically different forms of rule are stipulated for the two classes: 'the rule over freemen' in contradistinction to 'the rule over slaves', in order to bring the modes of government in conformity with *nature's* prescription, as indicated by the concepts of 'slavery by nature' and 'freedom by nature'.

It is highly significant that in Aristotle's view the established mode of social intercourse, with all its institutions, is sanctioned 'by nature'. Furthermore, the claimed fact of being sanctioned by nature confers at the same time the seal of unqualified approval on the thing in question: 'for what each thing is when *fully developed,* we call its nature. . . . Besides, the final cause and end of a thing is *the best*'.[30] Thus, the ideological need prevails all along the line, declaring that what happens to exist—the family, the village community, the state, slavery, etc.—is 'fully developed' and is 'the best', in accordance with the socio-historically specific practical embeddedness of

Aristotle's system of concepts.

And yet, when it comes to the phenomenon of commodity exchange, Aristotle stops at the point of declaring it to be 'non-natural' and refuses to condemn it. This is all the more significant since he does not hesitate for a moment to voice his condemnation, in no uncertain fashion, of what he considers to be 'against nature' in other spheres. He perceives the *dual* character of commodity (its 'use-value' and its 'exchange value'—or in Aristotle's own terminology: its 'natural use' and its 'non-natural use'). Moreover, he perceives that this 'unnatural' commodity exchange as an institution is some sort of a *challenge* to the prevailing social order. (Indeed, its 'real nature'—or 'fully developed form'—is quite incompatible with that order.) Since, however, the socio-economic phenomenon of commodity exchange does not represent a fundamental contradiction to the existing social hierarchy—not only in view of its *marginal* weight in the overall system of production but also because its impact is fully compatible with the class *structure* of society, and affects only the *specific form* of the latter, unlike the challenge of those who question the given social order as such[31]—he both criticizes and accepts it. And he resolves the underlying contradiction by postulating the 'makeshift' character of the whole process. Consequently, Aristotle is able to maintain his conception as a whole—centred around his concept of 'nature'—and at the same time also integrating into it, without major inconsistency, a contradiction that has *practically* appeared on the social horizon.

Aristotle's example clearly demonstrates that the ideological factor cannot be simply 'weeded out' from social theory by pinpointing the guilty 'ideological concepts'. For all social theory worth its name is constituted on the basis of, and in response to, a specific historical situation that requires the solution of a given set of practical tasks. A coherent response, naturally, is conceivable only in terms of a closely interlinked system of—directly or indirectly practice-orientated—concepts. This means that the ideological determinants are, of necessity, at work at all levels, throughout the system in question, and any advance on a determinate ideological position would require the modification of the *entire* conceptual framework of that social theory.

It must be stressed that we are concerned here with a fundamental *dimension* of all social theory, and not with isolated (or isolable) elements. Aristotle's 'derailing' concepts are functional necessities in his system as a whole, despite the apparent inconsistency of the support he lends to 'non-natural' commodity exchange, as we have seen above. For it is precisely through the 'derailing' concept of a 'makeshift for practical purposes' that Aristotle succeeds again in reconstituting the internal coherence of his system. Thus, he cannot possibly have an adequate concept of 'value' not only because of powerful socio-historical reasons (cf. the points stressed by Marx) but also in view of inherently conceptual determinations: in that his whole system would be thoroughly undermined and ultimately blown to pieces by the introduction of an adequate concept of value.

It is in this latter sense that we may sharply contrast the correct identification of the socio-historical determinants—the *ideological dimension*—of social theory with the *theoretical solution* of some specific problems at stake. In Marx's case, it was not enough to put into relief the social roots of the Aristotelian approach. At the same time, Marx also had to provide a coherent theoretical solution to the problems that defeated Aristotle, given the socio-historical as well as conceptual limitations of his system as a whole. (Indeed, one might even argue that the Marxian solution of the problem of value was a necessary condition of his concrete identification of the ideological determinants of the Aristotelian system. Here we can see the world of difference between the illuminating specificity of a social analysis based on a proper theoretical solution of the complex issues involved, and the *aprioristic* application of abstract sociological categories which hides its theoretical failure under blanket labelling devices.)

The critique of ideology, no matter how correct in its general orientation, is no substitute for solving the problems themselves. Identifying the causes of a shipwreck is not the same thing as eliminating such causes from the path of future shipping. Any given complex of problems has its *inner logic,* which means that—given a certain number of conditions anticipated in the original formulation—the problems are amenable, *in principle,* to a correct solution. The ideological dimension embraces both the formulation of the problems themselves and the elaboration of particular solutions to them. For what is possible *in principle* can only be realized if certain obstacles are first removed. And this is the point at which we can clearly see the interpenetration of ideological and theoretical factors. Marx states in *Capital* that:

> All commodities are *non-use-values* for their owners, and *use-values* for their non-owners. Consequently, they *must* all change hands. But this change of hands is what constitutes their *exchange,* and the latter puts them in relation with each other as *values,* and realises them as values. Hence *commodities* must be realised as *values before* they can be realised as *use-values.*[32]

This statement contains in a nutshell one of the central problematics of *Capital* which can be 'deduced' from it, provided that all the relevant operative concepts are 'activated' in their proper Marxian sense. But, of course, the problem of value cannot be formulated in these terms—let alone fully developed in the course of subsequent elaborations—without adopting the Marxian socio-historical vantage-point. Marx's line of attack, in accordance with that specific vantage-point, carries with it its own principles of selection of the relevant data. Without such principles the 'inner logic' of the above quotation cannot be made manifest, and the whole picture—which is merely adumbrated in our quote—cannot be properly worked out in its details.

Marx's specific socio-historical vantage-point enables him to produce solutions to the intricate problems of value which have eluded all his predecessors, from Aristotle to the classics of bourgeois political economy. This, however, does not mean that the Marxian system stands 'above ideology'. For all social theory is necessarily conditioned by the socio-historical situation of the particular thinkers. And it is precisely the specific set of socio-historical determinations which constitutes the ideological dimension of all social theory, irrespective of the historical vantage-point of the particular thinkers.

Unlike in natural science, the key concepts of social theory—be they 'man' and 'nature', 'individual' and 'society', 'culture' and 'community', 'scarcity' and 'surplus', 'supply' and 'demand', 'want' and 'utility', 'capital' and 'labour', 'property' and 'profit', 'status' and 'class interest', 'conflict' and 'equilibrium', 'polarization' and 'mobility', 'change' and 'progress', 'alienation' and 'revolution', etc., etc.—all remain *systematically argued and contested* concepts. Moreover, given the dynamic interrelationship of all social phenomena, no matter which particular points are in focus at any given time in any particular field of social enquiry, what is actually at stake is always the complex interrelationship between the specific point under scrutiny and the constantly changing totality of social intercourse. (In other words, the concepts of social theory are always 'totalizing' concepts, even when they appear in a grossly distorted form through the prisms of, say, 'logical atomism', 'methodological individualism', and the like. This 'totalizing' character, by the way, helps to explain why the fundamental concepts of social theory remain systematically contested concepts.) Furthermore, both the principles which guide the delineation of a specific field of enquiry from the complex totality of social phenomena, and those which determine the selection of a limited set of relevant data out of a virtually countless number of data available for the chosen range of problems, require their justification in terms of the entire system of a particular thinker as set against alternative systems of the past and the present. (The dangers of circularity in this connection are self-evident. Evasion of the task of justifying the fundamental principles and assumptions of a given system makes many a social scientist succumb to this danger.)[33] And again, the objects themselves of social theory—though widely differing as to their *relative time scale*—are all socio-historically specific and limited: in a sense they are all *'necessarily disappearing' objects.* (The historical necessity manifest in them is, in Marx's words, *'eine verschwindende Notwendigkeit':* a 'disappearing necessity'.) These are some of the principal reasons why all social theory is socio-historically conditioned both in its objects and in the specific mode of attack adopted by the particular thinkers in their attempts to get to grips with the problems of their age.

Stressing these points does not mean in the least that we are advocating a *relativistic* interpretation of ideology. The fact that any given set of practical problems is necessarily tied to a specific socio-historical situation does not prejudice at all the question as to which of a number of alternative solutions can claim for itself a higher degree of objectivity.

To defeat relativism it is vitally important to bear in mind all the principal constituents of this complex relationship, and not just *one* of them, as it happens in 'vulgar Marxism' and 'vulgar sociologism' alike—including much of so-called 'sociology of knowledge'—which one-sidedly concentrate on the question of social standpoint. This is why we insisted on the close interrelationship of three main factors:

(1) that a particular complex of problems appears *objectively-practically* on the social horizon, irrespective of the thinker's ability or failure to solve the given set of problems within the confines of his system (cf. Aristotle);

(2) the *inner logic* of the problematic in question which cannot be divorced from the *objective logic* of its practical foundations. (Cf. Marx's definition of the categories of thought as *'Daseinsformen'*—'forms of being'—which are subject to the dynamic laws of socio-historical development. Again, Aristotle's *theoretically-conceptually,* not just socially, limited grasp of the problem of value is a graphic example.)

(3) the reciprocal *interpenetration* of the theoretical and ideological factors in a particular system, and thus the importance of a higher socio-historical vantage-point in overcoming the limitations of previous systems. (This means that the problems and contradictions of particular systems must be identified and solved *theoretically,* in terms of their *inner logic,* in addition to correctly assessing the *ideological determinants* of the systems in question.) By contrast, a one-sided insistence on the determining role of the social standpoint carries with it not only crude mechanistic hypotheses but also a total inability to tackle such important issues as the 'change of standpoint'. (That is the question: how is it possible for a thinker—like Marx, for instance—to escape the narrow limits of his original class belonging.) For if our explanatory hypothesis for the specific characteristics of a particular social theory is the thinker's socio-economic standpoint *in and by itself,* there can be no reason for entertaining even the possibility of a change in class allegiance, except as a completely *gratuitous and irrational* act of 'horrid conversion'[34]—which is of course no explanation whatsoever. Nor can there be any rational justification for preferring one theory—the articulation of one specific standpoint—to another.

Karl Mannheim is a highly revealing case in this respect. He tries to overcome the mechanistic determinism and relativism of his approach by introducing the notion of the 'free-floating intelligentsia' *(freischwebende Intelligenz)* which is supposed to be the bearer of the adequate (non-relativistic) standpoint in virtue of the claimed 'empirical fact' that 'it subsumes in itself *all* those interests with which social life is permeated'[35] Of course, this 'empirical fact' is nothing but a *fictitious postulate,* 'established' by further postulates as, for instance, the one according to which the intellectual is 'the *predestined* advocate of the *intellectual interests* of the whole'.[36] (Suddenly 'all the interests of social life' have become 'the intellectual interests of the whole' for which the intellectual must be eminently suited, of course, by definition.) And if we wonder, why do 'free-floating intellectuals' associate themselves with the proletariat, for instance, we are offered a splendidly tautological 'explanation': 'This *ability* to attach themselves to classes to which they originally did not belong, was *possible* for intellectuals because they *could* adapt themselves to any viewpoint.'[37] Now we know.

The trouble with this approach is that it is made of empty postulates and assumptions within the structural framework of tautological cross-references. Since the key category—the 'free-floating intelligentsia'—is completely devoid of empirical foundations, the argument must be bolstered up at all its stages with assumptions leading to further assumptions and to mere postulates tautologically misrepresented as 'sociological facts' (or 'empirical facts'). Furthermore, even if, for the sake of argument, we assume that the 'free-floating intelligentsia subsumes in itself all those interests with which social life is permeated', this in itself means nothing whatsoever as regards the ways in which conflicting social interests are fought out and resolved *in reality.* And in fact a few paragraphs further on we are treated to yet another postulate as a 'solution': 'Their [the intellectuals'] *function* is to penetrate into the ranks of the *conflicting parties* in order to *compel them to accept their demands'.*[38] The 'function' in question is real enough. But not as an empirical fact 'amply shown' in history, as claimed (no example is given though, despite the 'ampleness'). It is very real and necessary, however, in Mannheim's framework of discourse, in that it fills an enormous gap in his argument and lends a semblance of reality to his key category.

The ideological function of Mannheim's 'freischwebende Intelligenz' which is supposed to be able to 'transform the conflict of interests into the conflict of ideas',[39] is obvious enough. What remains to be indicated are the fundamental theoretical and methodological characteristics of Mannheim's structure of argument as related to our problems. We have already seen how postulates follow assumptions in the general framework of tautological cross-references and definitional assumptions as well as postulates misrepresented as sociological facts. As to his key category: the 'free-floating intelligentsia' with its allegedly *'total orientation'*,[40] it is not too difficult to recognize its derivation from Lukács' concept of the '*standpoint of totality*'.[41] The basic difference is, however, that while in Lukács 'the standpoint of totality' is stressed as a crucial *methodological principle,* Mannheim turns it into a *fictitious sociological entity.* And while the concept of 'the standpoint of totality' is and remains a vital methodological principle of social science, irrespective of the particular use to which Lukács puts it in *History and Class Consciousness,* its apologistically-orientated conversion into the 'total orientation' of the 'free-floating intelligentsia' as the absolute embodiment and reconciliation of all actual social relativism and conflict, is a totally incoherent concept. (But of course in claiming empirical validity for categories which have only methodological status, Mannheim is neither the first nor the last in the field of social theory. Thus the importance of the problem goes well beyond the critique of his particular approach.)

In conclusion to this section we have to stress again that the identification of the ideological determinants of a specific social theory, however correct, is no explanation and solution on its own. Theoretical problems arise on the basis of objective social determinations which are to a greater or lesser extent 'visible' from a multiplicity of social standpoints. And since the various theoretical problematics have their inner logic, and since the totalizing character of social theory requires comprehensive solutions to the problems at stake, it is impossible to conceive the theoretical end-result simply in terms of strict sociological determination without grossly violating the actual sets of interrelationships. For while the thinker's specific socio-historical standpoint tends to determine this whole complex in accordance with the interests of the group to which he sociologically belongs, the inner logic of the various problematics as related to their practical foundations, and the methodological and theoretical conditions of the framework of social theory within which he attacks his task, tend to reveal the problematic features—indeed even the contradictions—of solutions too narrowly tied to that social group. Whatever his socio-historical limitations, the particular thinker—if he is a man of significance and not a mere apologist—will be induced to go beyond the immediate sociological determinations, to the point of exposing the *problematic* features of certain social relationships (cf. Aristotle's recognition of the 'non-natural' character of commodity exchange), or at a more advanced historical stage, to pinpoint the *contradictions* involved in them, even if he is incapable of supplying an adequate solution by himself (cf. Ricardo's account of the contradictions in the theory of value as inherited from his predecessors and further developed by him). Indeed, the perception of some major contradictions may very well induce some thinkers—like Marx and Engels, for example—to look for solutions in a direction that necessarily requires a change in social standpoint and class allegiance. This does not mean, of course, that the determinations of such a change arise from within theory itself. They originate on the basis of an immensely complex social practice of which the *inner logic* of theoretical problematics deeply rooted in their ontological foundations—i.e. coherent sets of socio-historically specific *'Daseinsformen'* as related to the given configuration of social *'Dasein'*—is a vital aspect. Our plea here, in opposition to some distorting approaches, was not in favour of a different type of theoretical one-sidedness but, on the contrary, for stressing the importance of recognizing and investigating in depth the entire complexity of factors which constitute these dialectical interrelationships.

8. THE SOCIAL STANDPOINT OF KEYNESIAN IDEOLOGY

Marx makes the point in his *Grundrisse* that 'only when the self-criticism of bourgeois society had begun, was bourgeois economy able to understand the feudal, ancient and oriental economies.'[42] The methodological importance of this observation for social science is quite fundamental. For if the comprehension of feudal, ancient and oriental economies requires a self-critical attitude towards bourgeois society, it is easy to see the vital necessity of a radically critical stance in adequately grasping and demonstrating the contradictions and inner laws of development of the social formation to which the social scientist himself belongs.

The consequences of failure in this respect are far-reaching. In bourgeois society 'capital is the economic power that dominates everything',[43] and an uncritical attitude toward such all-embracing power inevitably results in theoretical systems dominated by the mystifications of bourgeois *Dasein,* whatever the subjective intentions of particular thinkers with regard to some partial manifestations of that power. A graphic example is J. M. Keynes. He makes no bones about fully identifying himself with the standpoint of capital:

> 'How can I adopt a creed which, preferring the mud to the fish, exalts the *boorish proletariat* above the bourgeois and the intelligentsia who, with whatever faults, are the quality in life and surely carry the seeds of all human advancement? Even if we need a religion, how can we find it in the *turbid rubbish of the Red bookshops?* It is hard for an educated, decent, intelligent son of Western Europe to find his ideals here, unless he has first suffered some *strange and horrid process of conversion* which has changed all his values.'[44]
>
> 'When it comes to the *class struggle* as such, my local and personal patriotisms, like those of everyone else, except certain unpleasant zealous ones, are attached to my own surroundings. I can be influenced by what seems to me to be justice and good sense; but *the class war will find me on the side of the educated bourgeoisie.*'[45]

After such an identification with the bourgeoisie, it is not surprising to find that Keynes has to resort to mawkish sermonizing when he writes about what displeases him in capitalism: 'For at least another hundred years we must pretend to ourselves and to everyone else that fair is foul and foul is fair; for foul is *useful* and fair is not.'[46] The presumed *fatality* of the rule of 'usefulness' is opposed by an empty 'ought'; a moral indignation rendered completely impotent by associating 'foul' with 'useful'—by 'useful' meaning 'marketable' or 'profitable'; a typical mystification which hides the fact that in commodity-society *exchange-value* usurps the place of human *use-value* in that the production of *goods* is replaced by the production of *marketable commodities*—and by postulating the unavoidability of this association.

Similarly, in another work Keynes declares: 'One begins to wonder whether the material advantages of keeping *business* and *religion* in different compartments are sufficient to balance the moral disadvantages.'[47] As if the matter could be resolved through some kind of morally enlightened legislation—an idea *categorically* contradicted by Keynes' own account of socio-economic development which can only acknowledge—in the spirit of crude, mechanical determinism—the role of 'science and compound interest'. Thus, the moralizing question remains an idle wondering whether 'Moral Conscience' and 'Human Nature' can safely carry on their existence in separate universes: the former in the 'noumenal' world of metaphysical transcendentalism, and the latter in 'this phenomenal world of ours'.

The unmediated *dualism* of this reasoning is a *necessary* one. Socio-economic development must be explained as a fatality of Nature ('usefulness', 'the law of compound interest', 'productive techniques', etc.), while the prevailing values are considered separately, as 'intrinsic values'. The *practical intermediary* link between 'facts' (or 'techniques') and 'values'—namely, the established *social relations of production*—must remain unmentioned (and thus the conceptual structure must be a rigidly dualistic one) because pointing at them would reveal the socio-historical specificity (i.e. the 'disappearing necessity') of the bourgeois relations of production. Understandably, therefore, any departure from the bourgeois order must be explained in terms of the mysteries of religion. We have quoted above Keynes' remarks about the 'strange and horrid conversion of the zealous ones' who detach themselves from the rationality, naturalness, etc. of the perspectives of those who are 'the quality in life and carry the seeds of all human advancement'. The same structure of argument is in evidence in his approach to social trends he opposes:

> I feel confident of one conclusion—that if Communism achieves a certain success, it will achieve it, not as an improved *economic technique*, but as a *religion*... I do not think that it contains, or is likely to contain, any piece of *useful economic technique* which we could not apply, *if we choose*, with equal or greater success in a society which retained all the marks, I will not say of nineteenth century

individualistic capitalism, but of British bourgeois ideals.[48]

Thus, the issue can be 'confidently' prejudged—as early as 1925, when these lines first appeared—by begging the question. For if an alternative 'economic technique' cannot be used by bourgeois economics then it is not a 'useful economic technique' but an element of religion. At the same time, the historical—i.e. changeable—character of the capitalist social relations of production can be conveniently misrepresented as the system of 'useful economic techniques' which is, of course, its own justification. What disappears in this juxtaposition of 'fact and value', 'business and religion', 'technique and ideal', 'technique and religion', etc., is precisely the vital intermediary of the *social relations of production.* (We can note here the ideological function of conflating socio-historically specific 'structure' into timeless 'function'.)

'Technique as such' is, of course, compatible with different social systems of production. However, in so far as economic or productive techniques are embedded in a specific structure of social relationships—and to a greater or lesser extent they always are—they are not compatible with a rival system of production. This is why Keynes, significantly, has to add to his claim about the alleged neutrality of 'technique' two blatant escape clauses: '*useful* economic techniques' and '*if we choose* to apply them.'

This kind of reasoning enables all those who argue from the standpoint of capital to represent the crucial value-commitment, one's self-identification with the established social relations of production, as a purely rational and 'neutral' approval of 'useful economic techniques' (or of theories based on 'scientific facts,' 'descriptive models', 'pragmatic rules', 'sociological facts', 'empirical observations', etc., etc.) and to dismiss all rival approaches—especially those which dare to focus attention on the conspicuously unmentioned factor of the social relations of production—as 'zeal', 'religion', 'strange and horrid conversion', 'turbid rubbish of the Red bookshops', 'ideology', and the like.

9. THE IDEOLOGY OF PARSONIAN 'GENERAL THEORY'

The case of Talcott Parsons is equally significant, although in a rather different way, in that, unlike Keynes, he refrains from adopting an openly moralizing posture. His self-identification with the standpoint of capital (as we have seen earlier: with that of corporate capitalism) is as complete as his pretensions are to provide a 'universal theory of action'. Since, however, (strictly in the interest of 'universality', of course) the massive predominance of capitalist partiality must be hidden beneath thick layers of elaborately mystifying verbiage, the theoretical outcome of Parsons' efforts is, accordingly, a 'structural-functional analysis' of the 'universal structures' of bourgeois reification and of the apologetically defined self-perpetuating 'functions' of life confined 'within the action frame of reference' of alienated commodity society.

It would take up a great deal of space to attempt a detailed critique of Parsons' system, since cutting through the thick crust of bewildering verbiage to the core of his generic assertions would require the multiplication of the sort of 'translations' C. Wright Mills so admirably provided in *The Sociological Imagination*[49] on a smaller scale. But limitations of space compel us to concentrate, instead, on a few central points.

As C. Wright Mills rightly stresses, 'Grand theory is drunk on syntax, blind to semantics.... The grand theorists are so preoccupied by syntactic meanings and so unimaginative about semantic references, they are so rigidly confined to such high levels of abstraction that the 'typologies' they make up—and the work they do to make them up—seem more often an arid game of Concepts than an effort to define systematically—which is to say, in a clear and orderly way—the problems at hand, and to guide our efforts to solve them.'[50] To say, however, that 'In *The Social System* Parsons has not been able to get down to the work of social science because he is possessed by the idea that the one model of social order he has constructed is some kind of universal model; because, in fact, he has fetishised his Concepts'[51] is no explanation. Whether one single model, or one of a plurality of models, is rather beside the point. For if the model in question is constructed in the state of 'syntactic drunkenness' coupled with 'blindness to semantics', that sort of a model is useless both on its own and in the company of many. Furthermore, the coordination and unification of partial models in a comprehensive framework—though, of course, an 'open' one, both historically and structurally[52]—is a vital methodological requirement of all systems of social theory.

Parsons fetishises his concepts not because 'he is possessed by the idea' of having constructed a universal model—an idealistic suggestion—but because he *takes for granted* the fetishisms and reifications (the given stage of bourgeois *Dasein)* which constitute the practical foundations of his theoretical models. Thus, what Parsons is to be faulted on is not the—however illusory—ideas he might have about his own achievements, but the *apologetic nature* of the achievements themselves.

We may illustrate this with some of Parsons' key concepts as they appear in *Economy and Society*[53]: a work in which Parsons' customary lack of intelligibility is perhaps least in evidence. Unfortunately, it is necessary to start with a long quotation. But we can say in its favour that it shows, rather graphically, the method through which the socio-historically specific features of capitalist partiality are inflated into the sublime apologetic platitudes of the Parsonian 'general theory of social systems within the "action" frame of reference'. This is how the quotation goes:

> Let us summarize the model for institutional change as a series of logical steps in a cycle of change: (1) The process starts with a combination of 'dissatisfaction' with the productive achievements of the economy or its relevant sectors and a sense of 'opportunity' in terms of the potential availability of adequate resources to reach a higher level of productivity. (2) There appear symptoms of disturbance in the form of 'unjustified' negative emotional reactions and 'unrealistic' aspirations on the part of various elements in the population. (3) A covert process of handling these tensions and mobilizing motivational resources for new attempts to realize the implications of the existing value pattern takes place. (4) Supportive tolerance of the resulting proliferation of 'new ideas', without imposing specific responsibility for their implementation and for 'taking the consequences', is found in important quarters. (5) Positive attempts are made to reach specification of the new ideas which will become the objects of commitments by entrepreneurs. (6) 'Responsible' implementation of innovations is carried out by persons or collectivities assuming the role of entrepreneurs, either rewarded by entrepreneurial profit or punished by financial failure, depending on

consumers' acceptance or rejection of the innovations. (7) The gains resulting from the innovation and consolidated by their acceptance as part of the standard of living and their incorporation into the routine functions of production. In this final phase the new 'way of doing things' becomes institutionalized as part of the structure of the economy.

We suggest the following 'translation' into the terms of the separation of ownership and management in the corporate structure of the American economy; (1) There was diffuse dissatisfaction of responsible elements in the business world with the way the 'owner controlled' corporate system was working from the point of view of maximization of productivity, and an indirect feeling that the supply of capital was not wholly dependent on maintaining the status quo. (2) Symptoms of disturbance appeared; e.g., the 'technological' view of the destructive consequences of business (owner-dominated Veblen) machinations as interfering with 'efficiency': utopian exaggerations of the results to be obtained from abandoning 'business' altogether and becoming purely 'technological'. (3) Permissive-supportive attitudes toward the objections to the 'captain of industry' system, and toward the oppposite utopianism were found. (4) The 'new enterprise' of organizers of the corporate world, e.g., US Steel after Carnegie-Morgan: General Motors after Durant and Standard Oil after Rockefeller, gains in relative prominence. (5) New financial practices appear, tending to 'shake free' from the older family capitalistic control; e.g., free sale of securities to the general public; minority control practices, the holding company, etc. At the same time, there is rapid technological and organizational development of the firm into a kind of 'empire' in itself. (6) A new wave of profits follows, showing that the system can operate under the new conditions. For example, earnings of the post-Rockefeller Standard Oil Companies have been much greater than the Rockefeller fortune. (7) The new position is consolidated by its routinization, especially by the great output of new products to a high-wage consuming public: the 'new economy' has become independent both of the previous 'exploitation of labour' and the previous 'capitalistic control'.

There is thus in broad terms an encouragingly close fit between the outline of our theoretical model and the empirical facts of one recent change in the structure of the American economy. Of course, this is a mere starting-point for more intensive exploration of this and other cases.[54]

There is no space here to take this passage to as many pieces as we should. Let us only have a brief look at some of its most characteristic features.

It is interesting to note that exactly *seven* little boxes make up the Parsonian 'series of *logical* steps' and that the claimed 'empirical facts' readily fit into *exactly* seven little boxes. Moreover, as we are told in a footnote on page 271; 'The number and order of steps involved in this process corresponds with that postulated by Parsons and Bales in their paradigm of a cycle of internalization of a value pattern in the process of socialization (cf. *Family, Socialization, and Interaction Process,* Ch. VII). We feel that this correspondence is not fortuitous, but derives from certain general conditions and characteristics of the process of structural change in systems of action.' What an 'elegance'! What an 'economy'. The only remaining difficulty is that the seven little boxes are filled up to such a logico-empirical perfection that there can be no room in them for such factors as 'war', 'imperialism', 'colonial exploitation', 'class antagonism', 'economic crisis', etc., etc., which might otherwise perhaps have helped to explain the changes that have taken place 'in the corporate structure of American economy'.

The Parsonian account of the 'cycle of change' is based on the replacement of *objective* structural factors by mystifying *subjective* categories like 'negative emotional reactions', 'entrepreneurial attitudes', 'indirect feelings' (whatever they might be), 'utopianism and opposite utopianism',[55] and the like. Also, from time to time Parsons congratulates himself on how closely his paradigms and 'series of logical steps' *fit* the world of corporate capitalism—although he does not put it in quite this way (he calls it the 'close fit between our theoretical model and the empirical facts' etc.), and does not offer an explanation other than the implied perfection of his theoretical models. The plain truth, however, is a little more prosaic than that. The 'facts' fit his models because the latter are abstract 'translations' of the 'empirical facts' of corporate capitalism *as seen from the standpoint of monopoly capital.* This is why the representation of the available facts must be so revealingly *selective.* This is why he can 'retranslate' with such an ease the 'logical steps' of his 'paradigm' into the empirical sequences of—highly selective—events and 'structural changes'. (Though, of course, as a noble idealist he is convinced that his 'paradigms' come first and the 'empirical facts' oblige thereafter.) And this is why the promised 'more intensive exploration of this and other cases' never goes beyond the mere repetition of the inflated platitudes of Parsonian apologetics.

By way of demonstration, let us deal briefly with three closely interrelated points. (1) The total absence of *causal explanations* at key points of the analysis. The particular members of the sequence just *'appear', 'are found',* etc.—as if they came out of a large top-hat. Indeed, the basic apologetic function of the Parsonian 'series of logical steps' is to create the semblance of 'inner necessity' (better: 'logical necessity') for a state of affairs—a 'mere contingency' if there ever was one—which is simply taken for granted, ('as simply given'), is assigned the status of absolute necessity, and is projected into the 'paradigm' which in turn readily lends itself to being retranslated into the pseudo-empirical sequence of pseudo-causality. *Why* and *how* should 'dissatisfaction', 'disturbances', 'new ideas', 'innovations', 'new financial practices', etc. just 'appear'; why should the whole process be happily consummated in a 'new wave of profits', or for that matter why should the phenomenon of profit be associated with a *wave* character; and why should the pattern underlying the whole process be a *cyclic* one, postulating thus the necessary reproduction of the established relations of production in any 'new equilibrium', all these questions can find no place in the land of Parsons' paradigm. After all, the whole point of this 'paradigm' is to rule such questions—together with all their possible practical implications—*a priori* out of court.

(2) In a world founded on the 'structures' of Parsonian pseudo-causality anything goes, of course. And in fact, one of the sub-postulates of the general model is 'consumer sovereignty'. (It figures prominently in exactly these terms on page 160 and elsewhere in the book.) Accordingly, we are told that the whole process depends on '*consumers' acceptance or rejection* of the innovations'. Yet, the next—and last—'logical step' of the paradigmatic tale speaks only of '*acceptance*': the possibility of 'consumers' *rejection*' has magically disappeared from the picture. But this is as it should be—except for the claim that institutionalized acceptance is the *'final'* stage of a formerly fully open system of genuine alternatives. As a matter of fact, the latter cannot be the case even on Parsons' own showing. For if *acceptance* as such is the *necessary* condition of the 'final phase'—in that lack of acceptance would completely undermine and destroy the whole cyclic paradigm of our author, with who knows what cataclysmic consequences for his 'empirical facts'—then the possibility of a *rejection* at the preceding stage must be a completely *empty* notion: in other words a paradigmatic *fiction.* What makes the idea of 'consumer sovereignty'—'acceptance or rejection'—a mere resounding fiction is the very nature of the self-reproducing cyclic *system itself* which is quite unthinkable—as Parsons himself admits in the end—without the *institutionalization of acceptance* and, by implication, without the effective nullification of its alternative. And since *institutionalized acceptance*—the prosaic truth of high-sounding 'consumer sovereignty'—is a *structural necessity* of the

system itself (again, we have Parsons' own admission for this), the question of a *genuine alternative* (i.e. 'rejection' as a meaningful term) concerns the *system as such,* and not the possibility of isolated partial choices well within the system's boundaries. If, however, the question of genuine alternatives concerns the structure of the system *within* which the individual consumer—Parsons' 'sovereign'—is hopelessly trapped, effective rejection is conceivable only from *outside:* a possibility *a priori* ruled out by the self-perpetuatingly 'equilibrating' functionality of the Parsonian system. And furthermore, if the *individual subject* is necessarily trapped by the structure of institutionalized acceptance within which he is situated, a genuine alternative to the system necessarily requires both a *collective subject* and a subject whose 'sovereignty' is not confined to the sphere of mere *consumption.* But precisely for these reasons Parsons has to operate with the categories of subjective mystification, postulating the (fictitious) sovereignty of the individual consumer as an 'empirical fact', and claiming to *derive* from it the 'final phase of institutional acceptance' which he had in fact taken all the time *for granted:* indeed he has assumed it from the very beginning as the necessary climax—the identical omega and alpha—of his 'cycle of structural change'. The 'logical steps' of Parsons' deductions and derivations are thus gross violations of logic. As we can see, however, the objectionable points are not simply logical 'errors' and 'confusions'—although the substitution of subjective for objective factors and of individual for collective spheres of action is confusing enough—but necessary requirements of a theoretical system structured as a reified apologetics of the established relations of production.

(3) Thanks to the assumed framework of pseudo-causality, and thanks to the systematic confusion of subjective and objective factors as well as of individual and collective spheres of action, as a final consummation of Parsons' 'empirical translation' we are presented with these lines: *' "the new economy" has become independent both of the previous "exploitation of labour" and the previous "capitalistic control".'* The post-capitalist Millennium ('equilibrium') has thus arrived and it is here to stay. Our irresistible impulse to rejoicing is restrained only by the disturbing inverted commas. First, we become slightly anxious when we think that the 'new economy' is perhaps not a *new economy* after all, for it is put into inverted commas. And second, we are rather surprised to learn that the *'new*

economy' has become independent both of the previous ' "exploitation of labour" ' and of the previous ' "capitalistic control" ': we were never told before that it was *dependent* on them, let alone about how the miraculous change was so suddenly accomplished. The potentially explosive problems strangely 'appear' only at the point of their magic disappearance from the equilibrated picture. Besides, 'capitalism'—not to mention 'exploitation of labour'—figure in the book in inverted commas: they do not seem to have a proper ontological status. (Obviously, they are inventions of a certain Karl Marx who is 'refuted' in several sections of this learned book on the lines adopted by the passage we are talking about.) Which all adds up, unfortunately, to a not-so-reassuring proposition about the nature of Parsons' post-capitalist Millennium. Namely that the not-so-new-economy is 'independent' only of the unreal entities in inverted commas; it has the real stuff—*exploitation of labour and capitalistic control*—in greater abundance than ever before. Which in plain English simply means that at the end of our long and arduous logico-empirical journey we are back to square one in Parsons' truly circular *'cycle* of structural change.'[56]

Still, the journey itself was by no means a wholly wasted one. For we are now able to understand clearly that the 'striking fact' which Parsons could only report with self-admiring awe is not so striking, after all. 'The striking fact, in sum, is the correspondence—category for category—between the established economic classifications of the factors of production and the shares of income and a classification of the input-output categories of social systems which was arrived at in work on the level of general theory independently, without the economic categories in mind at all.'[57] But, of course, there was no need whatsoever to keep 'the economic categories in mind' in the course of elaborating the models of Systems Analysis: as Parsons himself says elsewhere, the models of 'modern' economists and General Theorists 'do not compete in the same methodological race',[58] and therefore they may be considered to be independent in this respect *from one another*. What the originator of the General Theory had to keep in mind though—and he did it in fact, as we have abundantly seen—was not 'the established economic *classifications'* but the *established relations of production* from which social theorists of all kinds are far from being independent. It is the latter correlation—the shared adoption of the standpoint of capital—which explains the profound structural affinity between the categories and models of apologetic economists and General Theorists. For in the non-methodological race involving the capitalist and the socialist perspectives of social control they compete side by side, against Marx's 'obsolete economic textbook' which they claim to be 'not only scientifically erroneous but without interest or application for the modern world.'[59]

The innermost structure of apologetic General Theory *necessarily* prevents it from realizing the task so frequently and loudly announced: namely the 'intensive exploration' of socio-economic reality—both past and present—in order to test the empirical validity of its models. All it is capable of doing is merely forcing social phenomena into the Procrustean bed of its own models and paradigms based on the structural features of corporate capitalism. (Particularly blatant examples of this way of proceeding are provided by the analyses of 'economic rationality'[60] and of the 'embryonic market structure'[61] of primitive societies in the book we discussed.) This is why in the end General Theory consummates itself as methodology for the sake of methodology, even when it assumes the guise of pseudo-empirical 'factuality'. The promised *Odyssey* of 'intensive explorations' is, thus, well beyond the powers of this General Theory. Its practitioners, it seems—with unending methodological invocations on their lips—are destined to remain forever locked into the prefabricated Trojan horse of the paradigmatic Parsonsiliad.

10. SOCIAL STRUCTURE AND SOCIAL THEORY

On the basis of what we have seen so far it seems to me that the ideologically most sensitive area of social science is the network of *fundamental principles and assumptions* within which the various sets of *particular theoretical propositions*—in a sense 'operational deductions'—are worked out. The former are *necessarily* linked—even if often unconsciously—to the *basic structural characteristics* of the given *socio-economic formation* which ultimately determine the categories, models, principles, methodological guidelines and inherent problematics—in short: the structure—of the specific fields of enquiry at any particular time in history. (This is why there can be such a thing as 'A Critique of Political Economy', and not just a critique of this or that particular tenet of a particular economist. But, of course, 'Political Economy' here stands for a socio-historically determinate type of theory, as contrasted with a generic 'discipline' whose subject matter would be the 'economic life of the society'. For it is only at a determinate time in history that the study of the metabolism between man and nature becomes the subject matter of *Political Economy.)*

The *specific* ideological character of a particular social theory is determined by the way in which the fundamental structural characteristics of the given social formation are articulated in it, from a particular social standpoint, in the form of some basic theoretical principles and assumptions (or premises) which constitute the points of departure, as well as the general framework of orientation of the particular lines of enquiry. (E.g. taking for granted 'Private Property', 'The Market', 'Exchange', 'The Division of Labour', etc.—from Adam Smith's 'propensity to exchange and barter' to present-day theorists who assume the structure and institutions of capitalist society 'as simply given'. Similarly with 'The State', 'The Family', 'Capital', 'Management', 'Banking', 'Money', 'Consumer Sovereignty', 'The Contract', 'Parliament', 'The Government', etc., etc. Equally, the necessary consequences for the whole structure of a theory of adopting as its key concepts 'social equilibrium', 'institutionalization' and 'socialization'.) Consequently, a basic criterion for assessing the scientific claims of a particular social theory must be its ability or failure to *submit to a constant critical evaluation and revaluation of its own fundamental principles and assumptions.* In this respect a close examination of what is *excluded* by a certain line of enquiry—whether on the grounds that 'it is an insoluble problem for the human reason', or that the dichotomy between 'facts' and 'values' *a priori* assigns the debated phenomenon to the realm of 'religion' and 'metaphysics', or that its discussion is incompatible with 'the proper methodological procedures', or again that it 'cannot be quantified' and 'reduced' into the categories adopted by a particular approach, etc., etc.—is of a paramount importance. Similarly, the never fulfilled promises, which are often unfulfillable *in principle* within the confines of the adopted approach (e.g. the ever-extended 'temporary' postponement of determinate tasks whose examination has a vital bearing on the assumptions and claims of the whole case: as, for instance, the 'temporary' neglect of the problems of large and comprehensive structures by the champions of 'small-group research'; or, again, the unfulfilled promises of General Theory discussed above) are highly revealing about the necessary structural limitations of certain types of social theory.

In social theory, it goes without saying, the 'übergreifendes Moment' (the factor of overriding importance) for making the necessary revaluations and readjustments is the prevailing socio-historical situation itself and the well-defined position of a particular thinker within it. Problems which must remain a complete mystery from a certain angle often turn out to be very simple indeed when approached from a social standpoint immune to the negative practical implications of the required theoretical solution. In this sense the adoption of the *historically* more advanced social standpoint is of a vital importance for social theory. It must be stressed, however, that a *historically* more advanced social standpoint is no guarantee *in itself* of the solution of the problems at stake. Nor is it justifiable to suggest, as many vulgarizers do, that a historically retrograde social standpoint is *ipso facto* the end of *all* scientific advance. The practically-critical attitude required for significant scientific achievements in the field of social theory, may be not only *compatible* with the interests of capital at some juncture but even *necessary* for its continued survival. Given the complex dialectics of social confrontation, the stakes are never summarily 'everything or nothing' in this sphere. This is why it becomes possible for a Keynes in the challenging circumstances of the General Crisis and its aftermath, to produce some *partial* scientific results *within* the boundaries of his overall approach, notwithstanding his *total* identification with the standpoint of capital as we have seen above. As a *general* theory and 'refutation' of the Marxian approach, his system is devoid of other than purely apologetic foundation. It represents, nevertheless, a genuine theoretical advance in the understanding and possible control of some *limited* factors *within* the overall framework of capitalist development at a *determinate* historical stage. (It becomes a total ideological mystification insofar as the *partial* results are turned into a *general* theory claiming *universal validity* to itself, eliminating at the same time also the *historical* dimension from the picture.) That in socio-economic practice this theory is put to *manipulative* uses, does not alter the fact that an important condition of, however partial, manipulative success was the theoretically successful identification of certain correlations and mechanisms of control which remained hidden from bourgeois economics at a previous stage. (Parsonian 'General Theory' is, of course, a very different proposition indeed: and precisely because it is *nothing but* apologetic General Theory, even when its immediate object is 'small-group research' or the analysis of 'the individual as a system'.) Although the scope of genuine achievements is strictly circumscribed by the requirements of approaching the problem *'from within'* the system itself, partial scientific advances are possible to the extent to which a new historical phase of the overall social confrontation necessitates some critical readjustments *in* the capitalist structures themselves. (Again, we can see a major difference: while Keynes successfully identifies some *mechanisms* of adjustment and control which temporarily enhance the power of the capitalist system, Parsons inflates the socio-historically limited conditions of manipulative structural readjustments into the 'universal model' of *structural change as such,* remaining always *within* the 'paradigms' of the established structures. This is what he modestly calls the 'Columbian' discovery of his General Theory in which 'the cycle of structural change' happily corresponds with 'the paradigm of a cycle of internalization of a value pattern in the process of socialization', thus producing, singlehanded, the 'new society' from which 'exploitation of labour' and 'capitalistic control' have disappeared in the course of the not-so-Columbian mystification.)

Another major aspect of this problematic is that the adoption of the historically more advanced social standpoint is not the same thing as a (thoroughly fictitious) final supersession of all ideology. We can only mention two principal factors in this context. (1) That in social theory even the greatest scientific advance—like Marx's solution of the problems of commodity production and exchange value—is tied to the conditions of its socio-historical relevance. What we have said above about the specific objects of social science as 'necessarily disappearing objects' applies to the Marxian problematic of value as well. If, however, no notice is being taken of the changing circumstances and of their implications for the sets of relationships as they appear in Marx's analyses, the repetition of the same terms which once registered the greatest scientific advance in the development of social theory becomes paralysing ideology. This is why one of the fundamental principles of the Marxian aproach stipulates that Marxist criticism 'must be constantly applied to itself'. (To hint very briefly at a problem of major importance whose elaboration is not possible here: Marx's demonstration of the *actual* terms and factors of '*contractual*' relationship between capital and labour which opposes his concept of 'labour power' to the mystifying and concealing explanations of Political Economy. It is easy to see that effective changes in the terms of these relationships—in accordance with the changing global relation of forces—have far-reaching implications for the whole theory as formulated by Marx at a particular juncture in history. Equally, it is easy to see that failure to follow up such implications in the form of adequate theoretical demonstrations, in accordance with the dynamically changing requirements of a historical period of transition from one social formation to another, is bound to have serious repercussions for both theory and associated social practice, even if the people involved have adopted, broadly speaking, the 'standpoint of labour'.) And (2), it must be remembered that Marxism is not only a critique of the capitalist social formation—its negation—but also a *strategy for instrumental-institutional readjustments* in a changed—actually and not fictitiously *post-capitalist*—socio-economic setting. In the latter respect, there are obviously a multiplicity of constraints and determinations at work, which are bound to interfere with the original—however correctly conceived strategies. (E.g., a particular country's position and relative power in the global framework; the limitations of the available instruments and productive powers vis-à-vis the given, and constantly changing, socio-economic tasks; the negative 'feedback' on the whole complex from the historically constituted and limited institutions under the pressure of social dynamism, etc., etc.) To pretend that such conditioning forces do not exist is nothing but the worst kind of ideological mystification. The answer is not the excogitation of timeless, *a prioristically* 'scientific' solutions but the recognition of the necessity of such a 'feedback', and the elaboration of strategies as well as of their vehicles of realization which—while necessarily adjusting themselves to the conditions of institutional feedback—remain in *overall* control even under the conditions of severe setbacks.

Thus, social theory is not *external* to the ideological determinants of socio-historical conditioning and institutional feedback but integral to it. It is this complex dialectic of simultaneously 'external' and 'internal', 'critical' and 'self-critical', 'detached' and 'fully involved', 'negative' and 'self-assertive', etc. character of historically significant and relevant social theory—as opposed to the thoroughly ideological claims of 'value-free social science'—which enables it to be both ideologically effective and scientifically valid, in accordance with the changing socio-historical conditions of its sphere of operation.

NOTES

1. This essay is an extended version of a paper presented to an Interdisciplinary Seminar of the Division of Social Science at York University, Toronto, in January 1972.
2. As I have shown elsewhere, this is by no means an isolated incident in Daniel Bell's work. He is equally at odds with facts when he 'analyses' Marx's writings. Cf. Chapter 8 ('The Controversy about Marx') of my book on *Marx's Theory of Alienation,* Merlin Press, London 1970.
3. Lukács has dealt with this line of argument as far back as 1924. After quoting Lenin's proposals about 'state capitalism', made at the beginning of 1918, he commented: 'These passages have been quoted in particular detail to refute wide spread bourgeois and social democratic myths according to which, after the failure of "doctrinaire Marxist" attempts to introduce communism "at one sweep", Lenin compromised and "clever realist that he was", deviated from his original political line. The historical truth is the opposite. So-called "War Communism"—about which Lenin said: "It was a makeshift" and: "It was the war and the ruin that forced us into War Communism. It was not, and could not be, a policy that corresponded to the economic tasks of the proletariat"—was itself a deviation from the path along which the development of socialism was to have run, according to his theoretical predictions.' Lukács, *Lenin: A Study on the Unity of His Thought,* New Left Books, London, 1970, pp. 76-7.
4. Lenin, *Collected Works,* Vol. XXXIII, p. 310. (The quotation from Lenin's opening speech is from pp. 277-8 of the same volume.) Throughout the volume italics are my own, unless

otherwise stated.

5. Cf. p. 435 of Theodore Draper, *The Roots of American Communism,* The Viking Press, New York, 1957.
6. Daniel Bell, 'Unstable America', *Encounter,* June 1970.
7. Max Weber, 'Objectivity' (1904), published in E. A. Shils and H. A. Finch (eds.), *The Methodology of the Social Sciences,* Free Press, New York, 1949, p. 99.
8. *Ibid.,* p. 91.
9. *From Max Weber: Essays in Sociology,* ed. H. H. Gerth and C. Wright Mills, Routledge & Kegan Paul, London, 1948, p. 229.
10. *Ibid.,* p. 216.
11. *Ibid.,* p. 215.
12. George C. Homans, *The Nature of Social Science,* Harcourt, Brace & World, New York, 1967, pp. 107-8.
13. *Ibid.,* p. 108.
14. *Ibid.*
15. *Ibid.,* p. 29.
16. *Ibid.,* pp. 49-50.
17. *Ibid.,* pp. 103-4.
18. Lewis Coser, *The Functions of Social Conflict,* Routledge & Kegan Paul, London, 1956, p. 20. (The quote is from Cooley, *Social Organization,* Scribner & Sons, New York, 1909, p. 199.)
19. Coser, *op. cit.*, p. 21.
20. *Ibid.,* p. 22.
21. *Ibid.,* p. 23.
22. Eager to find proofs to the soundness of the wishful thinking which postulated the definitive end of the antagonism between capital and labour in the age of 'the modern industrial society'—a wishful thinking shared by numerous 'men of the contemporary generation'—Parsons saw in the material supplied by this book (claiming the *'separation of ownership and control'* in the big corporations) the final refutation of Marx's theories. Yet nothing could be more amusing than this suggestion. For it was precisely Marx who predicted, well before anyone else, the *necessity of* such developments: as inherent in the trends of *concentration and centralization* of capital; trends resulting 'with the inexorability of a natural law' (Marx) in the corporate structures of advanced capitalism. But now the results of the trends he identified well before their maturation, are supposed to bury forever his theories about capitalism and—especially—about the *necessity* (not to be confused with some *mechanical inevitability*) of establishing a *socialist* social order.
23. Coser, *op. cit.,* p. 113.
24. Talcott Parsons, *The Social System,* p. 246. Quoted by Coser with approval on page 176 of his book.
25. Coser, *op. cit.*, pp. 118-19.
26. *Ibid.,* p. 176. Theoretically speaking this is, of course, a *non-sequitur.* For a *positive* factor—a specific American socio-

historical phenomenon—is 'explained' in terms of a mere *negativity:* a *lack* or *absence* of an allegedly strictly 'European' characteristic. The ideological function, however, is thoroughly 'sound' and rather obvious. For those who might worry are assured that they need not fear 'class struggle' in an America which is claimed to possess 'flexible adjustive structures'.

27. Coser, *op. cit.,* p. 157.
28. *Ibid.,* pp. 151-5.
29. Marx, *Capital,* Vol. I, pp. 59-60.
30. Aristotle, *Ethics,* Book I, Chapter 2. For our earlier quotations, cf. Aristotle, *Politics,* Book I, Chapter 2.
31. It is against the latter that he enunciates his principles about 'slavery by nature' and 'freedom by nature'.
32. Marx, *Capital,* Vol. I., p. 85.
33. We have seen some examples in the sections on Homans and Coser.
34. Cf. the quotation from Keynes referred to in note 45.
35. Karl Mannheim, *Ideology and Utopia,* Routledge & Kegan Paul, London, 1936. p. 140.
36. *Ibid.*
37. *Ibid.,* p. 141.
38. *Ibid.,* p. 142.
39. *Ibid.*
40. *Ibid.,* p. 143.
41. Cf. Lukács, *History and Class Consciousness,* Merlin Press, London, 1971,—especially the essay on 'The Marxism of Rosa Luxemburg'.
42. Marx, *Grundrisse der Kritik des Politischen Ökonomie*, Dietz Verlag, Berlin, 1953, p. 26.
43. *Ibid.,* p. 27.
44. J. M. Keynes, *A Short View of Russia* (1925).
45. Keynes, *Am I a Liberal?* (1925).
46. Keynes, *Economic Possibilities for Our Grandchildren* (1930).
47. *A Short View of Russia.*
48. *Ibid.*
49. Cf. Chapter 2 ('Grand Theory') of C. Wright Mills' book.
50. C. Wright Mills, *The Sociological Imagination,* Penguin Edition, pp. 42-3.
51. *Ibid.,* p. 58.
52. This is where we can see the importance of Lukács' methodological principle: 'the standpoint of totality' mentioned above.
53. Talcott Parsons and Neil J. Smelser, *Economy and Society: A Study in the Integration of Economics and Social Theory,* Routledge & Kegan Paul, London, 1956. Since it is frequently stressed in the book that Parsons is 'the Senior Author', and since all the important concepts are taken from his general system, for

the sake of brevity we refer to this book from now on under Parsons' name only.

54. *Ibid.*, pp. 270-2.
55. It is hard to believe, but this is the 'proof' of what is called 'opposite Utopianism', as supplied in a footnote on page 272: 'Anna Lee Hopson in a study of best-selling novels of the early 20th century found that the hero is unwilling to "knuckle under" to the "interests" and he is very generally rewarded by the idealistic love of the heroine who is regularly the daughter of one of these wicked men. Cf. Anna Lee Hopson, *Best Sellers, Media of Mass Expression,* unpublished PhD. dissertation, Radcliffe College, 1952.'
56. Since structure is defined as 'the essential internal conditions of a relatively stable equilibrium', (p. 248) the Parsonian concept of 'structural change' is a very peculiar notion indeed.
57. *Economy and Society,* p. 28.
58. *Ibid.*, p. 278.
59. Keynes, *Am I a Liberal?*
60. Cf. *Economy and Society,* pp. 175-8.
61. *Ibid.*, pp. 283-4.

II Contingent and Necessary Class Consciousness*

1. MARX'S APPROACH TO THE PROBLEM OF CLASS CONSCIOUSNESS

The following two quotations illustrate, better than anything else, the central dilemma of the Marxist theory of classes and class consciousness. The first comes from *The Holy Family*:

It is not a question of what this or that proletarian, or even the whole proletariat, at the moment considers as its aim. It is a question of *what the proletariat is,* and what, in accordance with this being, *it will historically be compelled to do.* Its aim and historical action is *irrevocably* and clearly foreshadowed in its own life situation as well as in the whole organization of bourgeois society today. There is no need here to show that a large part of the English and French proletariat is already conscious of its *historic task* and is constantly working *to develop that consciousness into complete clarity.*[1]

The second quotation, from a work by Gramsci, puts the emphasis on the vital need for developing class consciousness in an organizationally effective form:

It can be excluded that, by themselves, *economic crises* directly produce fundamental events; they can only create more *favourable ground* for the propagation of certain ways of thinking, of posing and solving questions which involve the whole future development of State life.

The decisive element in every situation is the force, permanently organized and pre-ordered over a long period, which can be advanced when one judges that the situation is favourable (and it is *favourable only to the extent to which such a force exists* and is full of fighting ardour); therefore the essential task is that of paying systematic and patient attention to forming and developing this force, rendering it even more homogeneous, compact, *conscious of itself.*[2]

* First published in *Aspects of History and Class Consciousness*, edited by István Mészáros, Routledge & Kegan Paul, London, 1971, pp. 85–127.

As we can see, the issue at stake is the relationship between historical necessity and class consciousness. On the face of it there seems to be a contradiction between Marx and Gramsci: the first speaks of the proletariat being *compelled* to fulfil its historic task, whereas the second insists that the historical situation itself is favourable only to the extent to which the proletariat has already succeeded in developing an organized force fully conscious of itself. However, for a more adequate understanding of the meaning of both quotations it is essential to notice that Marx, in his assertion of the historical necessity of class-conscious proletarian action, does not simply refer to 'economic crises'—the terms of Gramsci's polemics against 'vulgar economism'—but to the *'being'* of the class: i.e. he indicates the line of solution in terms of the complex determinants of a social ontology as contrasted with some economic mechanism. And this makes all the difference. For the 'being' of any class is the comprehensive synthesis of *all* factors at work in society, whereas the propounders of an 'economic determinism'—rightly castigated by Gramsci—single out *one* factor only, and crudely superimpose it on all the others.

If Marx's approach to the problem of classes and class consciousness is interpreted on the crude model of 'economic determinism', the dilemma mentioned above remains insoluble. Instead of a dialectical assessment of 'social being' we are given a schematic account and a pseudo-solution:

> It is apparent that Marx's theory of social classes, along with other parts of his doctrine, involved a basic ambiguity which has bedevilled his interpreters ever since. For, on the one hand, he felt quite certain that the contradictions engendered by capitalism would inevitably lead to a class conscious proletariat and hence to a proletarian revolution. But on the other hand, he assigned to class consciousness, to political action, and to his scientific theory of history a major role in bringing about this result. In his own eyes this difficulty was resolved because such *subjective elements* as class consciousness or a scientific theory were themselves a *by-product* of the contradictions inherent in capitalism.[3]

To treat class consciousness as mere *subjectivity* and *'by-product'* of capitalist economy is a caricature of Marx. This view arises from an approach which substitutes a one-sided, *mechanical* model of determination for Marx's complex *dialectical* model. Thus, in the end, consciousness is crudely subsumed under economy and its role becomes illusory: it cannot actively produce change, since it is itself the mere product (indeed, 'by-product') of capitalist economic development.

And here we come to a crucial question: the complexity of Marx's dialectical methodology. In a mechanical conception there is a clear-cut line of demarcation between 'determined' and its 'determinants'. Not so within the framework of a dialectical methodology. In terms of the latter: although the economic foundations of capitalist society constitute the 'ultimate determinants' of the social being of its classes, these 'ultimate *determinants*' are at the same time also '*determined* determinants'. In other words, Marx's assertions about the ontological significance of economics become meaningful only if we are able to grasp his idea of 'complex interactions' in the most varied fields of human activity. Accordingly, the various institutional and intellectual manifestations of human life are not simply 'built upon' an economic basis, but also actively *structure* the latter through an immensely intricate and relatively *autonomous* structure of their own. 'Economic determinations' do not exist outside the historically changing complex of specific mediations, including the most 'spiritual' ones.[4] In Marx's view 'the gods in the b e g i n n i n g are not the *cause* but the *effect* of man's intellectual confusion. Later this relationship becomes *reciprocal*.[5] Consequently, once beliefs of this kind—or indeed of any other kind—are held by man, they carry with them manifold repercussions for the totality of human life, including the 'economic fact' of 'allocating scarce resources' for the construction of cathedrals, for the maintenance of the Church and the clergy, etc. Similarly with consciousness in all its forms and manifestations which have a *relatively* autonomous structure of their own, determining thus, in the form of *reciprocity*, the economic structures of society while they are also determined by the latter. 'Supply and demand', 'production and consumption' are economic categories *par excellence*. But only on the surface. A closer look reveals that *none* of them makes any sense whatsoever without the historically changing category of '*human needs*', which cannot conceivably be accounted for in terms of one-sided economic determinations.

One cannot understand Marx's concept of class consciousness without understanding his view of social causation. According to

Marx, every human achievement introduces a new element into the complex set of interactions which characterize society at any given time. Consequently, what is the case 'in the beginning' cannot possibly remain the case at a later stage of development. The dialectical warning about the nature of economic determinations which prevail 'only in the last analysis' is meant to emphasize that while both structurally and genetically the concept of 'the material conditions of life' occupies a paramount position in the Marxian system—i.e. both as regards the historical *genesis* of the more complex forms of human interchange and in that material conditions constitute the structurally necessary *precondition* of human life in *all* conceivable forms of society—it is by no means capable of accounting for the complexities of social development on its own. Indeed, when Marx points to abundance—both material abundance and the free availability of time at the disposal of men—as the necessary *basis* of 'that development of human energy which is an end in itself, the true realm of freedom',[6] he does not suggest that this abundance produces 'the realm of freedom'. (If he did so he would be guilty of the contradiction of mechanically determining freedom.) On the contrary, by emphasizing the necessary basis and precondition of a truly free human development he indicates those conditions which—if satisfied—*enable* man to *overcome* those natural and material *determinations* which oppose 'that development of human energy which is an end in itself'.

This means that the role of consciousness becomes increasingly greater with the development of human productive powers. But precisely because of the relative autonomy of the various forms and manifestations of human consciousness, '*socialized man*' (i.e. 'the associated producers who rationally regulate their interchange with nature')[7] is by no means an *automatic* result of this development, although he is a *necessary* being at a certain stage of social interchange. Consciousness can be put at the service of alienated life, just as it can envisage the supersession of alienation.[8] The question whether the former or the latter forms of consciousness prevail in the society of potential abundance cannot even be tackled, let alone solved, in terms of a mechanical model of social causality which *must* deny the relative autonomy of social consciousness. ('Economism', 'fatalism', and 'immobilism' are the well-known political manifestations of this kind of mechanical approach to the problem of class consciousness.) On the other hand, the failure to understand the dialectic of reciprocal determinations can also result in assigning *absolute autonomy* to consciousness, postulating political structures and forms of organization in sharp contradiction to the *objective possibilities* of the given socio-historical situation. ('Subjectivism', 'voluntarism', 'adventurism', etc., are the equally well-known political manifestations of this undialectical conception.) In the case of mechanical determinism the possibility of a break in the chain of material determinations, in its Marxian sense, is *a priori* rejected, while in the case of undialectical voluntarism a break is arbitrarily postulated: without taking into account, that is, the conditions necessary for such a break. Marx, by contrast, on the one hand defines the *objective conditions* of a break in terms of the reciprocal determination of social being and social consciousness. (To illustrate this point: he insists that the productive forces had to reach a certain degree of development before it became possible to separate 'objectification' from 'alienation': a *possibility* that cannot become *reality* without the *conscious* implementation of the programme of 'de-alienating' the various forms and instruments of human 'self-objectification'.) On the other hand, Marx stresses the necessity of a *break* in the chain of economic determinations: a break without which he could not define the crucial characteristic of the proletariat as *'self-abolition'*, nor its class consciousness as awareness of the historical task of abolishing *all* class-limitations—the limitations of class-society—in the course of abolishing oneself as a class. 'Conscious self-abolition' as a result of economic determinism is a contradiction in terms. Consequently, either there is no alternative to reproducing the contradictions of class society in all conceivable forms of society, or the chain of socio-economic determinations must be broken. (We shall return shortly to this problem of 'conscious self-abolition'.) There can be no doubt as to where Marx stands on this issue.

Another major difficulty in fully grasping the meaning of Marx's theory of classes and class consciousness resides in the *multi-dimensionality* of his concepts. For *all* his categories are not only *structurally interrelated*, but also every one of them is conceived as *inherently historical.* This difficulty, thus, consists in adequately grasping the historical dynamism of structurally interconnected categories which are constitutive parts of a complex whole.

The structural aspect of this problem is well illustrated by Marx's warnings against isolating the specific categories of any particular field from the complex totality to which they belong: 'To try to give a definition of *property* as of an *independent* relation, a *category apart*—an abstract and eternal idea—can be nothing but an *illusion* of metaphysics.[9] The same goes, of course, for the concepts of 'classes' and 'class consciousness': they acquire their full meaning only as focal points of a multiplicity of structurally interconnected social phenomena. 'Do not say'—warns Marx—'that social movement excludes political movement. There is *never* a *political* movement which is not *at the same time social.*'[10] Consequently, 'class consciousness' cannot be understood simply in terms of the ideological and organizational factors of the political sphere, however important they may be. Isolating the issue of class consciousness from the complex problematics to which it objectively belongs can only give rise to voluntarism, subjectivism and adventurism. According to Marx, political devices on their own make no sense whatsoever; for men must change *'from top to bottom* the conditions of their industrial and political existence, and consequently *their whole manner of being'.*[11] *Strikes*, for instance, were enthusiastically greeted by Marx—in sharp contrast to his categorical condemnation of Luddism—not simply because they contributed to the development of working-class consciousness: he was quite aware of their limitations in that respect. (Limitations which were later appropriately termed by Lenin 'trade union consciousness'.) He insisted on their significance for the development of the productive forces in that they compelled the bourgeoisie to introduce labour-saving devices, mobilizing science in the service of higher productivity, and thus substantially hastening the maturation of both the productive potentials and the contradictions of capitalism.[12] The political factor thus acquires its significance in terms of a comprehensive set of reciprocal determinations: in virtue of its effective contribution to a profound structural modification of the totality of social processes—from the far-reaching transformation of the means of production to the creation of new ideas, new modes of organization, and new instruments of defensive and offensive action—carrying with it the impossibility of neutralizing or nullifying its total impact, notwithstanding the temporary success of measures devised for taming the trade union movement as a political force. In other words: the central significance of strikes is that they cannot be structurally integrated into the system of capitalist production in the long run, even if, paradoxically, they are bound to help remedy many a partial defect of capitalism in the short run. This objective dialectic of partial integrability and ultimate disintegration—i.e. both the negative and the positive aspects in their necessary interconnectedness—constitutes Marx's framework of reference, whereas concentrating on the partial and negative aspect alone lands one in a nightmare society of 'total alienation', with its 'fully integrated working class': a society to which nothing but the fictitious counter-example of a 'critical Utopia' can be opposed. Marx's approach always situates the partial movement in its global setting. This is why he can perceive already in the embryonic forms of working-class organization the developed forms, just as he can identify the reciprocal interchange of political and economic determinations in strikes embedded in the capitalist structure of production. Thus, it emerges that trade unionism simply cannot become an *exclusively* economic form of action, no matter how strongly this side of its nature predominates in a given historical period. (In this light the failure to create, *á la* George Woodcock, a 'non-political trade union movement'—that contradiction in terms—turns out to be a *necessary* failure.) Indeed, the logic of Marx's reasoning—in view of the point about the maturation of the productive forces under the impact of strikes, etc.—necessarily means that the more directly the capitalist system of production is involved as a whole in the given confrontation, the greater is the need to bring the political factors into the foreground, in a truly global framework of conflicts and collisions, when the non-integrability of forced concessions becomes particularly acute. And, again, the political factors cannot be separated from the socio-economic ones: fully developed *'internationalism'* and fully developed *'world market'*[13] necessarily imply each other. (We shall return to this problem later.)

The historical dynamism of the structurally interrelated particular factors has already been displayed in Marx's critical examples quoted above, and therefore need not retain us here much longer. Let it suffice to point at the general methodological validity of Marx's analysis concerning the structural interrelationship and, at the same time, historical specificity of *market* and *'division of labour'*, for instance. 'The extent of the market, its physiognomy, give to the division of labour at different periods a physiogonomy, a character', writes Marx, emphasizing 'the need to study the numerous influences which give the division of labour a definite character in every epoch.'[14] The same applies, it goes without saying, to 'classes' and 'class consciousness' which must be grasped as integral parts of a dynamic set of socio-historical factors. Thus, the modifications of the market, the further extension of the division of labour, the increase in society's productive powers, the concentration of capital, the far-reaching changes in the social pattern of consumption, the development of scientific knowledge, communication, transport, educational technology, etc.—all these factors have a vital bearing on the development of classes and class consciousness, just as the latter are bound to affect the former in one form or another.

Consequently, an adequate understanding of Marx's theory of classes and class consciousness requires the examination of his conception as a whole under one of its major aspects: an analysis whose focal point is the concept of 'social conflict and its complex determinants', assessed in accordance with the dialectic of reciprocal determinations.

2. CLASS POSITION AND CLASS INTEREST

Here we have to quote at a greater length a passage from *The Holy Family* which sums up the major points of Marx's view of classes and class consciousness:

Proletariat and wealth are opposites. As such they form a single whole. They are both begotten by the world of private property. The question is what particular place each occupies *within the antithesis.* It is not sufficient to declare them two sides of a single whole. Private property as private property, as wealth, is compelled to maintain itself, and thereby its opposite, the proletariat, in existence. That is the *positive side* of the contradiction, self-satisfied private property. The proletariat, on the other hand, is compelled as proletariat to abolish itself and thereby its opposite, the condition for its existence, that which makes it the proletariat, i.e. private property. That is the *negative side* of the contradiction, its restlessness within its very self, dissolved and self-dissolving private property... . Within this antithesis the private property-owner is therefore the conservative side, the proletarian, the destructive, side. From the former arises the action of preserving the antithesis, from the latter, that of annihilating it. In any case, in its economic movement private property drives towards its own dissolution, but only through a development which does not depend on it, of which it is *unconscious* and which takes place *against its will*, through the very nature of things, only inasmuch as it produces the proletariat as proletariat, misery *conscious of its spiritual and physical misery*, dehumanization *conscious* of its dehumanization and *therefore self-abolishing*. The proletariat executes the sentence that private property pronounced on itself by begetting the proletariat, just as it executes the sentence that wage-labour pronounced on itself by begetting wealth for others and misery for itself. When the proletariat is victorious, it by no means becomes the *absolute side* of society, for it is victorious only by abolishing itself and its opposite. Then the proletariat disappears as well as the opposite which determines it, private property.

When socialist writers *ascribe* this *historical role* to the proletariat, it is not, as Critical Criticism would have one think, because they consider proletarians as gods. Rather the contrary. Since the abstraction of all humanity, even of the semblance of humanity, is practically complete in the fully-formed proletariat; since the conditions of life of the proletariat sum up all the conditions of life of society today in their most inhuman and acute form; since man has lost himself in the proletariat, yet at the same time has not only gained theoretical consciousness of that loss, but through the no longer removable, no longer disguisable, *absolutely imperative need*—the *practical expression of necessity*—is driven directly to revolt against that inhumanity; it follows that the proletariat *can and must free itself*. But it cannot free itself without abolishing the conditions of its own life. It cannot abolish the conditions of its own life without abolishing all the inhuman conditions of life of society today which are summed up in its own situation.

Before embarking on a more detailed analysis, let us make a few brief comments on this important passage.

The first point to emphasize is the Marxian formulation of the problem of classes as an 'antithesis' (or structural antagonism) constituting—with its positive and negative sides—a single whole, whose elements cannot be absolutized (since they stand or fall together), nor indeed brought to a rest or 'reconciliation'. (The far-reaching implications of this idea will have to be discussed more in detail.)

The second point that needs stressing is the distinction between the two sides of this antagonism in terms of class consciousness which does not simply depend on *subjective* insight, but on *objective* factors: on one side, the *'unconscious'* character of capital determined by a specific form of social development which compels it, *'against its will'*, to produce its opposite; on the other, the *necessity*, through its manifestation in the form of *practical need*, which gives rise to self-consciousness. (The relationship between 'class interest' and 'false consciousness' must be understood as a complex interplay of these factors.)

Also, it is important to notice Marx's emphasis on the *'spiritual'* side of the misery of the subordinate class, for it is customary to misrepresent the Marxian view of 'increasing misery' as merely a material consideration. The fact is, however, that in Marx's thought, from the early writings to *Capital*, the material and intellectual-spiritual aspects are always linked together, and the worker's condition is described as growing worse *irrespective* of the material improvements (*'be his payment high or low'*[15]) precisely because of the inseparability of the two aspects.

Equally important is Marx's insistence that the '*self-abolition*' of the proletariat—defined as abolishing, at the same time, the conditions of dehumanization—cannot be achieved without the *conscious* action of the class that 'can and must free itself'. Indeed, the programme of '*self*-abolition' would be a contradiction in terms if things were left to the unconscious force of some mythical 'historical necessity'. (It is by no means accidental that further on we can read in *The Holy Family*: 'History does nothing... "history" is not, as it were, a person apart, using man as a means to achieve its own aims; history is nothing but *the activity of man pursuing his aims'.)* The *'absolutely imperative need'* mentioned by Marx has nothing to do with the Kantian 'categorical imperative', for it is *'the practical expression of necessity'*. But equally the latter has nothing to do with history personified or turned into some kind of a mechanistic 'economic determinism', for it cannot possibly prevail without the *human mediation* of 'absolutely imperative *n e e d*': the real human basis of an adequate *self-consciousness*, i.e. neither abstractly speculative nor crudely determined by unmediated empiria. In Marx's view it is not enough to say that there can be no 'self-abolition' without the maturation of its *objective* conditions. One must also add: the objective conditions themselves cannot reach their full maturity without the development of *self-consciousness* as consciousness of the need for de-alienation. Thus, the 'subjective' factor acquires an *over-riding* importance as the *necessary precondition* of success at that highly advanced stage of human development when the issue at stake is the '*self*-abolishing' abolition of the conditions of dehumanization. (We can see, again, the significance of a dialectical approach without which one must end up with irreconcilable 'antinomies' and 'dichotomies'.)

Finally, we have to draw attention to the often-ignored fact that Lukács' famous distinction between 'ascribed' or 'imputed' class consciousness and 'psychological' consciousness has its origin in the Marxian idea which opposes true or necessary class consciousness—one *'ascribed to the proletariat' in virtue of its being 'conscious* of its *historic task'* (as Marx writes a few lines further on, in the passage quoted at the beginning of this paper)—to the contingency of 'what this or that proletarian, or even the whole proletariat, at the moment considers as its aim'. (Even terminologically, the similarity is striking; Marx uses the term *'zuschreiben'*, and Lukács its closest synonym, *'zurechnen'*: which both mean 'to ascribe', 'attribute' or 'impute'.) Thus, Lukács' distinction between 'ascribed' and 'psychological' class consciousness is a reformulation of one of the basic tenets of the Marxian system. Indeed, as we shall see, it is quite impossible to make sense of Marx's theory of classes and class consciousness without this vital distinction. For any attempt to reduce Marx's theory to its 'sociologically sound'—or 'scientific'—elements, at the expense of its 'ideological concepts' (or 'merely philosophical ideas', 'logical constructs', etc.), turns the Marxian global vision into a haphazard assembly of disconnected fragments, in the spirit of flat empiricism and positivism. The separation of 'Marx the sociologist' from 'Marx the revolutionary' (or 'Marx the ideologue', etc.) can only contribute to a sterile stalemate in both theory and practice, whether the intention behind it is a conservative or an 'activist' one. This has been well known ever since Sorel—who opposed 'social science' to the function of 'shaping consciousness'[16]—though, of course, few of those who follow this line of reasoning today would wish to be associated with such a predecessor. All the same, breaking the dialectical unity of the Marxian set of concepts inevitably leads to this kind of polarization, which carries with it the unenviable choice between the 'scientific objectivity' of flat empiricism—the pedestrian assembly of the fragments of phenomenal immediacy, glorified as 'sound scientific principles'—and the inflated mythology of 'political activism as a category apart', which is supposed to be responsible, on its own, for 'shaping consciousness'. (It goes without saying that we can find a great variety of artificial polarization in the particular theories which share the methodology of a rigid, undialectical separation of the '*theoretical* concepts' from the '*practical*' ones, divorcing 'value-free theory', 'pure philosophy', 'scientific knowledge', and 'empirical theory' from 'ideology'; 'description' from 'evaluation'; 'analysis' from 'synthesis'; 'social facts' from 'ideal types'; 'rationality' from 'emotivism'; 'naturalism' from 'prescriptivism'; 'facts' from 'values'; 'necessity' from 'freedom'; 'is' from 'ought', etc. [17] Such theories, invariably, fulfil themselves in formulating unrealized—and, because of this methodology of rigid polarization, *a priori* unrealizable—programmes for *others*.)

Class consciousness, according to Marx, is inseparable from the recognition—in the form of 'true' or 'false consciousness'—of class interest based on the objective social position of the different classes in the established structure of society. This is why, in Marx's words: 'The English Established Church, e.g., will more readily pardon an attack on 38 out of its 39 articles than on 1/39th of its income. Nowadays atheism itself is *culpa levis*, as compared with criticism of existing property-relations.'[18]

It is this consciousness of one's class interest which explains the vehemence of Keynes' telling attack on Marxism:

How can I accept a doctrine which sets up as its bible, above and beyond criticism, an *obsolete economic textbook* which I know to be not only scientifically erroneous but *without interest or application for the modern world*? How can I adopt a creed which, preferring the *mud* to the *fish*, exalts the *boorish proletariat* above the bourgeois and the intelligentsia who, with whatever faults, are *the quality in life* and surely

carry the seeds of all human advancement? Even if we need a religion, how can we find it in *the turbid rubbish of the Red bookshops*? It is hard for an educated, decent, intelligent son of Western Europe to find his ideals here, unless he has first suffered some strange and horrid process of conversion which has changed all his values.[19]
When it comes to the *class struggle* as such, my local and personal patriotism, like those of everyone else, except *certain unpleasant zealous ones*, are attached to my own surroundings. I can be influenced by what seems to me to be justice and good sense; but *the c l a s s war will find me on the side of the educated b o u r g e o i s i e.*'[20]

This is clear and straight talking, overtly representing the class interests of a bourgeoisie confident of the stability of its power-position in the established order of society.[21]

The situation of those who are forced to notice, on the much more torn European mainland, the disappearance of the old stability, is quite different. Given the limitations of their social position, they interpret the undeniable social dynamism of their epoch as a movement that does not question the rule of capital. Thus, they postulate 'social mobility' as a 'convergence' of the classes, and consequently as the elimination of class conflict in a 'modern industrial society' smoothly managed by the 'unattached intelligentsia':

Max Scheler called our contemporary period the *'epoch of equalization'* (Zeitalter des Ausgleichs), which; if applied to our problems, means that ours is a world in which social groupings, which had hitherto lived more or less isolated from one another, each making itself and its own world of thought absolute, are now, in one form or another, *merging into one another.*[22]

Nearly half a century has gone by since the formulation of theories of this kind. Having, thus, persuaded themselves of the non-partisan character of their theories—in an epoch when, as a matter of fact, the distance between the 'haves' and the 'have-nots' continued to increase, and the only 'mergers' we could witness, on a global scale, were the results of take-over bids, producing giant monopolies, 'oligopolies', 'duopolies', 'conglomerates' and 'super-conglomerates'—representatives of the allegedly 'unattached intelligentsia' continued to write about 'equalization', 'the institutionalization of conflict', 'convergence', and the like. Within the confines of 'rigorously objective and impartial'—'value-free'—social science such 'emotive terms' as 'bourgeoisie' and 'proletariat' were ruled out of order, just as talking about 'capitalism' was considered 'obsolete' and 'ideologically biased'. The proper 'neutral' terms were: 'higher and lower income groups'—eliminating, semantically, the problem of classes—and capitalism was 'superseded' by 'modern industrial society', 'industrial civilization' and 'post-capitalist society'. (In the last few years even such terms as 'post-industrial society' were coined—whatever they might mean.) In this world of *semantic convergence*—in which the prevailing climate of wishful thinking induced some leading representatives of this 'value-free social and political science' to announce, with boundless optimism, nothing less than 'the end of ideology'[23]—the one and only legitimate use for these allegedly 'nineteenth century concepts' consisted in turning out an endless number of books and 'scientific research projects' on the *embourgeoisement* of the *proletariat.*

There is no space here for detailed analysis of these theories. We have to concentrate, therefore, on assessing only a few of their major tenets and methodological characteristics.

One of their striking features is the inflation of phenomena of necessarily *limited* significance into *universal* laws like 'equalization', 'convergence', 'institutionalization of conflict', 'embourgeoisement', etc. The smallest sign of *marginal* (limited, partial, isolated) equalization is eagerly greeted as *fundamental* or structural equalization. In such a generalized form these 'laws' amount to nothing more than an empty *postulate*, and, for that matter, a *self-contradictory* one. By projecting—as an objective social trend—the so-called 'equalization' and 'convergence' of the classes *within capitalism*, they postulate the 'supersession' of the actual *structural subordination* of labour to capital (a *necessary* feature of all conceivable forms of capitalism) without any need for the introduction of *radical structural changes* in the existing social relations of production. (The delicate renaming of capitalism as 'modern industrial society', etc., is one of the devices for hiding this contradiction. Another, theoretically far more important, one is the systematic confusion of all *structural* aspects of social phenomena with their *functional* aspects,[24] as we shall see at the end of this section.)

Having thus succeeded in squaring the circle—not by means of a 'logical construct' but through an *illogical* one—all that remains is to collect 'empirical evidence' in support of the *a priori* thesis of 'convergence'. And the more fragmentary and unrepresentative the data collected in a self-confirmatory fashion are, the better they succeed in concealing the *a priori* character and logical contradictoriness of this kind of 'value-free, scientific procedure'. The methodology of flat empiricism serves a dual purpose. On the one hand it hides the fact that all the available comprehensive sets of empirical data point to increasing polarization, growing inequality, and the concentration of the means of production in fewer and fewer hands, on a global scale—i.e. that they demonstrate the exact *opposite* of the claimed equalization, convergence, and structural integration of the classes. On the other hand, by stipulating the 'scientific' virtues of concentrating merely on the fragmentary details of phenomenal immediacy, it sets itself up—not by means of convincing arguments, but by simply rejecting, with self-complacent circularity, the methodology of 'generalizations' attributed to the 'ideological' adversary—as the one and only 'non-ideological' procedure. Thus, not only does it succeed in dispensing with the need of rendering explicit its—self-contradictory—assumptions, as indeed with the need to provide any justification for its adopted methodology; it also brings the additional bonus that this *a prioristic*, self-contradictory, *counter*-empirical, and blatantly ideological approach can be presented as the paradigm of presuppositionless, empirically founded, rigorous, scientific methodology—as non-partisan objectivity itself.

Thus, if Marx shows that capital and labour constitute a *structural antagonism* which *necessarily* excludes the possibility of a structural integration of the proletariat, this can be conveniently dismissed as an '*a priori* logical construct'. The fact is, though, that—in accordance with the programme Marx had consciously set himself already in his youth—his achievements have been obtained as a result of an '*empirical analysis* based on a conscientious critical study of political economy'.[25] The above-mentioned structural antagonism between capital and labour, far from being a mere logical construct, is necessarily inherent in the empirical reality of a mode of production which cannot function without the *ever-enlarging* reproduction of exchange value:

> The law of capitalist accumulation, metamorphosed by economists into a pretended law of Nature, in reality merely states that the very nature of accumulation excludes every diminution in the degree of exploitation of labour, and every rise in the price of labour, which could seriously imperil the continual reproduction, on an ever-enlarging scale, of the capitalistic relation. It cannot be otherwise in a mode of production in which the labourer exists to satisfy the needs of self-expansion of existing values, instead of, on the contrary, material wealth existing to satisfy the needs of development on the part of the labourer.[26]

This means that any increase in the price of labour must be *relative* to the general rate of *accumulation* (the result of increasing productivity, the concentration of capital coupled with some degree of rationalization, etc.) and *subordinated* to the latter; consequently, the *structural relations* of society remain fundamentally the same. (In other words, 'social mobility' is bound to remain *marginal* so long as the conditions of the structural subordination of labour to capital prevail.) Only particular individuals, not classes, can be integrated into an established structure of society which is constituted by the classes themselves. Given the structural antagonism between capital and labour, any talk about the 'integration' or 'embourgeoisement' of the proletariat in a society whose productive relations remain essentially the same is a contradiction in terms, no matter what kind of political intent may lie behind it.

The core of Marx's theory of classes and class consciousness is precisely this concept of the necessary structural subordination of labour to capital in commodity society. And no amount of increase in wages—for wages are wages are wages—could change that. (Not that there is any danger of significant increases. For even the latest Incomes Data Services survey states unmistakably that 'Poorly paid workers in Britain are getting poorer'.[27]) The class interest of the proletariat is defined in terms of changing this structural subordination. In Gramsci's words, it consists in 'the transformation of the *subordinate* into the *ruling* group'.[28] What is, thus, really at stake is not the issue of how to obtain 'a better wage for the slave' (Marx), nor indeed that of a change in the tone of voice—carefully filtered by 'human engineering'—which transmits the dictates of commodity production to the workers, but a *radical restructuring* of the established order of society.

Understandably, there are *qualitative* differences between the interests of the dominant group and those of the subordinate group. The most obvious of them is that the dominant group is interested in change only to the extent to which reforms and concessions can be integrated or institutionalized, whereas changes of this kind are *opposed* to the interests of the subordinate group in as much as they prolong its subordination. (A countervailing force is, of course, the impact of these reforms and concessions on the development of the productive powers of society, significantly contributing to the maturation of social contradictions, as already mentioned in the previous section.)

Another fundamental difference is that the individual self-interest of the particular members of the ruling group is directly related to the general objective of retaining the structurally dominant and privileged position the group as a whole enjoys in society. The 'transcendence of individual self-interest' in the direction of the collective interest of the class is, therefore, a mere fiction, since such a 'transcendence' in reality amounts to nothing but an effective safeguarding of crude self-interest. Consequently, 'the pursuit of self-interest' must be turned by bourgeois thinkers into a 'Natural Law'—the alleged law of 'Human Nature'—valid for this 'phenomenal world of ours', and the idea of its trancendence must assume the form of a fictitious 'ought', ideally but not effectively opposed to 'is', and confined to the equally fictitious 'noumenal' realm of metaphysical transcendentalism.[29]

All this is quite different with the subordinate group. Here the 'short-term' interests of particular individuals, and even of the class as a whole at a given time, can stand in radical opposition to the 'long-term' interest of structural change. (This is why Marx can and must point to the fundamental difference between contingent or 'psychological' and necessary class consciousness.) Thus 'the pursuit of individual self-interest'—leading to the integration of particular individuals in the established order of society—as well as the collective forms of reformist action in so far as they are straightforward extensions of this pursuit of particularistic self-interest, are opposed and transcended not in the form of an *a priori* impotent 'noumenal ought', but by the actuality of social development which in the long run necessarily condemns to failure such attempts at a structural integration of the subordinate class—a contradiction in terms—on any significant scale. This does not mean, of course, that the problem itself should be ignored, but that it must be kept in its proper perspective. To say that 'insofar as individuals seek their social betterment through individual rather than group action, to that extent class consciousness is weakened by status aspirations'[30] is a gross oversimplification. 'Group action' in itself is by no means a guarantee of an adequate class consciousness. It all depends on the actual nature of the objectives involved, i.e. on whether the achievements of group action can be successfully integrated or not. Group action devoid of strategically significant objectives can only strengthen 'group consciousness'—or 'trade union consciousness'—hooked on to the *partial* interests of a limited group of workers. In this it is *qualitatively* different from a group action like the Italian general strike of 1970, arising out of and further contributing to 'a crisis of authority which is in fact *the crisis of hegemony*, or crisis of the State in all spheres'.[31] Besides, the individual's 'betterment of his position' need not necessarily carry with it the weakening of class consciousness. Whether it does or not will depend to a large extent on the degree of class consciousness of the individual in question; a relationship implicitly denied by this mechanical-determinist view which first arbitrarily postulates a dichotomy between 'brute facts' and 'values' ('*Class* focuses on the divisions which result from the *brute facts* of economic organization. *Status* relates to the more subtle distinctions which stem from the *values* that men set on each other's activities'.[32]), and then concludes, with triumphant circularity, that aspirations at a 'betterment of one's position'—by definition (but only by this definition) involving a different set of values—necessarily weaken class consciousness. (Again we can witness the metamorphosis of arbitrary *apriorism* into a claim to empirical validity.)

The proletariat as merely the 'sum total' of its individual members (in Sartre's terminology: the class as a 'serial collective'[33]) at any given time is a sociological contingency, with specific aims and more or less limited powers and instruments for their realization. The *same* proletariat, though, is at the same time—in virtue of its necessarily subordinate class position with respect to the bourgeoisie—

also a constitutive part of the irreconcilable structural antagonism of capitalist society. The distance between these two aspects of the 'being of the proletariat', as reflected in the prevailing form of class consciousness, can be greater or lesser in different historical situations, and no linear progress in reducing the gap is implied by Marx's formulations of the problem of class consciousness. We shall discuss some of the related problems in the next section. Here we have to emphasize three points of major importance:

(1) That Marx was fully aware of the contradiction between the sociological contingency of the class (stratified and divided by sectional interests, etc.) at a given moment, and its being as constitutive of the structural antagonism of capitalism. He called it the contradiction between the *being* and *existence* of labour (i.e. the contradiction inherent in labour existing as *wage-labour*): a contradiction whose solution is a necessary prerequisite—in its dialectical sense—to a successful restructuring of society. The overriding factor in the resolution of this contradiction is, in Marx's view, the development of a class consciousness adequate to the social being of labour.

(2) Marx's concept of the proletariat as opposed to the bourgeoisie is not an 'ideal type', but a category of being: the *being* of the sociologically specific groups of proletarians who exist in a necessary structural subordination to capital at *all* stages of capitalistic development, whether the individuals concerned are conscious of it or not. Proletarian class consciousness is, therefore, *the worker's consciousness of his social being as embedded in the necessary structural antagonism of capitalist society, in contrast to the contingency of group consciousness which perceives only a more or less limited part of the global confrontation.* To assign to the concept of the proletariat merely the status of an 'ideal type' inevitably carries with it the conception of class consciousness and political action as an arbitrary 'ought', from Sorel's myth-conscious voluntarism to some contemporary advocates of a 'critical utopianism'. (Even some parts of Lukács' *History and Class Consciousness* are marred by the influence of Sorel's voluntarism and Max Weber's 'typology'.)

(3) The recognition of the contradiction between the 'being' and 'existence' of the proletariat carries with it the task of 'bridging the gap' between group consciousness and class consciousness, or, more exactly, the task of transcending the limits of group consciousness of

the given groups of workers in the direction of a global consciousness of their social being. According to Marx, this task is a realistic one only because it is in agreement with an objective trend of historical development. This fact, though, does not change its nature from being a *task* into a *mechanical historical inevitability*. The development of class consciousness is a *dialectical* process: it is a 'historical inevitability' precisely in so far as the task is *fulfilled* through the necessary intermediary of a self-conscious human agency. This, inevitably, requires some kind of organization—whether the constitution of parties, or of some other forms of collective intermediary—structured in accordance with the specific socio-historical conditions that prevail in a particular epoch, with an overall strategic aim of dynamic interventions in the course of social development. (The latter alone are capable of leaving a lasting mark—in contrast to the ephemeral success of mere political agitation—on the consciousness of the proletariat as a whole, since they involve objective modifications in its social being.) In other words, the 'spontaneous' and 'direct' development of proletarian class consciousness—whether under the impact of economic crises or as a result of individual self-illumination—is a utopian dream. However much (in view of some negative past experiences) one might wish the contrary, the question of political organization cannot be bypassed. The real issue is, therefore, the creation of organizational forms and institutional intermediaries which are *adequate* to the global strategic objectives, considering (*a*) the socio-historical limitations that objectively circumscribe the possibilities of action in every epoch, and (*b*) the necessary limits and distorting effects of the institutional form itself. For an undue amount of 'negative feedback' from (*a*) and (*b*)—which is unavoidable to some extent—can not only nullify hardwon achievements, but also turn the originally dynamic institution into a powerful break and a major obstacle to all further advance. The paradoxical element in the dialectic of institutions is that structuring themselves in accordance with necessary limitations mentioned in (*a*) constitutes both their positive features and their negative characteristics of petrification and self-perpetuation. The institution's ability to meet the challenge of a specific historical situation—its *raison d'être*—requires structural firmness and stability; its impact, though, on socio-historical development produces not only advance, but, at the same time, also an element of institutional obsolescence. (This point underlines the superficiality and evasiveness of all talk about 'personality cult' as an explanatory hypothesis.) The institution is dynamic only so long as it *struggles* with its task, and acquires a more or less extensive layer of inertia the very moment it gains the upper hand. Thus, the *victory* of a specific institutional form over the historical limitations which were at its roots is at the same time also the well-deserved *defeat* of this form: a defeat which is, nevertheless, often transformed into a Pyrrhic triumph of the obsolete, but powerfully ossified, institution—at the expense of the social body that originally brought it into being. Correctives against this kind of development can and must be incorporated either into the structure of a particular institution, conceived on its own (a strictly limited possibility), or into the institutional set-up as a whole whose parts reciprocally interact with one another, or indeed both into the particular institutions and into the total institutional structure of society. Development will largely depend on the effectiveness of the given set of correctives in *minimizing* the negative institutional feedback mentioned above.

It goes without saying that the concept of irreconcilable structural antagonism does not imply anything like a 'homogeneous class consciousness', nor indeed 'occupational uniformity' and the like. Also, given the dynamic interchange of a multiplicity of factors in socio-historical development, it would be utterly foolish to postulate a static hierarchy of the strategic position of particular social groups. Groups which occupied a strategically more important position at a certain stage of development of the productive forces may very well find their erstwhile power significantly curtailed as a result of changes in patterns of production and consumption, and vice versa. What is inconceivable, though, is a permanent nullification of the effects of the withdrawal of labour, whichever groups' labour falls into the category of strategically more important labour. Categories like 'working-class occupations' must be treated *dynamically*, otherwise the dangers of mistaking technological advances for the 'integration of the working class' become acute. Similarly, it would be fallacious to suppose that traditionally 'trouble-free' groups will remain docile, notwithstanding significant shifts towards an increasing strategic importance of withdrawing *their* labour, which was negligible in the past. (Such phenomena as teachers' strikes were unheard-of in the not so distant past; they are likely to gain in importance in the future.) The same goes for the efforts to turn into a *general law* the relative integrating impact of technological change associated with more pleasant working conditions in *some* factories: a projection which ignores the crucial fact that such an impact is largely dependent on the *exceptional* status of the marginal groups in question. We could go on, almost indefinitely, with these examples. The significant thing about their *logic* is that they want to have it *both ways*: a shift in power from a prevalently manual occupational structure to one that is increasingly intellectual, coupled with the docility of powerless intellectual occupations; the assertion of universal conformity to a pattern of behaviour rooted in the ethos of exceptional status, etc. Their *methodology* is equally telling: it consists in an arbitrary projection of some wishfully selected aspects of the established order of society as *permanent* features of all future society, at the same time fictitiously *postulating* a transformation of all the contrasting characteristics of—divided, polarized, conflict- and crisis-ridden—society into the pre-selected (and often even misdescribed) *partial* phenomena, elevated to the status of a *universal 'model'*, in conformity to the (no doubt velvet-gloved) 'iron law of convergence'.

In Marx's view no degree of capitalistically embedded technological development can eliminate the necessary structural subordination of labour to capital, no matter what particular kinds of modification are made in the occupational pattern of society. It is no use to expect the voluntary acceptance of the soulless routine of commodity production on the ground that it is 'a discipline inherent in the working process itself', which therefore applies 'to superiors and subordinates alike'. For the issue at stake is not *technology itself*, but its *mode of application*, i.e. *commodity production* that imposes the discipline of soulless routine on 'superiors and subordinates alike', in so far as it does. And to the extent to which it does, if it does, there is an identity of interest between these 'superiors and subordinates' in changing the prevailing system of production: a point which shows that the 'superiors' in question are not the ruling class to which labour is *structurally* subordinated and opposed. Thus, again, we are given a *semantic* solution, produced by the mystifying confusion of *functional*—technical, instrumental—subordination with *social-structural* subordination. (The same kind of reasoning characterizes the confusion of the social-structural division of labour with its functional-instrumental-technological division: a mystifying confusion from which one can conveniently deduce that the Marxian programme to abolish the social-structural-hierarchical division of labour is nothing but 'day-dreaming'.)

'Class position', 'class interest', 'capital', 'labour', 'class antagonism', 'class consciousness', etc., have no meaning whatsoever if taken apart from one another. (They acquire their meaning, as we have seen, only relative to the general framework of reference of which they are constitutive parts.) As a coherent and interdependent set of concepts, they are designed to grasp the dynamic structure of capitalist society, so as to enable one to assess the multiplicity of constantly changing phenomena in their proper perspectives. The fact, though, that these concepts are the most fundamental categories of capitalist society does not mean that they are some kind of an abstract 'blue-print' of capitalism in general, unaffected by the historical modifications of social phenomena. A higher level of generality is not the same thing as standing above history, though of course, historical change does not exercise a uniform rate of influence on concepts of varying degree of generality. While the most fundamental concepts are a necessary prerequisite to an adequate understanding of changing phenomena, the latter carries with it a greater concretization of some particular elements of the basic set, and, through the interdependence of the various sets of concepts, of the entire conceptual apparatus. (To give an example: the concept of 'trade union consciousness'—which could not emerge before a certain stage of historical development—greatly concretized Marx's original conception as a whole.) Thus, the Marxian conception is characterized by the dialectical reciprocity between the different degrees of generality of the closely interrelated concepts, corresponding to the structural differences and interactions of the various social factors. Without a coherent set of fundamental concepts the ephemeral phenomena cannot be separated from those of lasting significance (fragmentary empiricism and positivism). And without a dynamic interchange between the various levels of the conceptual framework, including those which notify the apparently unimportant 'capillary changes' of social phenomena, Marxism can degenerate into a catechism of dogmas with fixed and absolutized meaning (e.g. the dead scholasticism of Stalinist formulas). In contrast to both, the Marxian conception, far from taking refuge in the realm of *a priorism*, provides the necessary conceptual framework for empirically founded theoretical study as well as for social and political action.

3. THE DEVELOPMENT OF CLASS CONSCIOUSNESS

Marx makes the point in *The Poverty of Philosophy* that 'Labour is organised, is divided differently according to the instruments it disposes over. The hand-mill presupposes a different division of labour from the steam-mill.'[34] This fact, though, should not be interpreted in the sense of a crude technological determinism; for 'The separation of the different parts of labour. . . exists only in modern industry under the sway of competition',[35] 'where the authority, Capital, groups and directs the work'.[36] In other words, the problem is the reciprocal determination of all the factors that characterize the unfolding of capitalist society. Marx repeatedly stresses the interdependence of structural class antagonism with the development of the division of labour: 'Industry and commerce, production and the exchange of the necessities of life, themselves determine distribution, the structure of the different social classes and are, in turn, determined by it as to the mode in which they are carried on'.[37] The individuals, like it or not, are subordinated to the 'independent existence' which classes acquire in the course of this development:

> the class in its turn achieves an independent existence over against the individuals, so that the latter find their conditions of existence predestined, and hence have *their position of life and their personal development assigned to them by their class*, become subsumed under it. This is the *same phenomenon* as the subjection of the separate individuals to the *division of labour* and can only be removed by the abolition of private property and of labour itself.[38]

Thus, the issue at stake is just as much the emancipation of the particular individuals *from their own class* as that of the emancipation of the *subordinate* class from the ruling class. The 'other' to which the individual is subjected in an alienated society is not simply 'the other class', but also his own class—i.e. the constitution of human relations within class boundaries—insofar as it circumscribes the limits of his development. 'Competition', 'division of labour' and 'private property' are conditions under which the individuals are bound to be grouped together in the form of antagonistic class relations, and the continued existence of the classes can only maximize the power of the 'division of labour', etc., over *all* individuals in society. Consequently, the resolution of the contradictions inherent in class society is inconceivable without the abolition of *all* those objective conditions—like the division of labour—which inevitably reproduce one form or another of 'particularism' even if the juridical form of 'private property' is already abolished.

We have to quote here an important passage in which Marx describes the development of the subordinate class as follows:

Large-scale industry concentrates in one place a crowd of people unknown to one another. Competition divides their interests. But the maintenance of wages, this common interest which they have against their boss, unites them in a common thought of resistance—c o m b i n a t i o n. Thus combination always has a double aim, that of stopping the competition among themselves, in order to bring about a general competition with the capitalist. If the first aim of resistance was merely the maintenance of wages, combinations, at first isolated, constitute themselves into groups as the capitalists in their turn unite in the idea of repression, and in face of always united capital, the maintenance of the association becomes more necessary to them than that of wages... In this struggle—a veritable civil war—are united and developed all the elements necessary for a coming battle. Once it has reached this point, association takes on a political character.

Economic conditions had first transformed the mass of the people of the country into workers. The domination of capital has created for this mass a common situation, common interests. This mass is thus already a *class as against capital*, but not yet *for itself*. In the struggle, of which we have noted only a few phases, this mass becomes united, and *constitutes itself as a class for itself*. The interests it defends become class interests. But the struggle of class against class is a political struggle.[39]

As we can see, Marx introduces here a number of important terms, emphasizing that the objective 'end' of this development is the self-constitution of the proletariat as a 'class-*for-itself*'. This term is crucial for the understanding of Marx's theory of classes and class consciousness. Unfortunately, though, it has proved to be a major stumbling-block for commentators. Frequently it is suggested that the difference between class-in-itself and class-for-itself is that the latter term denotes a politically organized group in a situation of conflict, whereas the former does not. If this were so, there would be no difference between the bourgeoisie and the proletariat; nor could Marx make his point about the future of class society as transcended through the action of the 'class-for-itself'. For if there is no intrinsic difference between the ruling and the subordinate classes, then the latter's action can only be conceived as merely a reversal of the terms of their relationship, with no structural consequences for the development of society as a whole. In other words, the central theme of Marx's theory of classes—the abolition of class society itself— is thrown overboard.

Now the fact is that, ever since 1843, Marx had made a fundamental distinction between the proletariat and all the other classes in history, emphasizing that 'labour' is not so much a class-in-itself (or an estate proper) as the necessary foundation of bourgeois society itself, as the condition of existence of the bourgeois order,[40] i.e. a class standing in a non-symmetrical and non-reversible relationship to its opposite. (A reversal could only change the names of the actors, but not the roles themselves.) A few months later, continuing the same line of reasoning, he spoke of the proletariat as 'a class which is the dissolution of all classes', in virtue of which it has a truly '*universal* character'.[41] References to the *political* form of the struggle should not mislead us into believing that it is the culmination or ultimate 'end' of this process. According to Marx, direct political action is only the *first step* taken on the road to a 'self-transcending self-realization' of the 'class-for-itself'. For 'every class which is struggling for mastery, even when its domination, as is the case with the proletariat, postulates the abolition of the old form of society in its entirety and of domination itself, must *first* conquer for itself *political power* in order to represent its interest in turn as the general interest, which *in the first moment it is forced to do*'.[42]

The Poverty of Philosophy discusses the matter in the same spirit:

> The organisation of revolutionary elements as a class supposes the existence of all the productive forces which could be engendered in the bosom of the old society. Does this mean that after the fall of the old society there will be a new class domination culminating in a new political power? No. The condition for the emancipation of the working class is the abolition of every class, just as the condition for the liberation of the Third Estate, of the bourgeois order, was the abolition of all estates and all orders. The working class, in the course of its development, will substitute for the old civil society an association which will exclude classes and their antagonisms, and there will be no

> more political power properly so-called, since political power is precisely the official expression of antagonism in civil society. Meanwhile the antagonism between the proletariat and the bourgeoisie is a struggle of class against class, a struggle which carried to its highest expression is a total revolution.[43]

Thus, the point is that proletarian political action heralds the end of political power and of the political form which characterizes 'the struggle of class against class'. In terms of this negative political confrontation, the proletariat remains a 'class as against capital', i.e. only a class-in-itself. The concept of the proletariat as also a class-for-itself implies *self*-constituting *universality*, i.e. a conscious opposition not merely to bourgeois particularism but to any particularism whatsoever, including the one that necessarily goes with all forms of 'political power properly so-called', even if vested in the proletariat.

The notion of 'in-and-for-itself' is Hegelian in its origin, and is defined in terms of both *universality* and *self-mediation*: 'it mediates itself with itself through its negativity, and is thus posited for itself as the universal'.[44] While Marx rejects the Hegelian idea of the 'for-itself' as an independent moment—we should remember that he speaks of the proletariat becoming *also* a class-for-itself, in addition to being 'a class as against capital'—he retains the criteria of 'universality' and 'self-mediation' as characteristics of the class in-and-for-itself. This is why the bourgeoisie, unlike the proletariat, cannot be described as a class in-and-for-itself. It cannot 'mediate itself with itself through its negativity', for it stands in an antagonistic relation to the proletariat, its negation. Also, it cannot 'posit itself for itself as the universal', since it is constituted as an inherently exclusivistic social force, in the self-contradictory form of 'partiality universalized', i.e. partial self-interest elevated into the general organizing principle of society. In this the bourgeoisie is particularism *par excellence*: the former Third Estate becoming the 'estate in-and-for-itself'—the principle of the Estates, 'definite and limited privilege' (Engels), mediated through its negativity (i.e. one type of partial privilege mediated through other types of partial privilege), and universalized as the fundamental governing principle of society and as the expropriation of all privilege for itself (cf. the conversion of feudal land-ownership into capitalistic agriculture)—but only a 'class-in-itself'. The bourgeoisie is a class which acquires its class character by subsuming the various forms of privilege under its own mode of existence, becoming thus a class of the estate type, or a class of all estates, arising out of them and carrying their principle to its logical conclusion. Consequently, it can be opposed by a class of a radically different type ('a class with radical chains, a class *in* civil society which is not a class *of* civil society'): one which—as a universal class in-and-for-itself—at one and the same time must oppose not only the bourgeoisie (a class *of* civil society), but also the principle of privilege and particularism itself. The estate in-and-for-itself constituted as merely a class-in-itself, or a class *of* civil society, is incapable of self-transcendence, whereas the universal class in-and-for-itself necessarily defines itself in terms of its self-abolition as a particular—proletarian—class, as a class *in* civil society. The proletariat is constituted *in* civil society in the process of the alienation of labour, as a being opposed by alienated labour. Its existence as a 'class-in-itself' is, therefore, a pseudo-positivity: a 'mere semblance of existence', a 'positivity' made of negation. This contradiction can only be resolved by negating the pseudo-positivity of its own existence, which necessarily implies both the negation *of* civil society in which the proletariat is constituted as it is, and its *own* negation as a particular class *in* civil society. (As we have already seen, in Marx's view 'the condition for the emancipation of the working class is the abolition of every class'). The bourgeoisie is the estate-for-itself precisely because it can envisage its own self-transcendence as a particular estate as well as the transcendence of all estates in the form of a class-in-itself, carrying with it the establishment of a new order of society in accordance with the being of this class-in-itself. By the same token, it cannot develop from a class-in-itself into a class in-and-for-itself, since its mode of existence as the privileged class-in-itself necessarily presupposes the preservation of the structural subordination of the proletariat to the bourgeoisie within the established order of society. Equally, the proletariat is a class in-and-for-itself only insofar as it is objectively capable of establishing a viable *historical alternative* to its own structural subordination as well as to the necessity of subordinating *any* class to any other. (The abolition of the classes carries with it, of course, an end to the necessary structural subordination of the individual to the class, a relationship replaced by the non-contradictory unity of part and whole: the *self*-mediating *social individual.*)

The increasing structural-historical complexity of the interchange between the contradictions inherent in the social division of labour on the one hand and the various forms and institutionalized manifestations of antagonistic self-interest on the other can be summed up, in an ascending order, as follows:

(1) the antagonism of individuals against individuals—*bellum omnium contra omnes*: the war of each against all—gives rise to the individual's subordination to his class, and to all individuals' subsumption under some class or other;

(2) the conflict among individuals constituting one and the same class within the general framework of an antagonistic structural division of labour in society as a whole—engenders sub-groups, sub-classes, estates, etc., on either side of the basic social antagonism;

(3) the antagonism between the fundamental classes of society—such as the contradiction between the bourgeoisie and the proletariat as classes-in-themselves, unfolding in the first place in a form that does not call into question the established structure of society—carries with it:

(4) the conversion of some particular estates and sub-classes into peripheral groups, i.e. into groups affected by, but not frontally involved in, the all-encompassing structural antagonism, or indeed, partaking in it, in one form or another, on both sides (petty bourgeoisie, impoverished gentry, intellectuals, etc.); their opposition is thus directed not so much against a specific social group as against the social framework itself, but in the form of an *abstract negation*—a powerless or ineffective opposition—since their strength is also their weakness: a peripheral position which, while allowing them to assume a generically critical attitude towards society, necessarily condemns them to an impotence graphically expressed in the self-fulfilling character of their ideologies (from some later representatives of the Enlightenment to anarchism, and from the manifold varieties of 'populism' to the countless forms of utopianism, both 'positive' and 'negative' or 'critical');

(5) the intensification of the fundamental social antagonism produces the proletariat as a class in-and-for-itself—a class both

belonging to class society and opposing it in its own being—thus generating an *effective negation* of class domination, necessitating both the self-abolition of the proletariat as a class and the establishment of a classless society.

The various modes of being involved in these antagonisms are:

(1) the '*isolated individual*' ('*der vereinzelte Einzelne*') or 'abstract universal' ('*abstrakter Allgemeine*'), motivated by immediate self-interest (it is an 'abstract universal' because its 'universality' is constituted by the indeterminate, abstract generic 'self');

(2) the *partial group* (estates, sub-classes, strata, etc.) held together by 'definite limited privileges';

(3) the *conservative hegemonic group*, tied to its interest in preserving the established structural relations;

(4) the *peripheral group*, motivated by its interest in preventing further polarization and therefore opposed to the intensification of the basic social antagonism;

(5) the *dynamic (self-transcending) hegemonic group* or the class in-and-for-itself, interested in the development of the 'social individual' ('*sozialer Einzelne*') or the 'concrete universal' ('*konkreter Allgemeine*') human being. ('Concrete universal' since its universality is not defined in terms of the generic 'self' or 'ego', but with reference to actual, historically specific, social relationships).

The respective modes of consciousness are in keeping with these modes of being, namely:

(1) abstract self-consciousness, or consciousness of merely individual self-interest;

(2) status consciousness or the consciousness of specific privileges;

(3) exclusivistic class consciousness or the consciousness of self-fulfilment in terms of class-dominance;

(4) non-class self-consciousness or (illusory) being-above-class consciousness;[45]

(5) the effective unity of *class self*-consciousness and class *non-self*-consciousness, devoid of illusions of standing above classes, but also inherently opposed to the alienated reality of class existence. (In other words: proletarian class consciousness has nothing to do with the fiction of a 'homogenous class consciousness', which never existed, nor could ever exist, let

alone become 'obsolete'. Self-consciousness of the class in-and-for-itself cannot be other than the consciousness of its 'historic task' of constituting an actual historical alternative to the established order of society: a task effectively rooted in the irreconcilable contradictions of its own socio-historical being.)

The Marxian dynamic analysis of the structural antagonism of capitalist society—in which the higher order and more comprehensive structures retain and intensify the contradictions of the lower stages—far from being a form of *a priorism*, is diametrically opposed to all forms of *a priorism*. For the methodology of *a priorism* does not grow on some special philosophical tree, out of the soil of nothing, but arises from the insoluble contradictions of a determinate social being: one which is forced to *reverse* in imagination the actual structural relationships of society so as to produce an *'a priori proof'* of the 'rational order' of society depicted upside-down, of history conceived in the reverse. This is clearly displayed in the Hegelian constructions:

> The rational consideration of a topic, the consciousness of the Idea, is concrete, and to that extent coincides with a genuine practical sense. Such a sense is itself nothing but the sense of rationality or the Idea... The concrete state is the whole, articulated into its particular groups. The member of a state is a member of such a group, i.e. of a social class, and it is only as characterized in this objective way that he comes under consideration when we are dealing with the state. His mere character as universal implies that he is at one and the same time both a private person and also a thinking consciousness, a will which wills the universal. This consciousness and will, however, lose their emptiness and acquire a content and a living actuality only when they are filled with particularity, and particularity means determinacy as particular and a particular class-status... Hence the single person attains his actual and living destiny for universality only when he becomes a member of a Corporation, a society, &c., and thereby it becomes open to him, on the strength of his skill, to enter any class for which he is qualified, the class of civil servants included.[46]

As we can see, *actual* particularism is derived by means of an *a priori deduction* from the '*Idea*' of universality, so as to be successfully reconciled with the latter through the fictitious 'mediation' of an *abstract* 'possibility'—an empty postulate—of the individual acquiring universality by entering *any* class 'on the strength of his skill'. We are allowed to perceive the contradiction between particularism and universality at the point of its magic disappearance: particularism arrives on the stage as an *a priori* postulate destined to fill the emptiness of universality and immediately ceases to be mere particularism. Thus, the contradiction between particularism and universality—now you see it, now you don't—is gone forever, while actual particularism is here to stay, so as to fulfil its 'living destiny for universality'. This method of *a priori* deduction, based on an imaginary reversal of the actual relations, enables Hegel (*a*) to substitute illusion for reality, misrepresenting the fact that it is the 'universal' political sphere which is fundamentally determined by the particularism of private property and class conflict, and not vice versa, thus elevating into an *a priori* law the state's 'illusion of being the *determinant* where it is in fact *determined*';[47] (*b*) to produce a speculative 'solution' to the contradiction between particularism and universality, 'actuality' and 'form'; and (*c*) to conceal the real nature of the political sphere: its inherent particularism transubstantiated into a formal universality directly emanating from the 'Idea'.

In Marx's case 'universality' is not an Idea—let alone an *a priori* fixity concealing the speculative transubstantiation of partial interests—but an *actual movement*: a historical necessity inherent in the objective conditions and contradictions of tangible, empirically verifiable, social development. 'Communism'—writes Marx:

> is for us not a state of affairs which is to be established, an ideal to which reality will have to adjust itself. We call communism the real movement which abolishes the present state of things. The conditions of this movement result from the premises now in existence. Moreover, the mass of propertyless workers . . . presupposes the *world market through competition*. The proletarian can thus only exist world-historically, just as communism, its activity, can only have a 'world-historical' existence. World-historical existence of *individuals*, i.e. existence of individuals which is directly linked up with world history.[48]

This conception of world history, world market, and the development of the actual social individual—three closely interrelated aspects of the problematic of movement towards universality—is prominent in *all* of Marx's works from 1844 onwards. Indeed, it is so fundamental to his theory as a whole that, according to his plans, *Capital* should have reached its climax in Book VI, dedicated to the analysis of the *world market.* (See his letter to Engels, 2 April 1858). Unfortunately, however, many past interpretations of his work systematically ignored this, assessing the validity of the particular theses within the framework of a pseudo-totality of their own creation, producing, thus, a hopelessly one-sided view of Marx.

To take one example, Marx's idea that the emancipation of the working class necessarily involves the abolition of all classes becomes a mere postulate—a categorical imperative—if it is confined within the boundaries of one state only. The matter is, though, radically different in its Marxian framework of assessment:

The further the separate spheres, which act on one another, extend in the course of this development, the more the original isolation of the separate nationalities is destroyed by the developed mode of production and intercourse and the division of labour between various nations naturally brought forth by these, the more history *becomes* world history. Thus, for instance, if in England a machine is invented, which deprives countless workers of bread in India and China, and overturns the whole form of existence of these empires, this invention becomes a *world-historical fact*... From this it follows that this transformation of history into world history is not indeed a mere abstract act on the part of the 'self-consciousness', the world spirit, or of any other metaphysical spectre, but a quite material, *empirically verifiable act*, an act the proof of which every individual furnishes as he comes and goes, eats, drinks and clothes himself.[49]

Another important aspect of this problematic is the development of the instruments of production under the conditions of *international* division of labour and its repercussions on global socio-economic development:

Thanks to the application of machinery and of steam, the division of labour was able to assume such dimensions that large-scale industry, detached from the national soil, depends entirely on the *world-market*, on international exchange, on an *international division of labour*.[50]

Equally, in *Capital*, Marx sums up the inner laws of this development in world perspectives:

This expropriation [of the expropriators] is accomplished by the action of the immanent laws of capitalistic production itself, by the *centralisation of capital*. One capitalist always kills many. Hand in hand with this centralisation, or this expropriation of many capitalists by few, develop, on an ever-extending scale, the co-operative form of the labour-process, the conscious technical application of science, the methodical cultivation of the soil, the transformation of the instruments of labour into instruments of labour only usable in common, the economising of all means of production by their use as the means of production of combined, *socialised labour*, the entanglement of all peoples in the net of the *world-market*, and with this, the *international* character of the capitalist régime.[51]

Thus, development towards universality, from partial structures like the Estates to comprehensive classes, from local limitations to world history, etc., is inseparable from the development of large-scale industry and world trade, from the concentration of capital and the corresponding establishment of a truly all-embracing world market, and from the development of the division and socialization of labour on a world scale.

Ultimately the whole problematic culminates in the vital question of the division of labour, since the division of society into classes has its roots in alienated productive activity that assumes the form of a social division of labour. Consequently, de-alienation of productive activity, abolition of classes and abolition of the division of labour are only different aspects of one and the same process. To postulate, then, a 'classless society' while the division of labour is maintained and enforced is nothing but the 'wood-iron' ('das hölzerne Eisen'—Marx) of communism round the—ever-receding—corner'.

So long as 'activity is not *voluntarily* divided',[52] but regulated, instead, by some kind of 'natural' process, in the framework of international competition and confrontation, there must be in existence social structures capable of imposing on the individuals who constitute society a structural (not merely functional) division of labour. And the structures of such an enforced social-hierarchical division of labour are precisely the classes.

The supersession of the structural division of labour, clearly, does not depend on the goodwill of enlightened individuals, but on the maturation of some specific, objective conditions on a global scale. The relationship between a purely *functional* (voluntary) and the (enforced) *structural* division of labour is the same as that between *objectification* and *alienation*. Human advancement is inconceivable without objectification necessarily interconnected with a functional division of labour. Furthermore, up to a certain stage in human development, self-objectifying productive activity cannot take place without assuming an alienated form, without, that is, the functional division of labour necessarily becoming also a social-structural one.

This *historical* necessity of a fusion between objectification and alienation, functional and structural division of labour culminating in the structural subordination of labour to capital, is however, 'a *disappearing* necessity' ('eine verschwindende Notwendigkeit'—Marx), as indeed all historical necessities are. It disappears in the course of productive development that brings with it not only the concentration of capital, but, simultaneously, also the socialization of the labour process on a formerly unimaginable scale, transforming the earlier necessary social-structural regulators of the productive process—the classes—into anachronistic shackles of all further productive advance. (The arms race, with all its global repercussions, is one of the most fundamental factors to be considered in this connection.)

The production of the social individual is the same process as the emancipation of society from the classes which are but an alienated objectification of the individual's social dimension. Since, however, the classes themselves are constituted and continue to develop in accordance with the more and more internationally articulated structural division of labour, this emancipation of the social individual from the conditions of his alienated self-objectification in class-society necessarily implies, in its turn, the growing supersession of the social division of labour on a world-wide scale.

4. CONCLUSION

What is, then, an objective theory of class consciousness? According to the author of *History and Class Consciousness* it is

> the theory of its objective possibility... [i.e.] whether it is actually possible to make the objective possibility of class consciousness into a *reality*. Hitherto this question could only occur to extraordinary individuals (consider Marx's completely non-utopian prescience with regard to the problems of dictatorship). Today it has become a real and relevant question for a whole class: the question of the inner transformation of the proletariat, of its development to the stage of its objective historical mission. It is an *ideological crisis* which must be solved *before* a practical solution to the world's economic crisis can be found.[53]

No one should doubt that stressing the conditions of objective possibility is vitally important in these matters. But an objective theory of class consciousness cannot be other than its—dialectically qualified—historical *necessity*, not merely *possibility*. An 'objective possibility' which is not formulated in terms of an actual historical necessity is neither objective nor possible. Equally, we are not facing an '*ideological* crisis' which must be solved '*before* a practical solution can be found'. The problem is our global social crisis whose solution necessitates *also* the solution of the ever-deepening ideological crisis as one of its fundamental *moments* and co-determinants; and not *before* but *en route* towards the elaboration of viable practical remedies.

An objective theory of class consciousness implies above all the assessment of its problematic in terms of the Marxian global conception of capitalism as an actual world system. This means that even the apparently purely local phenomena of social conflict must be related to the objective totality of a given stage of socio-economic development. Without a conscious attempt to link the specific social phenomena to the general trends and characteristics of capitalism as a global system, their significance remains concealed or appears disproportionately magnified, and even the general laws—such as the law of pauperism, the diminishing rate of profit, etc., valid only in globally qualified terms—appear to be nothing but speculations and abstractions. Marx repeatedly stressed that all laws are significantly modified by the manifold specific circumstances interchanging with them in their field of action which embrace—through complex dialectical mediations—the totality of the social system in question. And, given the prevalence of sufficiently powerful modifying forces, exceptional solutions may very well arise, without affecting in the least the validity of the general laws themselves. For instance: Marx expected the outbreak of socialist revolutions in the most advanced capitalist countries, although he also stressed the possibility of a revolution in Russia and in the Far East. For the latter, special conditions had to prevail—such as the artificial closure of the socio-economic boundaries of Tsarist Russia during the First World War, which intensified its internal contradictions to the point of explosion on the eve of defeat, when the means of displacing or diffusing the accumulated pressure via external channels had been drastically foreclosed—resulting in a break in the capitalist world system in a backward country. Similarly with China. Thus, to conclude that these revolutions 'refute' Marx, confining the validity of his analyses to underdeveloped countries (where, it is said, misery was powerful enough to affect the political consciousness of people in favour of revolutionary action) is a failure to notice the obvious: namely, that these revolutions broke out at the end and in the immediate aftermath of an imperialist world war, and became successful under conditions when, as a result of internal and external contradictions, the major capitalist powers could not act in unison against them. Marx's general analysis remains as valid as ever, since it does not concern the 'developed' countries, nor the 'underdeveloped' ones, taken separately, but the capitalist world system as a *whole*, with all its inherent structural contradictions, whatever particular forms of 'exception' they may—indeed must—assume at different times and in different socio-economic settings characterized by varying degrees of industrialization. In an objective dialectical framework of reference, working 'exceptions' constitute the general 'rules' which, in an unending interchange, are made into new 'exceptions' and new 'rules', thus both modifying (concretizing) and confirming the general conception itself.

The nature and role of the various social groups can only be grasped in this comprehensive framework of analysis which highlights the fact powerfully stressed by Lukács that:

> Bourgeoisie and proletariat are the only pure classes in bourgeois society. They are the only classes whose existence and development are entirely dependent on the course taken by the modern evolution of production and only from the vantage-point of these classes can a plan for the total organisation of society *even be imagined*. The outlook of the other classes (petty bourgeois or peasants) is ambiguous or sterile because their existence is not based exclusively on their role in the capitalist system of production but is indissolubly linked with the vestiges of feudal society. Their aim, therefore, is not to advance capitalism or to transcend it, but to reverse its action or at least to prevent it from developing fully. Their class interest concentrates on *symptoms of development* and not on development itself, and on elements of society rather than on the construction of society as a whole.[54]

This principle is valid precisely with reference to the global-international social setting, and in this respect its practical strategic importance is paramount. For assessing the respective strategic importance of the various social groups within the limited boundaries of a national community, however large, can only produce illusory strategies insofar as the local power relations are out of phase with global trends which in the end are bound to nullify the—however spectacular—temporary successes of a world-historically peripheral social group. (See the tragic failure of the Mexican revolution.) Peasant-based social movements in the age of world capitalism could only succeed in countries in which the elemental spontaneity of peasant revolt had been adequately *fused* with the strategy of the proletariat as the one and only globally valid historical alternative to the capitalist system of production. (China, Cuba. This is all the more remarkable in view of the fact that the numerical and institutional strength of the working class in these countries was almost negligible at the time when they embarked on the road to a successful revolution.)[55] It is by no means accidental that 'populist' ideologies either degenerated everywhere into a sterile form of intellectual Oblomovism, or developed into systems of ideas—e.g. from Chernyshevsky to Plekhanov in Russia—which could easily be linked to Marxism. Thus, necessary class consciousness is the recognition of the objective socio-historical prevalence of the strategic world perspectives of the working class in both its negative and positive aspects: i.e. both as a radical negation of the capitalist world system and as a positive organizational principle of production based on a structural emancipation of labour.

It cannot be stressed enough: all this does not mean 'homogeneity' and 'uniformity'. The mystifying entanglement of the functional and social-structural factors mentioned above is not merely a feature of theory, but of social practice itself. It manifests itself in the form of complex social stratifications, with definite partial interests reflected in the contingency of stratum-consciousness at any particular time. But, again, it is essential to consider these problems against the dynamic background of transformations which have been, and continue to be, taking place on a massive scale. For the objective tendency inherent in the nature of capital—its growth into a global system coupled with its concentration and increasingly greater technological and science-intensive articulation—undermines and turns into an anachronism the social-structural-functional subordination of labour to capital. Indeed, we can witness already that the traditional forms of hierarchical-structural embeddedness of the functional division of labour tend to disintegrate under the impact of the ever-increasing concentration of capital and socialization of labour. In this paper I can merely point to a few indicators of this striking change:

(1) The escalating vulnerability of contemporary industrial organization as compared to the nineteenth-century factory. (The so-called 'wild-cat strikes' are inconceivable without the underlying economic and technological processes which both induce and enable a 'handful' of workers to bring to a halt even a whole branch of industry, with immense potential repercussions.)

(2) The economic link-up of the various branches of industry into a highly stretched system of closely interdependent parts, with an ever-increasing imperative for safeguarding the *continuity of production* in the system as a whole. (The more the system is stretched as regards its cycle of reproduction, the greater is the imperative of continuity, and every disturbance leads to more stretch as well as to an ever-darkening shadow of even a temporary breakdown in continuity.) There are increasingly fewer 'peripheral branches', since the repercussions of industrial complications are quickly transferred, in the form of a chain-reaction, from any part of the system to all its parts. Consequently, there can be no more 'trouble-free industries'. The age of paternalistic enterprise has been irretrievably superseded by the rule of 'oligopolies' and 'super-conglomerates'.

(3) The growing amount of socially 'superfluous time' (or 'disposable time'),[56] customarily called 'leisure', makes it increasingly absurd, as well as practically impossible, to keep a large section of the population living in apathetic ignorance, divorced from its own intellectual powers. Under the impact of a number of weighty socio-economic factors the old mystique of intellectual elitism has already disappeared for good. Also, side by side with a growing intellectual unemployment—both potential and actual—as well as a worsening of the cleavage between what one is supposed to be educated for and what one actually gets in employment-opportunities, it becomes more and more difficult to maintain the traditionally unquestioning subordination of the vast majority of intellectuals to the authority of capital.

(4) The worker as a consumer occupies a position of increasingly greater importance in maintaining the undisturbed run of capitalist production. Yet he is as completely excluded from control over both production and distribution as ever—as if nothing had happened in the sphere of economics during the last century or two. This contradiction introduces further complications into the established productive system based on a socially stratified division of labour.

(5) The effective establishment of capitalism as an economically interlocking world system greatly contributes to the erosion and disintegration of the traditional, historically formed and locally varying, partial structures of stratification and control, without being able to produce a unified system of social and political control on a world-wide scale. (So long as the power of capital prevails, 'world government' is bound to remain a futurologist pipe-dream.) The 'crisis of hegemony, or crisis of the State in all spheres' (Gramsci) has become a truly international phenomenon.

In the last analysis all these points are about the question of *social control.* In the course of human development, the function of social control had been alienated from the social body and transferred into capital, which thus acquired the power of grouping people in a hierarchical structural-functional pattern, in accordance with the criterion of a greater or lesser share in the control of production and distribution. Ironically, though, the objective trend inherent in the development of capitalism in all spheres—from the mechanical fragmentation of the labour process to the creation of automated systems,[57] from local accumulation of capital to its concentration in the form of an ever-expanding and self-saturating world system, from a partial and local to a comprehensive international division of labour, from limited consumption to an artificially stimulated and manipulated mass-consumption in the service of an ever-accelerating cycle of reproduction of commodity society, and from 'free time' confined to a privileged few to the mass production of social dynamite, in the form of 'leisure', on a universal scale—carries with it a result diametrically opposed to the interest of capital. For in this process of expansion and concentration the power of control invested in capital is being *de facto* re-transferred to the social body as a whole, even if in a necessarily irrational way, thanks to the inherent irrationality of capital itself. That the objectively slipping control is described from the standpoint of capital as 'holding the nation to ransom' does not alter in the least the fact itself; for nineteenth-century capitalism could not be 'held to ransom' even by an army of 'trouble-makers', let alone by a mere 'handful' of them. Here we are confronted with the emergence of a fundamental contradiction: that between an effective loss of control and the established form of control, capital, which, by its very nature, can be nothing *but* control, since it is constituted through an alienated objectification of the function of control as a reified body apart from and opposed to the social body itself. No wonder, therefore, that in the last few years the idea of *workers' control* has been gaining in importance in many parts of the world.

Now the fundamental difference between contingent and necessary class consciousness is that whereas the former perceives merely some isolated aspects of these contradictions, the latter comprehends them in their inter-relatedness, i.e. as necessary features of the global system of capitalism. The former remains entangled in local skirmishes even when the scale of the operation is relatively large, whereas the latter, by focusing attention on the strategically central issue of *social control*, is concerned with a comprehensive solution even when its immediate objectives appear to be limited ones. (e.g. an attempt to keep alive, under workers' control, a factory falling to the axe of capitalist 'rationalization').

The historical necessity of the development of this consciousness resides in the objective contradictions of the socio-economic system, to which it has to provide a global strategic alternative. In this sense, necessary class consciousness is the consciousness of the necessarily global character of any viable historical alternative to the established order of productive relations. Those who want to deny the development of this consciousness must first prove either that the global system of capitalism is devoid of significant contradictions, or that it is capable of mastering its contradictions under all circumstances.

The development of necessary class consciousness does not imply its constitution as a 'homogeneous *psychological bond*'—which is a fiction, as we have seen—but the elaboration of strategically viable *programmes of action* embracing a multiplicity of specific social groups in whatever variety of organizational forms may be required. The non-appearance of the Godot of a common psychological bond is completely beside the point. What cements various social groups together in a favourable historical situation—for instance, at the time of a general strike—is not some mysterious psychological power but significant practical programmes arising from the empirical reality of the common structural subordination of the groups concerned to the power of capital. And the historically necessary development of class consciousness consists precisely in this practical elaboration of a set of strategic aims corresponding to the objective structural position of the various social groups which formulate them.

In conclusion it must be stressed that the historical necessity in question has nothing whatsoever to do with any form of mechanistic fatalism. For although the socio-historical setting in which necessary class consciousness arises inescapably determines one's *field* of action as well as the general *direction* of development, it does not define the *rate* and *forms* of change, nor indeed the nature and amount of human *sacrifices* that go with great social upheavals and transformations. These factors primarily depend on the available programmes and institutional forms of action for which the given, more or less self-conscious, human agencies have to assume responsibility. But even so, self-conscious political action becomes meaningful only in terms of the socio-historical necessities which give rise to it. For, given the fact stressed by Marx that the objective trend of development towards universality (this 'totalizing' historical *necessity*) is inseparable from the individual's existential '*need* for universality and integrality of self-development', true social consciousness is constituted—in an inescapable response to socio-historical challenge—as an *inner necessity*: a dialectical unity of subjective and objective, internal and external determinations.

NOTES

1. Marx's stresses are indicated by spaced lettering; my own are italicized. Similarly with other quotations. Spaced and also italicized lettering indicates stresses both by the authors concerned and by myself.
2. Antonio Gramsci, *The Modern Prince and Other Writings*, Lawrence & Wishart, London, 1957, pp. 172–3.
3. Reinhard Bendix and Seymour Martin Lipset (eds.), *Class, Status, and Power*, 2nd ed, Routledge & Kegan Paul, London, 1967, p.11.
4. I have discussed these problems at a greater length in Chapter 3 of my book on *Marx's Theory of Alienation*, Merlin Press, London, 1970.

5. Marx, *Economic and Philosophic Manuscripts of 1844*, Lawrence & Wishart, London, 1959, p. 80.
6. Marx, *Capital*, Vol. III, Chapter 48.
7. *Ibid.*
8. As is well known, Marx had put to his own use Hegel's insights into the structure of capitalist society. Equally, who could deny that Marx's diagnosis of the contradictions of capitalism had been instrumental in bringing about 'counter-moves' and reforms which helped to retard the maturation of some contradictions identified by him? Needless to say, the views which express a determinate social position can only be used within certain limits by the social adversary. To the extent, though, to which they can be used, paradoxically they contribute to a, however temporary, neutralization of the denounced contradictions. Such a deadlock, once perceived, can only be broken by an appropriately modified social consciousness which, in its turn, will again be subject to the dangers of manipulative use by the adversary. Since social consciousness is not a conspiratorial instrument, but the expression of dynamic social relations—comparable to chess rather than to a game of cards—the readjustment of one's strategic programmes in accordance with changing situations is vitally important.
9. Marx, *The Poverty of Philosophy*, Lawrence & Wishart, London n.d., p. 130. This is why Marx scorns Proudhon for imagining that 'competition' or 'monopoly' are straightforward 'economic categories' (*ibid.*, pp. 127–8) or for his attempts at assigning to 'machinery' the same status: '*Machinery*', writes Marx, '*is no more an economic category than the bullock that drags the plough.* Machinery is merely a *productive force.* The modern workshop, which depends on the *application* of machinery, is a *social productive relation*, an economic category' (*ibid.*, pp. 112–13). Those who imagine that at an advanced stage of production—characterized by automated machinery—the production of surplus-value is transferred to 'fixed capital' (machinery) as the embodiment of 'scientific knowledge' are guilty of the same inability to distinguish between the *means of production* and their socially specific *application.* Marx anticipated their arguments when he wrote in the *Grundrisse*, in the section dealing with the problems of machinery and automation: 'For the thesis [cf. Lauderdale, etc.] which wants to make capital as such create value separately from labour, and thus also s u r p l u s - v a l u e (or profit), fixed capital—namely that capital whose material existence or use value is machinery—is still the form which gives the most credence to their *superficial fallacies.*' Dietz Verlag, Berlin, 1953, p. 590.
10. *The Poverty of Philosophy*, p. 147.
11. *Ibid.*, p. 123. (It should be noted that the operative term is, again, 'their whole manner of being'—i.e. 'social being'—and not simply 'economics').

12. *Ibid.*, pp. 140–4.
13. See, for instance, the following passage from *The Poverty of Philosophy* (p. 144): 'The economists want the workers to remain in society as it is constituted and as it has been signed and sealed by them in their manuals. The [utopian] Socialists want the workers to leave the old society alone, the better to be able to enter the new society which they have prepared for them with so much foresight. In spite of both of them, in spite of manuals and utopias, combination has not ceased for an instant to go forward and grow with the development and growth of modern industry. It has now reached such a stage, that *the degree to which combination has developed in any country clearly marks the rank it occupies in the hierarchy of the world market.* England, whose industry has attained the highest degree of development, has the biggest and best organized combinations.' Thus, the significance of trade unionism is seen by Marx in its world perspectives: as a crucial aspect of the irreversibly global development of the capitalist system of production.
14. *Ibid.*, pp. 108–9.
15. *Capital*, Vol. I, Chapter 25, Section 4. And in the same section, after formulating the general law of capitalist accumulation carrying with it the growth of pauperism, he adds: '*Like all other laws, it is modified in its working by many circumstances*, the analysis of which does not concern us *here*'.
16. 'Autre chose est faire de la science sociale et autre chose est former les consciences', i.e. 'It is one thing to do social science, but it is quite another to shape social consciousness'.
17. In contrast to this undialectical separation, Gramsci emphasized that ' "too much" (and therefore superficial and mechanical) political realism, often leads to the assertion that the man of State must work only within the sphere of "effective reality", not interest himself in "what should be", but only in "what is". This would mean that the man of state must have no perspectives longer than his own nose. . . the point is, in other words, to see whether "what should be" is an arbitrary or necessary act, concrete will or a hopeless wish, a desire, a yearning for the stars. . . To apply the will to the creation of a new balance of the really existing and operating forces, basing oneself on that particular force which one considers progressive, giving it the means to triumph, is still to move within the sphere of effective reality, but in order to dominate and overcome it (or contribute to this). "What should be" is therefore concrete, and is moreover the only realistic and dynamic interpretation of reality. . . The Savonarola-Machiavelli opposition is not an opposition between what is and what should be. . . but between two should-be's, the abstract and cloudy one of Savonarola and the realistic one of Machiavelli, realistic even if it did not become immediate reality', *op. cit.*, pp. 162–3.
18. Marx, *Preface* to the first edition of *Capital*, 1867.
19. J.M. Keynes, *A Short View of Russia*, 1925.
20. J.M. Keynes, *Am I a Liberal?*, 1925.

21. Keynes correctly characterized G.E. Moore's ethical theory as rooted in self-reassuring and self-complacent Edwardian stability. His own intellectual formation was, of course, very similar to Moore's.
22. Karl Mannheim, *Ideology and Utopia*, Routledge & Kegan Paul, London, 1936, p. 251.
23. Ironically, even a leading propagandist of 'the end of ideology', Daniel Bell, had to speak recently of the '*dismal record*' of this social science, adding that 'In the areas of education, welfare, social planning, there has been little knowledge that one can draw upon for policy purposes. Social scientists have reluctantly begun to admit that the problems are more "complex" than they thought.', 'Unstable America'. *Encounter*, June 1970.
24. The recent vogue of those forms of 'structuralism' which are characterized by a systematic ambiguity as regards 'function' and 'structure' is inseparable from the ideological need to find a respectable methodological foundation for these 'metaideological' theories.
25. *Economic and Philosophic Manuscripts of 1844*, p. 16.
26. *Capital*, Vol. I, Chapter 25, Section I.
27. *Sunday Times Business News*, 26 July 1970.
28. Gramsci, *op. cit.*, p. 154.
29. The case of J.M. Keynes offers some instructive insights. We have already seen that when it comes to discussing Marxism, political swearwords take over from reasoning ('turbid rubbish of the Red bookshops', etc.). It is equally significant that he has to resort to mawkish sermonizing when he writes about what displeases him in capitalism: 'For at least another hundred years we must pretend to ourselves and to everyone that fair is foul and foul is fair; for foul is *useful* and fair is not' (*Economic Possibilities for Our Grandchildren, 1930*). The presumed *fatality* of the rule of 'usefulness' is opposed by an empty 'ought': a moral indignation rendered completely impotent by associating 'foul' with 'useful'—meaning 'marketable' or 'profitable': a typical mystification which hides the fact that in commodity-society *exchange-value* usurps the place of human *use-value* in that the production of *goods* is replaced by the production of *marketable commodities*—and by postulating the unavoidability of this association. Similarly, in another work Keynes declares: 'One begins to wonder whether the material advantages of keeping *business* and *religion* in different compartments are sufficient to balance the moral disadvantages' (*A Short View of Russia*). As if the matter could be resolved through some kind of morally enlightened legislation—an idea *categorically* contradicted by Keynes' own account of socio-economic development which can only acknowledge the role of 'science and compound interest'. Thus, the moralizing question remains an idle wondering: 'Conscience' and 'Human Nature' can safely carry on their existence in separate universes. The unmediated *dualism* of this reasoning is a *necessary* one. Socio-economic development must be explained as a fatality of Nature ('usefulness',

'the law of compound interest', 'productive techniques', etc.), while the prevailing values are considered separately, as 'intrinsic values'. The practical *intermediary* link between 'facts' or 'techniques' and 'values' —namely, the established *social relations of production*— must remain unmentioned (and thus the conceptual structure must be a dualistic one) because pointing at them would reveal the socio-historical specificity of the bourgeois relations of production. Understandably, therefore, any departure from the bourgeois order must be explained in terms of the mysteries of religion. We have quoted above Keynes' remarks about the 'strange and horrid conversion of the zealous ones' who detach themselves from the rationality, naturalness, etc., of the perspectives of those who are 'the quality in life and carry the seeds of all human advancement'. The same structure of argument is in evidence in his approach to social trends: 'I feel confident of one conclusion—that if Communism achieves a certain success, it will achieve it, not as an improved *economic technique*, but as a *religion*. . . I do not think that it contains, or is likely to contain, any piece of *useful economic technique* which we could not apply, *if we choose*, with equal or greater success in a society which retained all the marks, I will not say of nineteenth century individualistic capitalism, but of British *bourgeois ideals*' (*A Short View of Russia*). Thus, the issue can be 'confidently' prejudged—as early as 1925, when these lines first appeared—by begging the question: for if an alternative 'economic technique' cannot be used by bourgeois economics then it is not a 'useful technique' but an element of religion. At the same time, the historical—i.e. changeable—character of the capitalist social relations of production can be conveniently misrepresented as 'useful economic technique' which is, of course, its own justification. What disappears in this opposition of 'fact and value', 'business and religion', 'technique and ideal', 'technique and religion', etc., is precisely the vital intermediary of the *social relations of production*. (We can note, again, the ideological function of conflating socio-historically specific 'structure' into timeless 'function'). 'Technique as such' is, of course, compatible with different social systems of production. However, insofar as economic or productive techniques are embedded in a specific structure of social relationships—and to a greater or lesser extent they always are—they are not compatible with a rival system of production. This is why Keynes, significantly, has to add to his claim about the alleged neutrality of 'technique' two blatant escape-clauses: '*useful* economic techniques' and '*if we choose* to apply them'.

This kind of reasoning enables all those who argue from the standpoint of capital to represent the crucial value-commitment: one's self-identification with the established social relations of production as a purely rational and 'neutral' approval of 'useful economic techniques' (or of theories based on 'scientific facts', 'descriptive models', 'pragmatic rules', 'empirical observations', etc.) and to dismiss all rival approaches—especially those which dare to focus attention on the conspicuously unmentioned factor of the social relations of production—as 'zeal', 'religion', 'horrid conversion', 'turbid rubbish of the Red bookshop', 'ideology', and the like.

30. David Lockwood, *The Blackcoated Worker. A Study in Class Consciousness*, Allen & Unwin, London, 1958, p. 210.
31. Gramsci, *op. cit.*, p. 174.
32. Lockwood, *op. cit.*, p. 208.
33. See Sartre, *Critique de la raison dialectique*, Gallimard, Paris, 1960.
34. *The Poverty of Philosophy*, p. 112.
35. *Ibid.*, p. 113.
36. *Ibid.*, p. 115.
37. Marx-Engels, *The German Ideology*, Lawrence & Wishart, London, 1965, p. 58.
38. *Ibid.*, pp. 69–70.
39. *The Poverty of Philosophy*, p. 145.
40. See Marx's *Critique of the Hegelian Philosophy of Right.*
41. Marx, Introduction to the *Critique of the Hegelian Philosophy of Right.*
42. *The German Ideology*, p. 46.
43. *The Poverty of Philosophy*, pp. 146–7.
44. Hegel, *Science of Logic*, Allen & Unwin, London, 1929, Vol. II, p. 480.
45. The pseudo-empirical character of theories which insist on the special mediating role of the 'unattached intelligentsia' can be clearly perceived in the following passage: 'Participation in a *common educational heritage* progressively tends to suppress differences of birth, status, profession, and wealth, and to unite the individual *educated people* on the basis of the *education* they have received'. Thus *freischwebende Intelligenz* is born out of a *tautological postulate* declared to be nothing less than 'a *purely empirical investigation* through description and structural analysis'. Once born, no task is too great for this intelligentsia, for 'it subsumes in itself all those interests with which social life is permeated'. The function of its representatives is 'to penetrate into the ranks of the conflicting parties in order to compel them to accept their demands', and who would be so mean as to ask the question 'How?' (Mannheim, *op. cit.*, pp. 138–42, and 239). Marx criticized the manifestation of a similar illusion in these words: 'He wants to be the synthesis—he is a composite error. He wants to soar as a scientist above the bourgeois and the proletarians; he is merely the petty bourgeois, continually tossed back and forth between capital and labour' (*The Poverty of Philosophy*, p. 107).
46. Hegel, *Philosophy of Right*, Clarendon Press, Oxford, 1942, pp. 200–1.
47. *Critique of the Hegelian Philosophy of Right*, MEW, Vol. 1, p. 305.
48. *The German Ideology*, p. 48.
49. *Ibid.*, pp. 60–1.

50. *The Poverty of Philosophy*, p. 118.
51. *Capital*, Vol. 1, Chapter 32.
52. *The German Ideology*, p. 45.
53. Georg Lukács, *History and Class Consciousness*, Merlin Press, London, 1971, p. 79.
54. *Ibid*., p. 59. This important idea has its origin in three of Marx's detailed analyses of contemporary French history: (1) *The Class Struggles in France, 1848 to 1850*; (2) *The Eighteenth Brumaire of Louis Bonaparte*; and (3) *The Civil War in France*.
55. Mao Tse-tung's approach to the problem of classes and class consciousness shows a significant advance even with respect to Lenin's theory.
56. See *Grundrisse der Kritik der politischen Ökonomie*, pp. 593–4.
57. 'Nothing is more absurd than to see in machinery the *antithesis* of the division of labour, the *synthesis* restoring unity to divided labour. The machine is a unification of the instruments of labour, and by no means a combination of different operations for the worker himself. . . . Simple tools; accumulation of tools; composite tools; setting in motion of a composite tool by a single hand engine, by man; setting in motion of these instruments by natural forces, machines; system of machines having one motor; system of machines having one automatic motor—this is the progress of machinery. The concentration of the instruments of production and the division of labour are as inseparable one from the other as are, in the political sphere, the concentration of public authority and the division of private interests. . . . What characterizes the division of labour in the *automatic work-shop* is that labour has there completely lost its specialized character. But the moment every special development stops, the *need for universality*, the tendency towards an *integral development of the individual* begins to be felt. The automatic workshop wipes out specialists and craft idiocy', *The Poverty of Philosophy*, pp.117–21.

III Marx 'Philosopher' *

Marx's striking pronouncement on philosophy: 'The philosophers have only interpreted the world, in various ways; the point is to *change* it[1]—is often understood in a one-sided way: as a radical rejection of philosophy and a call for its supersession by 'scientific socialism'. What is not appreciated in such interpretations is that Marx's idea of such an *Aufhebung* is not envisaged simply as a theoretical shift from philosophy to science but as a complex practical programme whose realization necessarily implies the dialectical unity of 'the weapon of criticism and the criticism of weapons'[2], which means that philosophy remains an integral part of the struggle for emancipation. As Marx put it: '*you cannot supersede philosophy without realising it*',[3] which cannot be accomplished *in* science itself, but only in practical reality or social praxis—which includes, of course, the contribution of science. Furthermore, the original proposition cannot be divorced from Marx's assertion of the necessary interconnection between this 'realization of philosophy' and the proletariat. For:

> Just as philosophy finds its *material* weapons in the proletariat, so the proletariat finds its *intellectual* weapons in philosophy... Philosophy cannot realise itself without the transcendence [*Aufhebung*] of the proletariat, and the proletariat cannot transcend itself without the realization [*Verwirklichung*] of philosophy.[4]

———

* First published in *The History of Marxism, Vol.1, Marxism in Marx's Day* edited by Eric Hobsbawm, Harvester Press, Brighton, 1982, pp. 103–36.

The two sides of this dialectical interrelationship thus, according to Marx, stand or fall together.

But are such assertions to be taken seriously, or should they be considered no more than colourful examples of youthful exuberance and rhetorics? Can we assign any meaning—and if so, what exactly—to the idea of 'realizing philosophy' without which 'the proletariat cannot transcend itself'? And since we cannot help seeing that the proletariat did not succeed so far in the historical task of transcending itself, should we turn our back to the embarrassing problem by pretending that Marx's programme has been accomplished in 'theoretical practice', through the supersession of philosophy by the *idea* of 'scientific socialism', 'the science of history', etc.? What role, if any, is left to philosophy in the constitution of a socialist consciousness and in the realization of the practical tasks facing us once Marx's critical remarks on past philosophy and on the relationship between philosophy and social life are consistently applied to the assessment of post-Marxian trends of development? These and similar questions are essential for our understanding of Marx's significance for philosophy as well as of philosophy's significance for the kind of social praxis which Marx himself had advocated.

1. THE REALIZATION OF PHILOSOPHY

Following his father's wishes, like Lukács seventy years later, Marx dedicated himself at first to the study of law. Soon, however, he felt the 'urge to wrestle with philosophy', realizing that in view of the profound link between philosophy and his chosen field of study 'there could be no headway without philosophy'. He wrote half-apologetically to his father from Berlin in 1837: 'I became even more firmly bound to the modern world philosophy from which I had thought to escape'.[5] Philosophy for him was not a substitute for getting laboriously acquainted with the details of the technical literature: his reading of tedious juridical texts was just as phenomenal as his note-taking in his later years. He wasn't looking for some speculative *a priori* alternative to the minutiae of legal knowledge but for a guiding thread—an adequate theoretical foundation—to tie them together. He realized that the only way to gain a proper understanding of any object of study was to grasp it in the network of its dynamic interconnections, and he proudly stressed the principle according to which '*the object itself must be studied in its development*'.[6] The refusal to uncritically assume the existent as simply given, and the demand for relating the particular points to their manifold dialectical interconnections in the overall process, understandably, led Marx to question rigorously the limits of his subject of study. Thus the transition from studying the empirical aspects of law ('administrative science',[7] as he called it) to Jurisprudence and from the latter to philosophy in general was natural for him and coincided with the deepening of his understanding of the problems at stake.

To be sure, this kind of progression is not a peculiarity valid for Marx alone. True, the depth and extent to which Marx was able to draw the philosophical conclusions from a critical examination of the empirical material (legal case studies as well as discussions of civil procedure, criminal law and the law of property, among other things) revealed a fast-maturing immense talent with a Gargantuan appetite for knowledge matched by an unequalled power of generalization and an ability to perceive the most far-reaching implications of any point at issue. An extraordinary single-mindedness of purpose coupled with a conscious effort to integrate life and work, the part and the whole, was clearly in evidence from the first moment of his recorded reflections, as we can see in his famous letter to his father to whom he wrote: 'allow me to review my affairs in the way I regard life in general, as the expression of an intellectual activity which develops in all directions, in science, art and private matters.'[8] No wonder, therefore, that witnessing Marx's Promethean determination to fuse life and work—that is, his way of addressing himself to the problems of philosophy with such an intensity that he didn't just study them but at the same time also lived them—made Moses Hess (by six years Marx's elder) write of him to a friend with boundless admiration and enthusiasm:

> prepare yourself to make the acquaintance of the greatest, perhaps the *only* now living *true philosopher*, who soon, wherever he may appear (in print or on the lecture platform), will draw the eyes of Germany upon himself. Dr Marx—that is the name of my idol—is still a very young man (perhaps 24 years old at the most) who will deliver the last blow to the religion and politics of the Middle Ages. He combines the sharpest wit with the deepest philosophical earnestness. Think of Rousseau, Voltaire, Holbach, Lessing, Heine and Hegel united in one person; I say *united*, not thrown together—and there you have Dr. Marx.[9]

All this is very true: the depth of insight of a Marx cannot be set up as a norm for all. Nevertheless, the general direction of the undertaking must be the same in that the inner logic of any particular field of study points beyond its own partiality and demands to be inserted into increasingly broader contexts until the point is reached where the full range of dialectical interconnections with the whole is adequately established. And philosophy is ultimately nothing but the comprehensive framework of such connections without which the analysis of particular areas is bound to remain fragmentary and hopelessly one-sided.

Nor could it be sensibly argued that Marx's subsequent critique of speculative idealism and contemplative materialism alike radically changed his attitude to the importance of philosophy itself. To talk about Marx's 'youthful philosophical phase' as opposed to his later submergence in 'science' and in 'political economy' is a crude misrepresentation based on an appalling ignorance or distortion of quite elementary facts.[10] The target of his criticism of philosophy was from the very beginning its remoteness from and opposition to the real world, and the impotence that necessarily followed from such an idealistic separation. This is why he wrote already in 1837: 'From the idealism which, by the way, I had compared and nourished with the idealism of Kant and Fichte, *I arrived at the point of seeking the idea in reality itself*.'[11] He was conscious of the fact that the problematical development of philosophy as an alienated universality was the manifestation of an objective contradiction and he was trying to find a solution to this contradiction. Thus when he reached the conclusion—in a critical rejection of the impotence of mere philosophical *interpretations*—that the problem did not arise from within philosophy itself but from the relationship between the latter and the real world, and that consequently the solution was in the *changing* of this world, he did not advocate a capitulation to fragmentariness and partiality, nor turning of one's back to the philosophical search for universality. On the contrary, he insisted that the measure of emancipation must be the degree to which social praxis regains its universal dimension: a task he also called 'the realization of philosophy'.

Of course, Marx denied the legitimacy of an independent, self-oriented philosophy,[12] just as he scorned the idea of a separate existence of politics, law, religion, art, etc., in that all these areas ('ideological reflexes') had to be understood in relation to the objective development of the forces and relations of production as an integral part of the totality of social praxis. Equally, he rejected the idea that philosophy could have a privileged domain of its own and a separate medium of existence[13] which could be opposed to real life. And he stressed the role of the *division of labour*[14] in the formation of the illusions which philosophy had about itself. But he hastened to add that such developments whereby philosophy etc. come into contradiction with the existing relations 'can only occur because existing social relations have come into contradictions with existing forces of production'.[15] Thus the problem was identified as a profound contradiction of the social division of labour itself which made philosophy usurp—together with some other ideological forms—the dimension of universality. This did not mean in the slightest that the demand for universality itself was to be dismissed: only its speculative and imaginary realization. This is why Marx insisted on the reintegration of philosophy with real life in terms of the *necessity of philosophy* as the necessity of its realization in the service of emancipation. Thus philosophy, with these qualifications, continued to inform and orient Marx's work in a most significant sense to the very end of his life.

The idea of universality appeared in philosophy before Marx as an abstract principle. Another term of the same problematic, *totality*, was likewise articulated as a speculative philosophical and methodological concept. Marx revealed the true significance of these categories by putting into relief their real ground of existence and by treating them as the most general *Daseinformen* ('forms of existence')[16] which were reflected in philosophy 'as in a *camera obscura*, in an inverted form' so as to be able to deduce actuality from the 'idea'. Marx described the real bases of universality and its historical corollary, 'world history', in the following terms:

(1) 'the universal development of productive forces':

(2) 'the actual empirical existence of men in their *world-historical*, instead of local being';

(3) 'universal competition' and the development of universal interdependence ('*universal* intercourse between men. . . makes each nation dependent on the revolutions of others');

(4) the development of the 'universal class', the proletariat which 'can only exist *world-historically*, just as communism, its activity, can only have a "world-historical" existence', in other words, a 'world-historical existence of individuals, i.e. existence of individuals

which is *directly* linked up with world history.'[17]

Consequently, the problem of universality, though at first perceived in a fictitious form in philosophy, was not simply a speculative philosophical perversion, but a real issue with a vital bearing on the life of every single individual now *directly* linked to world history in its actual unfolding. This is why it was not 'youthful rhetorics' to talk about the 'realization of philosophy' as the work of actual historical development through the agency of real social individuals and their collective manifestations.

Marx raised the problem of universality and its realization also under its other vital aspect: as *appropriation.* Again in place of mere conceptual transformations and solutions he presented us with the objective dialectic of real existence. And again in opposition to a speculative philosophical projection of the grandiose unfolding of the Idea, the picture drawn was that of the harsh reality and potential liberation of actual historical development. For:

things have now come to such a pass, that the individuals must appropriate the existing totality of productive forces, not only to achieve self-activity, but, also, merely to safeguard their very existence. This appropriation is first determined by the object to be appropriated, the productive forces, which have been developed to a totality and which only exist within a universal intercourse. From this aspect alone, therefore, this appropriation must have a universal character corresponding to the productive forces and the intercourse. The appropriation of these forces is itself nothing more than the development of the individual capacities corresponding to the material instruments of production. The *appropriation of a totality of instruments of production* is, for this very reason, the *development of a totality of capacity in the individuals* themselves. This appropriation is further determined by the persons appropriating. Only the proletarians of the present day, who are completely shut off from all self-activity, are in a position to achieve a *complete* and no longer *restricted* self-activity, which consists in the *appropriation of a totality of productive forces* and in the thus *postulated* development of a *totality of capacities.* All earlier revolutionary appropriations were restricted; individuals, whose self-activity was restricted by a crude instrument of production and a limited intercourse, appropriated this crude instrument of production, and hence merely achieved a new state of limitation. Their instrument of production became *their property,* but they themselves remained *subordinate to the division of labour* and to their *instrument of production.* In all appropriations up to now, a mass of individuals remained subservient to a single instrument of production; in the appropriation by the proletarians, a mass of instruments of production *must* be made subject to *each individual,* and property to *all.* Modern *universal* intercourse can be controlled by *individuals,* therefore, only when controlled by *all.*[18]

Thus the philosophical concepts of universality and totality were shown by Marx to be closely linked to and dependent upon the possibility of a full appropriation which they anticipated in an abstract form in opposition to and in a speculative supersession of the deficiencies (partiality and conflict-ridden character) of empirical existence. Marx rejected this abstract negation and clearly identified the objective conditions, forces and tendencies of the social development which itself defined appropriation as the production of a totality of capacities in the individuals in conjunction with the development of a totality of productive forces and instruments of production in the framework of a universal intercourse. And in the same spirit later, in the *Grundrisse,* he projected the *'free development of individualities'*[19] and in *Capital* he anticipated for men 'conditions most favourable to, and *worthy of, their human nature*. . . ; that development of human energy which is an *end in itself,* the *true realm of freedom*'.[20] The universality of such appropriation was characterized by Marx not only in terms of the highest level of the totality of productive forces and the corresponding all-round development of capacities in the individuals within a universal intercourse, but also in the radically new modality of property ownership: namely the exclusion of individuals as separate individuals from the ownership of the means of production in order to make possible their effective control by the totality of associated producers.

Guardedly, Marx used the expressions: '*postulated* development of a totality of capacities' and '*must* be made subject to *each* individual and property to *all*' (referring to the means of production). In this way he not only emphasized the necessary interdependence of the all-round development of the individuals and their conscious control of property and production, but also put into relief that so long as such developments are not actually accomplished in real life, philosophy is bound to continue to live a separate existence instead of being integrated in everyday life and thus 'realized'. For the separateness of philosophy is only the manifestation of an inner contradiction of a social praxis which as yet failed to realize its potential of developing the totality of capacities in the individuals appropriating the totality of productive forces under their combined control. This is the negative aspect of the problem. The positive is that philosophy, under such circumstances, is not merely the necessary manifestation of this failure—which itself cannot be swept under the carpet by pseudo-scientific verbal devices like 'theoretical practice', nor by haughtily dismissing Marx's theory of fetishism as Hegelianism and the outgrowth of 'German cultural Romanticism'—but at the same time also a vital reminder of a positive potentiality for transcending that failure. If partiality continues to prevail under our present-day circumstances, making the demand for universality appear extremely remote from reality, that is not philosophy's fault. The question is whether we resign ourselves to the triumph of partiality, elevating it to a permanent condition of existence, as Marx's critics tend to do, or negate it whichever way we can, including the form in which the philosophical 'weapon of criticism' can and must contribute to the success of a practical negation. There can be no doubt as to where Marx stands on this issue, with his advocacy of the 'development of free individualities' and of the 'true realm of freedom . . . worthy of human nature'. By contrast, the speculative verbal supersession of philosophy by 'Theory', 'Theoretical Practice', by the so-called 'rigorous scientific concepts of experimental reasoning', and the like, can only lead to a conservative rejection of the unity of theory and practice and to the sceptical dismissal of Marx's values as unrealizable dreams.

2. 'THE POSITIVE SCIENCES' AND MARX'S 'POSITIVE SCIENCE'

Marx's philosophical development towards a radical watershed in the entire history of philosophy was staggeringly fast. It goes without saying that he did not simply break away from the great heritage of the past. On the contrary, he continued to make generously positive references to the classics of philosophy—from Aristotle to Spinoza and from Vico to Hegel—throughout his almost half-a-century-long literary activity. But the ideas of past philosophers, however fully acknowledged, were closely integrated by him, as 'superseded-preserved' elements, into a monumental conception of exemplary originality. He worked out the basic outlines of this conception as a very young man, in his early twenties, and he went on articulating and developing the new world view in all its dimensions through his major works of synthesis.

Engels wrote of Marx in 1886: 'Marx stood higher, saw further, and took a wider and quicker view than all the rest of us'.[21] Whatever we may think of Engels' own significance in the elaboration of Marxism, there can be no doubt about the fundamental validity of his statement. What Moses Hess perceived and enthusiastically described in the letter quoted above, and what Engels summed up in four equally enthusiastic words ('Marx was a genius')[22] was clearly in evidence from the outset. Marx's rightly famous letter to his father—written at the age of barely nineteen—revealed an incommensurable passion for synthesis coupled with an ability to treat not only the material under his scrutiny but also his own efforts with remorseless criticism, moving forward from one comprehensive framework of assessment to the next in a relentless fashion, refusing to rest on the laurels of his own achievements, though soberly acknowledging the relative merit of the enterprise. Talking of his own first attempt at sketching a philosophy of law he wrote: 'The whole thing is replete with tripartite divisions, it is written with tedious prolixity, and the Roman concepts are misused in the most barbaric fashion in order to force them into my system. On the other hand, in this way I did gain a general view of the material'.[23] The next step revealed that he was simply unable to proceed in less than comprehensive fashion: 'I drafted a new system of metaphysical principles, but at the conclusion of it I was once more compelled to recognise that it was wrong, like all my previous efforts.'[24] Intense dissatisfaction with this line of approach made him look for a solution in a very different direction:

> I arrived at the point of seeking the idea in reality itself. If previously the gods had dwelt above the earth, now they became its centre. I had read fragments of Hegel's philosophy, the grotesque craggy melody of which did not appeal to me. Once more I wanted to dive into the sea, but with the definite intention of establishing that the nature of the mind is just as necessary, concrete and firmly based as the nature of the body. My aim was no longer to practise tricks of swordsmanship, but to bring genuine pearls into the light of day.[25]

But before this phase could be considered closed, the rather one-sided rejection of Hegel, based on no more than a fragmentary knowledge of his work, gave way to a much more balanced—though by no means uncritical—reassessment at the end of which again a yearning for a positive totalization came to the fore:

> While I was ill I got to know Hegel from beginning to end, together with most of his disciples . . . In controversy here, many conflicting views were expressed, and I became ever more firmly bound to the modern world philosophy from which I had thought to escape, but all rich chords were silenced and I was seized with a veritable fury of irony, as could easily happen after so much had been negated.[26]

To be sure, these remarks, together with others contained in the same letter, did not amount to a coherent world view as yet. They were significant, nevertheless, as indications of an intense search for a new framework of totalization; one capable of a dynamic comprehension of a growing and deepening range of knowledge. The moment the principle of 'seeking the idea in reality itself' appeared on Marx's horizon, a tension had been created which could not be resolved within the confines of philosophy as such. From this insight two further steps followed with compelling necessity, even if they were fully spelled out a few years later. First, that the insoluble character of past philosophical problematics was inherent in the philosophers' attempt to find the solutions in philosophy itself (that is, within the self-imposed limitations of the most abstract form of theory). And second, that the constitution of an adequate form of theory must be conceived as an integral part of the unity of theory and practice.

This latter principle in its turn made all theoretical solutions strictly transient, incomplete, and 'other-directed' (as opposed to the 'self-referential' coherence of past philosophy): in one word it made them *subordinate*—though, of course, *dialectically* subordinate—in the overall dynamism of self-developing social praxis. It had to envisage the historical supersession of all philosophical conceptualizations, including that of the new conception itself inasmuch as it was tied to a particular configuration of social forces and their antagonisms: an aspect which induced precisely those interpreters of Marx who could not understand the dialectic of theory and practice to attribute to the new world view nothing more than purely heuristic value, and, of course, even that of a very limited kind. We shall see in a moment the way in which Marx reached his radical conclusions, but first we have to glance at a few salient features of his new synthesis, worked out in a conscious opposition to the philosophical systems of his predecessors.

Engels, in his essay on Feuerbach, summed up his position on the problematical nature of past philosophical systems as follows:

With all philosophers it is precisely the 'system' which is perishable; and for the simple reason that it springs from an imperishable desire of the human mind—the desire to overcome all contradictions. But if all contradictions are once for all disposed of, we shall have arrived at so-called absolute truth—world history will be at an end. And yet it has to continue, although there is nothing left for it to do—hence, a new, insoluble contradiction. As soon as we have once realised—and in the long run no one has helped us to realise it more than Hegel himself—that the task of philosophy thus stated means nothing but the task that a *single philosophy* should accomplish that which can only be accomplished by the *entire human race* in its progressive development—as soon as we realise that, there is an end to all philosophy *in the hitherto accepted sense of the word.* One leaves alone 'absolute truth', which is unattainable along this path or by any single individual; instead, one pursues attainable *relative truths* along the path of the *positive sciences,* and the summation of *their results* by means of *dialectical thinking.*[27]

The important point in Engels' analysis is that the new world view, conscious of the fundamental contradiction in the way in which past systems treated the relationship between absolute and relative truth, had to be an *open system* replacing the *lonely philosopher* by the *collective subject* of successive generations that continue to advance knowledge in the progressive development of mankind. Indeed, Marx's completely unparalleled influence in the whole of human history cannot be separated from the fact that he had radically redefined philosophy as the collective enterprise to which many generations contribute their share in accordance with the requirements and potentialities of their situation. (In this sense in which we are talking about a radical reorientation of the whole framework of knowledge as a great collective enterprise, there can be only Marxism and not 'Marxisms'. The latter are socio-political specificities sharing the same basic orientation, and it is inherent in the spirit of the new world view that it must find its articulation through constant redefinitions and innovations, as the conditions of its further development significantly change through history and through the advancement of knowledge.) Thus it is not in the least surprising that the burden of producing a radically redefined general framework of orientation while undertaking the elaboration of socio-historically specific tasks made impossible for Marx to complete *any one* of his major works, from the *Economic and Philosophic Manuscripts of 1844* to the *Grundrisse* and to *Capital*,—not to mention countless other projects which he hoped to undertake but could not carry out. Nor should this worry us unduly, since the unfinished character of Marx's lifework is inseparable from the world historical novelty of his undertaking and from the challenging openness of his system. It goes without saying that not even the greatest talent can escape the consequences of historical and personal limitations. But much of today's talk about the 'crisis of Marxism' reveals a crisis of one's own convictions rather than some well-identified lacunae in Marx's vision.

On the other hand, Engels' characterization of 'the end of all philosophy'—which deeply affected many subsequent interpretations—is disturbing in two major respects. The first is that even if philosophy is rightly defined as a collective enterprise, it is nonetheless one that is realized through the partial accomplishments of particular individuals—like Marx himself—who try to resolve the contradictions they perceive, to the best of their abilities, circumscribed not only by personal talent but also by the vantage point attainable at any given time in the progressive development of mankind. Thus nothing could be more Hegelian than Engels' idea of assuming 'the entire human race' as the materialist equivalent to Hegel's 'absolute mind' in possession of 'absolute truth',—although it is presented as the polar opposite to Hegel. In reality philosophy is advanced in the form of partial totalizations which of necessity constitute, at any given point in time, including the post-Hegelian phase of development, some kind of a *system* without which the very idea of 'relative truths' would make no sense whatsoever. The alternative to the Hegelian concept of absolute truth is not 'the entire human race' as the notional possessor of some such 'absolute truth', but the totalizing synthesis of attainable levels of knowledge progressively superseded in the collective enterprise of particular systems. Consequently, no matter how consciously open was the Marxian world view in its inception and general orientation, it had to be *systematically* articulated at different stages of Marx's development—from the *Paris Manuscripts* to *Capital*—if it was to qualify as an adequate totalization of knowledge.

The second respect in which Engels' analysis is extremely problematical is closely connected with the first. For having expelled from philosophy its vital function as the given system of totalizing knowledge (that is, as a system which not only *arranges* but also *constitutes* knowledge, anticipating and furthering developments as well as following and synthesizing them) he was left with a positivistic reduction of philosophy to a mere *'summation* of the results of the *positive sciences.'* Furthermore, the ambiguity between this vision of the 'positive sciences' and the Hegelian notion of 'positive knowledge'—wrongly attributed to Marx by Colletti and others—followed as an afterthought to this analysis when Engels asserted that 'though unconsciously, Hegel showed us the way out of the labyrinth of systems to real positive knowledge of the world.'[28] Although it was no part of Engels' conscious intentions, the tendency inherent in the shift we have seen in his analysis is that the criterion of truth is retransferred within the confines of *theory as such*—an orientation from which Marx so emphatically freed himself—and, modelled upon the 'positive sciences', becomes the foundation of a fictitiously self-sustaining 'theoretical practice' more or less openly opposed to Marx's principle which announced the dialectical unity of theory and practice as the real watershed between his line of approach and that of his predecessors. And, ironically, since no solid supporting evidence can be found in the whole body of Marx's massive work[29] to maintain the claimed adherence to the model of 'the positive sciences', he can now be also accused of 'Hegelianism' (or of an ambiguous wavering between empiricist scientism and romantic Hegelianism) for failing to provide the positivistic evidence required by the neat reductionist scheme.

In point of fact, Marx's development followed a very different route. He explicitly rejected modelling philosophy on the natural sciences, since he considered them 'abstractly material'[30] and subject to the same contradictions in the totality of social praxis which both divorced theory from practice and produced an ever-increasing fragmentation of theoretical and practical activities, sharply opposing them among themselves, instead of sustaining their unified development in an integrated framework. His references to 'positive science' were neither idealizations of natural science, nor concessions to Hegelianism—let alone an uneasy mixture of the two—but expressions of a programme firmly anchoring theory to 'real life' and to the 'representation of practical activity' which could appear in the natural sciences, constituted on the basis of the social division of labour, only in an abstractly material and one-sided form. In opposition to speculative philosophy he wrote:

We set out from *real, active men,* and on the basis of their real life-process we demonstrate the development of the ideological reflexes and echoes of this life-process. The phantoms formed in the human brain are also, necessarily, sublimates of their *material life-process,* which is *empirically verifiable* and bound to material premises . . . This method of approach is not devoid of premises. It starts out from the real premises and does not abandon them for a moment. Its premises are men, not in any fantastic isolation and rigidity, but in their *actual, empirically perceptible process of development* under definite conditions. As soon as this *active life-process* is described, history ceases to be a collection of *dead facts* as it is with the *empiricists* (themselves still *abstract),* or an *imagined activity of imagined subjects,* as with the idealists.[31]

And he emphatically added a clear definition of his meaning of 'positive science': 'Where speculation ends—in real life—there *real, positive science* begins: the representation of the *practical activity,* of the *practical process of development of men.*'[32] The same view is amplified a few pages further on:

This conception of history depends on our ability to expound the *real process of production* . . . to explain all the different *theoretical products and forms of consciousness,* religion, philosophy, ethics, etc. etc., and trace their origins and growth *from that basis;* by which means, of course, the whole thing can be *depicted in its totality* (and therefore, too, the *reciprocal action* of these various sides on one another). It has not, like the idealistic view of history in every period to look for a *category,* but remains constantly on the *real ground of history;* it does not explain practice from the idea but explains the *formation of ideas from material practice;* and accordingly it comes to the conclusion that all forms and products of consciousness cannot be dissolved by *mental criticism* ['theoretical practice'] . . . but only by the *practical overthrow* of the actual social relations which gave rise to this idealistic humbug;

that *not criticism but revolution is the driving force of history,* also of religion, of philosophy and all other types of theory.[33]

As we can see, Marx's concern with *'real, positive* science' was meant as an unmistakably clear and radical reorientation of philosophy towards *'real, active* men'; towards their *'actual,* empirically perceptible process of development'; towards their 'material life-process' dialectically grasped as an *'active* life-process'; in sum: towards the representation 'of the *practical activity,* of the *practical* process of development of men'. This was very much in line with the youthful inspiration of 'seeking the idea in reality itself', though, of course, grasped at a much higher level, in that the later formulation indicated in the references to social praxis also the *solution,* whereas the early one amounted to no more than a—however genial—intuition of the *problem* itself. Even the imagery used on both occasions revealed a striking similarity. The youthful letter, after the sentence which spoke of seeing the idea in reality itself, went on like this: 'If previously the gods had dwelt above the earth, now they became its centre.' And the paragraph quoted above (see note 31) from *The German Ideology* opened with these words: 'In contrast to German philosophy which descends from heaven to earth, here we ascend from earth to heaven. That is to say . . . we set out from real, active men.[34] And again we can witness that the higher level of conceptualization resolves the almost enigmatic ambiguity of the original imagery which reflected not only the problem—and the programme—of demystifying religion on the ground of earthly reality but at the same time also the young student's inability to do so satisfactorily, whereas *The German Ideology* firmly located religious and other fantastic conceptions as necessarily arising out of the contradictions of determinate modes of social praxis, and thus requiring for their solution the *practical overthrow* of the actual social relations of production.

The other point we cannot stress enough is the shift from Marx's singular—'positive science', in the sense we have seen—to the empiricist plural of 'positive sciences', with the suggestion that the new philosophy simply 'summarizes' the results of such 'positive' (natural) sciences ('their results') 'by means of dialectical thinking'. This is by no means a minor slip. On the contrary, its implications are very serious and far-reaching. For this is the Marxian passage so significantly transformed by Engels: *'Self-oriented* philosophy loses its medium of existence with the *representation of reality.*[35] It is replaced at the outset by a synthesis of the most general results which can be abstracted from surveying the historical development of men.'[36] Clearly, then, the 'results' mentioned by Marx are not those of the 'positive sciences' which leave to philosophy nothing but the role of 'summarising their results by means of dialectical thinking'. (Which itself is rather baffling. For how can thinking be dialectical if its role is not the production of ideas and results but merely the 'summarising' of what is handed down to it? Nor is it possible to see how the whole enterprise could turn out to be dialectical if the partial results were themselves not constituted dialectically, so as to make necessary some sort of a superimposition of the dialectic on them, as it were, from the outside.) In Marx's view, on the contrary, the results in question are themselves produced by the theory which also synthesizes them, and they are produced through surveying the actual historical development of men, putting into relief their most significant objective—practically constituted—characteristics. Furthermore, this surveying is obviously not a matter of simple observation, but a dialectical process of taking hold of the immensely rich *'active life-process'* (in sharp contrast to the 'collection of dead facts as it is with the *empiricists,* themselves *still abstract*') within a well defined, *praxis-oriented theoretical framework,* elaborating the great variety of factors involved in the surveyed practical activity of historically developing men in accordance with determinate *'material premises'* and thus actively dialectically reconstituting the theoretical framework itself which again encompasses the next round of survey. This is what Marx means by 'positive science' which is of necessity *totalizing* and therefore cannot possibly exist in the plural—not in Marx's sense of the term. He makes this amply clear when he insists that in his conception—which explains all theoretical manifestations in relation to their material ground in conjunction with the principle of the unity of theory and practice—'the whole thing can be depicted *in its totality*', whereas 'the positive sciences' inevitably leave the vital task of totalization untouched since it lies beyond any one of them. And the other, equally important, point stressed by Marx is that the dialectical interchange of the complex material factors with all the different theoretical products and forms of consciousness—'the *reciprocal action* of these various sides on one another'—can only be grasped in such a framework of totalization. Whether one calls it a new form of philosophy or—in a deliberate polemical opposition to speculative philosophy—'positive science' is of little importance. What does matter, however, is that we cannot have a dialectical conception of history without such a framework of totalization which 'the positive sciences' cannot possibly displace or replace.

Ironically for those who pay scant attention to historical evidence, the only time Marx treated philosophy approvingly as a *theoretical practice* was when he was still trapped within the confines of an idealist outlook. In his doctoral dissertation, written between early 1839 and March 1841, he argued that:

> the *practice* of philosophy is itself *theoretical.* It is the *critique* that measures the individual existence by the essence, the particular reality by the Idea. But this *immediate realisation* of philosophy is in its deepest essence afflicted with contradictions, and this its essence takes form in the appearance and imprints its seal upon it.[37]

But even this approval, as we can see, was not unqualified. For it was coupled with a hint about some contradictions inherent in philosophy's opposition to the world, even though the author of the doctoral dissertation could not offer a precise definition of their nature, let alone an adequate solution to them. Given the limitations of his outlook then, he could depict the tensions and oppositions in question only as a most uneasy *stalemate:*

> When philosophy turns itself at will against the world of appearance, then the system is lowered to an abstract totality, that is, it has become one aspect of the world which opposes another one. Its relationship to the world is that of reflection. Inspired by the *urge to realise itself,* it enters into tension against the other. The inner self-contentment and completeness has been broken. What was inner light has become consuming flame turning outwards. The result is that as the world becomes philosophical, philosophy becomes worldly, that its realisation is also its loss, that what it struggles against on the *outside* is its own *inner deficiency,* that in the very struggle it falls precisely into those defects which it fights as defects in the opposite camp, and that it can only overcome these defects by falling into them. That which opposes and that which it fights is always *the same as itself,* only with factors inverted.[38]

The contradictions could not be firmly identified because they were grasped as emanating from philosophy itself and thus tending toward a 'diremption [splitting up] of individual self-consciousness in itself' as regards the predicament of particular philosophers, and to an 'external separation and duality of philosophy, as two opposed philosophical trends'[39] as regards philosophy as a whole. The idea that the problem might arise out of the 'inadequacy of the world which has to be made philosophical'[40] appeared for an instant, but in terms of the problematic confined to the opposition of two philosophical trends it had to be subsumed as a 'moment' of the overall scheme of an ultimately self-oriented theoretical practice.

All the same, the problem itself appeared on the horizon and its unresolved character represented a challenge for Marx. His development in the years that immediately followed the completion of his doctoral dissertation consisted in the realization:

1 that the subjective aspect of the problem cannot be confined to the consideration of *individual* subjectivity alone, in terms of which the dissertation tackled it,[41] but must be complemented by a dialectical conception of the actual historical development that produces a *collective agency* in relation to which the *actual realization*—which necessarily escapes 'individual self-consciousnesses'—may be envisaged; and
2 that this demand for the realization of philosophy—arising out of the 'inadequacy of the world' concretely defined as an antagonism inherent in a determinate mode of social praxis—must be linked to the programme of radically reconstituting theory in the *unity of theory and practice* and in a supersession of the prevailing *social division of labour.*

Such steps as were necessary to reach these conclusions were taken by Marx in circumstances of pressing practical problems. As he recalled it later: 'In the year 1842–43, as editor of the *Rheinische Zeitung,* I first found myself in the embarrassing position of having to discuss what is known as material interests.'[42] And indeed in his 'Justification of the Correspondent from the Mosel' he articulated a strikingly important point. He wrote that:

> In investigating a situation *concerning the state* one is all too easily tempted to overlook *the objective nature of the circumstances* and to explain everything by the *will* of the persons concerned. However, there are *circumstances* which determine the actions of private persons and individual authorities, and which are *as independent of them as the method of breathing.*[43]

How hollow philosophical abstractions must have sounded to the ears of a man who arrived at holding such convictions. No wonder, therefore, that he was eager to set a standard to theory in accordance with the objective requirements of the actual circumstances. In a letter written in August 1842 he insisted that '*True theory must be developed and clarified within the concrete circumstances and in relation to existing conditions.*'[44] And in the spirit of his own principle, he undertook a meticulous study of the objective conditions and forces that manifest themselves in the concrete circumstances, with a view of understanding the dynamic of their interrelations and the possibilities of a conscious intervention in their development. The results of this undertaking were incorporated in his *Critique of the Hegelian Philosophy of Right,* in his essays 'On the Jewish Question', in his system *in statu nascendi* known as the *Economic and Philosophic Manuscripts of 1844,* and in his celebrated 'Theses on Feuerbach' linked to his vital share in *The German Ideology.* These works not only made the final reckoning with speculative philosophy but simultaneously also elaborated the framework of a new type of totalization of actual historical development, with all its manifold, dialectically interacting factors, including even the most esoteric forms and manifestations of consciousness. Having identified in the proletariat the collective agency and material force through which 'the realisation of philosophy' could be reformulated in a radically new form and at a qualitatively higher level, he continued to insist that 'the proletariat finds its *intellectual* weapons in philosophy.'[45] Thus, situating his type of philosophy in relation to a concrete socio-historical force, and defining its function as both integral and necessary to a succcessful struggle for emancipation, enabled Marx to formulate the demand for the *practical* overthrow of the actual social relations' as the guiding principle and measuring rod of the meaningfulness of the new philosophy. A philosophy which arises at a particular juncture in history from a determinate social praxis. A philosophy which—in accordance with the unity of theory and practice—vitally contributes to the unfolding and full realization of the potentialities inherent in this emancipatory praxis.

3. MARX'S RELATION TO HEGEL

Marx's relation to the Hegelian philosophy was quite unique. In one sense, Hegelianism represented for him the polar opposite of his own approach which advocated ascertainable 'material premises' in contrast to 'self-oriented' philosophical speculation: an approach articulated from a dynamic vision of 'the standpoint of labour',[46] as against Hegel's adoption of the uncritical and ultimately ahistorical partiality of the standpoint of political economy'.[47] In another sense, however, Marx never stopped stressing the gigantic character of Hegel's achievements, brought to realization at an immensely important juncture of historical development in the aftermath of the French Revolution, in response to the most complex and dynamic interplay of social forces—including the emergence of labour as a hegemonic movement—in world history.

Marx's critical appropriation of this philosophy was very far from being confined to a youthful phase. Quite the contrary. For once he settled his accounts not only with Hegel himself but also with his 'neo-Hegelian' followers—basically in his *Critique of the Hegelian Philosophy of Right,* the *Economic and Philosophic Manuscripts of 1844,* and *The German Ideology*—the road was cleared for putting to a positive use those acquisitions of the Hegelian philosophy which Marx considered to be of a fundamental value. Indeed, references to Hegel in the *Grundrisse* and in *Capital* were numerous and on the whole highly positive—much more so than in the early works. For reasons which we shall see in a moment, important affinities came to the fore precisely at a time when Marx was struggling with the task of synthesizing some of the most intricate aspects of his conception of capital and of the manifold contradictions inherent in its dialectical and historical[48] unfolding. As Lenin himself insisted: 'It is impossible completely to understand

Marx's *Capital,* and especially its first chapter, without having thoroughly studied and understood the *whole* of Hegel's *Logic.* Consequently, half a century later none of the Marxists understood Marx!'[49] Another half a century later still, alas, Marx's relation to Hegel is no less subject to prejudices and aprioristic preconceptions than at the time Lenin jotted down this famous aphorism.

The blatant misreading of Hegel's significance for the development of philosophy, and with it the total incomprehension with which Marx's relationship to this great thinker is treated, is by no means accidental. It reveals the stubborn persistence of attempts at discarding dialectics in favour of tempting simplifications of one kind or another. As Marx observed in a letter in this regard: 'The gentlemen in Germany . . . think Hegel's *dialectic* is a *"dead horse"*. Feuerbach has much to answer for in this respect.'[50] And he sarcastically commented in another letter:

> Herr Lange wonders that Engels, I, etc., take the *dead dog Hegel* seriously when Büchner, Lange, Dr Dühring, Fechner, etc., are agreed that they—poor dear have buried him so long ago. Lange is naîve enough to say that I 'move with rare freedom' in empirical matter. He hasn't the least idea that this 'free movement in matter' is nothing but the paraphrase for the method of dealing with matter—that is, the *dialectical method.*[51]

Thus an adequate evaluation of Marx's relationship to Hegel is not a minor matter. In a way it sums up Marx's relation to philosophy in general and his conception of dialectics in particular.

As we have already seen, Marx's original wholesale rejection of the Hegelian philosophy—on account of its idealistic remoteness from social reality—soon gave way to a much more differentiated appreciation. To be sure, he emphatically condemned 'that philosophic dissolution and restoration of the empirical world'[52] which he identified in an embryonic form already in the *Phenomenology.* But at the same time he insisted with no less emphasis that it is an outstanding achievement that Hegel 'grasps the essence of *labour* and comprehends objective man—true, because real man—as the outcome of man's *own labour.*'[53] Just how great an achievement this was, may be appreciated by bearing in mind that now for the first time in history the possibility of elaborating a truly comprehensive historical conception had been created, in sharp contrast to the fragmentary insights of earlier thinkers. Why Hegel himself could not consistently live up to the standard of his own great achievement will be clear when we compare his conception of history with that of Marx. This comparison will also show why Marx had no need whatsoever to treat Hegel as a 'dead dog' and his dialectic as a 'dead horse' in order to go radically beyond him. He could generously acknowledge that *'Hegel's dialectic is the basic form of all dialectic'*[54] precisely because he could 'strip it of its mystical form' at the crucial points where the 'standpoint of political economy' turned the basic form of all dialectic into a forced construction, so that the 'mystical veil' should make the antagonistic social contradictions disappear from sight through their merely conceptual resolution.

The first major step Marx took in his critical appreciation of the Hegelian philosophy was concerned with politics, his primary preoccupation at the time. It was his political radicalism which separated him from his young Hegelian friends, and already in March 1843, he was also critical of Feuerbach, for the latter's inadequate treatment of politics. The point Marx firmly made was that Feuerbach refers *'too much to nature and too little to politics,* although that is the only link through which present-day philosophy can become true.'[55] Thus he found Feuerbach wanting in this crucial respect right from the beginning and therefore he could put the author of *The Essence of Christianity* only to a very limited use. When he later emphasized that Feuerbach had much to answer for the production of an anti-dialectical climate in Germany, he explained the positive impact of Feuerbach's principal work by comparing it with Proudhon's best work, *What is Property? (Qu'est-ce que la propriété?):*

> Proudhon's relation to S. Simon and Fourier is about the same as that of Feuerbach to Hegel. Compared with Hegel, Feuerbach is very poor. All the same he was epoch-making *after* Hegel, because he laid stress on certain points which were disagreeable to the Christian consciousness but important for the progress of criticism, and which Hegel had left in mystic semi-obscurity.[56]

As the 1843 critique shows, this assessment was no hindsight.

Belabouring nature and heavily underscoring politics, clearly, could not really help Marx in accomplishing what he had set out to do: the elaboration of a dialectical conception of actual social development in place of Hegel's idealistic synthesis of ingenious conceptual transformations. He insisted that 'The entire mystery of the *Philosophy of Right* and of Hegelian philosophy in general' is contained in paragraphs 261 and 262 of this work[57] which justifies the political state by presenting the conditions 'as the conditioned, the determining as the determined, the producing as the product of its product.'[58] And he did not stop at simply stressing the *'pantheistic mysticism'*[59] involved in speculatively deriving the family and civil society from the idea of the state, thus overturning the actual relations in a way whereby 'The fact, which is the starting point, is not conceived to be such but rather to be the mystical result.'[60] Pointing to such reversals could not resolve by itself anything at all. On the contrary, it could only serve to give the semblance of a new-found rationality to extremely problematical, indeed contradictory, social structures by insisting that they are at the roots of the various ideological pictures. Such work of demystification—as, for instance, pointing out the connection between the earthly and the 'holy family'—must be complemented, if it is not to be turned into a new form of mystification, by an adequate analysis of the social contradictions manifest in those problematical social structures themselves which in turn generate the mystifying images of false consciousness. The real object of criticism is always the *fundamental determinant*—in this case the specific mode of social metabolism which assigns the individuals to determinate (indeed, one could say 'predestined') functions within the boundaries of the unholy triad of the family, the civil society and the state—and not merely the however correct assertion of the *immediate determination* between the family and civil society on the one hand, and the political state on the other, which would leave all three just as massively standing as Feuerbach's critique of religion does not affect in the slightest the earthly family. The suggestion that one could have one side without the other naïvely and undialectically severs their necessary connections, giving the illusion of a solution in the form of a one-sided, false rationality: a great impoverishment with respect to Hegel—and this is why 'compared to Hegel, Feuerbach is very poor'—who undoubtedly puts into relief the dialectical interconnections, even if in a speculative form, as a set of 'logical-metaphysical determinations.'[61]

How can one avoid the 'dialectical circularity'[62] which characterizes the Hegelian solution in that the development of dialectically interconnected moments is 'predestined by the nature of the concept'?[63] This is all the more important since all such 'dialectical circularity' leads a very uneasy existence on the very border of undialectical tautology.[64] Marx's answer consisted in breaking the circle while not only retaining the dialectical framework of explanation but simultaneously also revealing its real ground of determination. He showed that Hegel was forced into the kind of solution he gave because of the *'unresolved antinomy'*[65] between *external necessity and immanent end* in his conception of the actuality and ideality of the state. Since 'the standpoint of political economy' makes the solution of this antinomy impossible, though insisting on its solution (thus introducing another contradiction and determining the feasible lines of reasoning) 'empirical *actuality* is admitted *just as it is* and is also said to be *rational;* but not rational because of its own reason, but because the empirical fact in its empirical existence has a significance which is other than it itself . . . The actual becomes phenomenon, but the Idea has no other content than this phenomenon.'[66] Thus it is the necessary retention of the underlying social contradiction which sunders the Idea from its content, degrading actuality to the status of mere phenomenality which of course calls for ideality as its counterpart and in its otherness its own ground of rationality. In this way an *'Idea-Subject* which is differentiated from the fact itself'[67] is speculatively generated, and in turn it produces the identical Subject-Object through which 'that philosophic dissolution and restoration of the empirical world (with all its actual contradictions) to which we referred earlier can be accomplished.

As we can see, Marx did not stop at the point of asserting the 'upside-down' character of the Hegelian conceptual framework, but pressed on to demonstrate its revealing ideological function, identifying the—for Hegel insoluble—contradiction as its fundamental ground of determination. Such an analysis pointed in the direction of the most radical *practical* conclusions. Just as he wrote one year earlier in his 'Comments on the Latest

Prussian Censorship Instruction' that 'The real, *radical cure for censorship* would be its *abolition'*,[68] he could see no solution to the problems of the state short of its radical negation and supersession, with all the necessary implications for the family and civil society. Indeed, it was in view of the insoluble contradictions of the 'civil society' (inseparably linked to the family) that the conclusion about the radical supersession of the state asserted itself as inescapable. Thesis X on Feuerbach—'The standpoint of the old materialism is civil society; the standpoint of the new is human society, or social humanity'—put in a nutshell one of the most striking innovations of the Marxian philosophy. For the *whole*[69] of bourgeois philosophy treated as a self-evident axiom the constitution of human society as 'civil society', based on the irreconcilable antagonism of its individual members, which in turn predicated with an equally axiomatic validity the unquestionable necessity of the state as the benevolent manager of the pre-existing antagonisms, and consequently as the absolute *precondition* of social life as such. The outrageous logic of all such reasoning—which not only dualistically severed the rule-constituting political sphere from its material base, but simultaneously also established the absolute primacy of the political over social life of which it was in fact a historically specific manifestation and dimension—had to be called by its proper name, even if such logic of political legitimation assumed in Hegel an immensely complex and rather opaque form as compared to the relatively naîve transparency of the Hobbesian scheme. To envisage the reintegration of the political dimension with the material life-process of society, it was necessary to negate both the political state itself and that fictitious individualistic 'human nature' (the alleged producer of the irreconcilable antagonism) which reciprocally postulated one another in the self-sustaining ideological circle—a vicious circle if there ever has been one—of bourgeois rationality. 'Human society, or social humanity' as the standpoint of the new philosophy was the only basis on which an objectively unfolding process of social recuperation could be conceived, in opposition to the arbitrarily frozen historical dynamism as encapsulated in the various self-legitimating schemes of the state and civil society.

Another point that clearly emerges from the Marxian critique of Hegel's philosophy of right is that—contrary to Lukács' *History and Class Consciousness* and its followers—the 'identical Subject-Object' could not play a positive part in Marx's reasoning. On the contrary, it was precisely his critique of this problematic which helped Marx to reconstitute the dialectic on a radically different footing. Marx not only demonstrated the apologetic function of the identical Subject-Object in the Hegelian scheme of things—namely 'that philosophic dissolution and restoration of the empirical world' which we have seen above—but also put into relief that in order to make this ideological function possible, the objective dialectical factors had to be artificially dissolved by Hegel into the 'Idea-Subject and the fact itself' so as to be reunited again in the prefigured construct of legitimation. This is no place to enter into a discussion of the far-reaching implications of this complex of problems in any detail. Let it suffice to indicate simply the diametrically opposed tendencies manifest in Marx's and in Hegel's approach. For insofar as the problematic of the identical Subject-Object can embody a movement, it is one tending towards a point of *rest:* the resolution of the originally postulated teleological end. In Marx, on the contrary, the movement is *open-ended* and its fundamental intent is subversive, not reconciliatory. And as far as the synthesis of the complex forces is concerned which makes intelligible the dynamism of social tranformations, Marx's explanation—quite unlike Hegel—concentrates on:

(1) The unity of the *individual and the collective subject* (of which the 'übergreifendes Moment' is the latter, even if it is given the most subtle conceptual and historical qualifications); and

(2) the unity of *the ideal and the material,* mediated through the dialectic of *theory and praxis.*

Clearly, in both instances the feasible points of rest are of necessity strictly transient, amounting to a relative unity only, but never to identity,[70] while the superseding drive forward retains its ultimately overriding importance[71]—notwithstanding the partial stabilization of determinate phases, and notwithstanding the institutional inertia which tends to petrify them—in the course of historical development.

Thus Marx's conception of the dialectic went beyond Hegel right from the moment of its inception in two fundamental respects, even if he continued to maintain that Hegel's dialectic is the basic form of all dialectic. First, the critique of the Hegelian transformation of the objective dialectic into a speculative conceptual edifice (through the dualistic opposition of the Idea-Subject to empirical existence degraded to mere phenomenality) established the interplay of objective forces as the true framework of dialectics and as the real ground of determination of even the most mediated subjective factors. And second, the demonstration of the ideological determinants of Hegel's speculative-conceptual dialectic—the 'philosophic dissolution and restoration of the empirical world' as an ahistorical construct which contradicted the profoundly historical potentialities of the Hegelian conception itself—emphatically put into relief the irrepressible dynamism of the actual historical developments, together with a precise indication of the necessary levers through which the revolutionary agency is enabled to intervene in accordance with its conscious aims in the positive unfolding of the objective dialectic. These accomplishments were *structurally incompatible* with Feuerbach's philosophy, and they were worked out by Marx in the years 1843–4 when, according to a crude schematism, he was supposed to be a 'Feuerbachian humanist'.

However stressing the exemplary originality of Marx's approach should be no reason for minimizing the immense philosophical significance of the Hegelian dialectic. Attempting a demonstration of the validity of the Marxian solutions merely in terms of the opposition to Hegel hopelessly distorts and underscores not only the historical importance of the Hegelian philosophy but also the real scope to Marx's own discourse, making it out to be thoroughly dependent on the theoretical problematic of his great predecessor. Such an assessment, in other words, only manages to attack Hegel in the name of Marx while undermining Marx's own significance. In truth it was finding his own angle—a standpoint radically different from the standpoint of political economy—which enabled Marx both to understand 'the entire mystery of Hegelian philosophy' and to appreciate its historical achievements notwithstanding its all too obvious mystifications. The radical negation of Hegel cannot be the measure of Marx's greatness, just as the lasting importance of the Hegelian achievements cannot simply be confined to their relative consonance with Marx.

While the unsparing critique of the Hegelian philosophy of right and of its unquestioning attitude towards the state was a necesssary precondition for an adequate theoretical grasp of the historical dialectic, some of the more positive acquisitions of Hegel's conception became visible to Marx only after he had reached his own conclusions on the problems concerned. Thus to view such matters in terms of 'Hegelian influence' or an alleged liberation from it would be totally beside the point. To give a typical example, one of Marx's major discoveries concerned the role of *labour-power* as a commodity in the development of capitalism. Marx stressed in this respect the specificity of the capitalistic production relations in that the owner of labour-power could only sell his labour-power for a limited period, otherwise he would convert himself from the owner of a commodity into a commodity (a slave), thus undermining the necessary form of reproduction of the new mode of production. Obviously, Marx drew qualitatively different conclusions from this insight than Hegel could from the standpoint of political economy. However, the limitation of the Hegelian standpoint does not diminish in the least the importance of the fact itself that Hegel succeeded in identifying with great clarity the specificity mentioned above, and Marx did not hesitate for a moment to acknowledge this when he quoted in *Capital* the relevant passage from none other than the *Philosophy of Right:*

> I may make over to another the use, *for a limited time,* of my particular *bodily and mental aptitudes and capabilities;* because, in consequence of this restriction, they are impressed with a character of alienation with regard to me as a whole. But by the alienation of all my labour-time and the whole of my work, I should be converting the substance itself, in other words, my general activity and reality, my person, into the property of another.[72]

Similarly, the instrument of production as the crucial mediatory factor in human development has a paramount importance in Marx's theory:

> An instrument of labour is a thing, or a complex of things, which the labourer interposes between himself and the subject of his labour, and

which serves as the conductor of his activity. He makes use of the mechanical, physical, and chemical properties of some substances in order to make other substances subservient to his aims.[73]

Clearly, the problem at stake involves a principle of the highest order, with the most far-reaching consequences for the understanding of the historical dialectic, and for the reasons which we have seen earlier it would be most unreasonable to expect the philosopher who assigns to empirical existence the status of mere phenomenality to articulate it along the same lines as Marx. What is significant, however is that even if in a highly abstract form (indeed, with a touch of mysticism in the mode of its expression) the crucial dialectical principle of mediation is defined by Hegel at the highest level of philosophical generality as the interplay of factors which follow their own inherent logic of unfolding, as we can see in the footnote Marx added to his own formulation: 'Reason is just as cunning as she is powerful. Her cunning consists principally in her *mediating activity,* which, by causing objects to act and re-act on each other *in accordance with their own nature,* in this way, without any direct interference in the process, carries out reason's intentions.'[74]

We can notice a significant change in Marx's orientation with respect to Hegel's *Logic* in particular. In the *Critique of Hegel's Philosophy of Right* he treated with utmost sarcasm 'the holy register of the Santa Casa (the *Logic*)'[75] and he complained that 'Hegel's true interest is not the philosophy of right but logic. The philosophical task is not the embodiment of thought in determinate political realities, but the evaporation of these realities in abstract thought. The philosophical moment is not the logic of fact but the fact of logic.'[76] Which was all right as far as it went, but it did not go deep enough. For it remained oblivious to a vital dimension of the *Logic,* namely the systematic elaboration of the principles which constitute 'the basic form of all dialectic', even if shrouded in mystical veil.

The Hegelian logic was in fact the outcome of two fundamental determinations: one extremely problematical and the other far less so. (That is to say, the second was problematical only to the extent to which it was necessarily tied to the first and therefore was bound to suffer its consequences.) The author of the *Critique of Hegel's Philosophy of Right* was acutely aware of the first—namely the ideological transubstantiation of determinate social-political realities into logical-metaphysical determinations so that they can evaporate in one sense only to be restored in another—but he had at the time very little concern for the other. Once, however, he identified the task as the systematic investigation of the nature of capital and of the manifold conditions of its socio-historical supersession—which inevitably put the earlier prevalent concern with politics in perspective, as 'the political-legal superstructure' the contradictions of which cannot be unravelled on their own but only in the context of a precise understanding of the material base and of its complex dialectical interactions with the totality of highly mediated social structures—the need for a dialectical totalization of the whole complex became imperative. For now Marx had to investigate not only the given realities (and still less only the 'determinate political realities') but also various embryonic forces and tendencies, together with their most far-reaching ramifications and implications, in the framework of a rigorous dialectical assessment. Working out the full implications of complex problems, putting into relief the rich connections of their inner determinations, following consistently and systematically their developments to their logical conclusions 'in accordance with their own nature', anticipating their future developments on the basis of their objective determinations as opposed to simply postulating uselessly abstract possibilities— all this had to be done in *Capital,* and to do it was conceivable only in the form of a dialectical totalization. Significantly enough, the constantly recurring category in the *Grundrisse* and in *Capital* is *'Sichsetzen'*[77] or 'self-positing', which in a way sums up the mode in which objective determinations appear and assert themselves in the course of actual socio-historical development. The inspiration in the use of this and similar categories[78] is, of course, Hegel. Not in the sense of some problematical 'influence' which would leave a foreign element in the body of Marxian thought, but categories considered as *'Daseinsformen'*[79] in the framework of a profoundly original theory are transferred from Hegel into Marx's universe of discourse and reactivated there with a qualitatively different meaning.

All the same, Marx was anxious to stress, more than anybody else, that it was Hegel who first produced a coherent system of dialectical categories—even if in a highly abstract and speculative form—which put him far above his predecessors and contemporaries. In a letter to Engels Marx stated that Comte is '*miserable* compared to Hegel. Although Comte, as a professional mathematician and physicist, was superior to him, i.e. superior in matters of *detail,* even here Hegel is *infinitely greater as a whole.*'[80] It was Hegel's unprecedented ability to make his totalizing conception of dialectical categories bear on all matters of detail—whenever, that is, ideological determinations did not structurally prevent him from doing so—which made him infinitely superior to all positivist worshippers of reified 'fact' and lifeless 'science'.[81]

In a letter quoted above, Marx made a similar point about his own work. As we have seen, he stressed that 'Lange is naîve enough to say that I "move with rare freedom" in empirical matter. He hasn't the least idea that this "free movement in matter" is nothing but the paraphrase for the *method* of dealing with matter—that is, the *dialectical method.*'[82] The 'free movement in matter' when, as in Hegel's case, the matter in question has been transposed into the homogeneous medium of a speculative-conceptual universe, was relatively easy, as compared to the task Marx himself had to accomplish. For he could not merely explore the intricate logic of his concepts on their own, but constantly had to refer them back to empirical reality. Having masterfully succeeded in doing so, in the framework of a dialectical philosophical conception firmly anchored to actuality, is the true measure of Marx's intellectual greatness.

NOTES

1. K. Marx, *Theses on Feuerbach*, Spring, 1845. Italics indicate emphases added by myself.
2. K. Marx, *Introduction to the Critique of the Hegelian Philosophy of Right*, December 1843–January 1844.
3. *Ibid.*
4. *Ibid.*
5. The last three quotations are from Marx's letter to his father,

Berlin, 10 November 1837.

6. *Ibid.*
7. *Ibid.*
8. *Ibid.*.
9. Letter by Moses Hess to Berthold Auerbach, Berlin, 2 September 1841.
10. In this respect see Chapter 8, 'The Controversy about Marx' of I. Mészáros, *Marx's Theory of Alienation*, London, 1970.
11. From Marx's letter to his father quoted above.
12. 'There is no history of politics, law, science, etc., of art, religion, etc.' (Marx's note on the manuscript of *The German Ideology*, Lawrence & Wishart, London, 1965, p. 671):

    Since the young Hegelians consider conceptions, thoughts, ideas, in fact all the products of consciousness, to which they attribute an *independent existence*, as the real chains of men (just as the Old Hegelians declared them the true bonds of human society) it is evident that the Young Hegelians have to fight only against these illusions of the consciousness.;... Morality, religion, metaphysics, all the rest of ideology and their corresponding forms of consciousness,... no longer retain the *semblance of independence*. They have no history, no development; but men, developing their material production and their material intercourse, alter, along with this their real existence, their thinking and the products of their thinking. .... If these theorists treat really historical subjects, as for instance the eighteenth century, they merely give a history of the ideas of the times, torn away from the facts and the practical development fundamental to them. (*Ibid.* pp. 30, 38, 53.)
13. 'When reality is depicted, *philosophy as an independent branch of knowledge* loses its medium of existence.' (*Ibid.* p. 38).
14. Division of labour only becomes truly such from the moment when a division of material and mental labour appears. From this moment onwards consciousness *can* really flatter itself that it is something other than consciousness of existing practice, that it *really* represents something without representing something real; from now on consciousness is in a position to emancipate itself from the world and to proceed to the formation of 'pure' theory, theology, philosophy, ethics, etc. (*Ibid.* p.43).
15. *Ibid.*
16. The expression is from Marx's Introduction to the *Grundrisse*, but the idea itself dates back to the early 1840s.
17. These quotations are from *The German Ideology, op. cit.* pp. 46-8. A marginal note by Marx to *The German Ideology* reads as follows: 'Universality corresponds to (1) the class versus the state. (2) the competition, world-wide intercourse, etc., (3) the great numerical strength of the ruling class. (4) the illusion of the *common* interests (in the beginning the illusion is true), (5) the

delusion of the ideologists and the division of labour.' (*Ibid.* pp. 62-3). As we can see, Marx is talking about very important objective factors, and one should not misinterpret the terms 'illusion' and 'delusion' in a subjectivistic-voluntaristic sense. For he himself explicitly states that 'common interest' is very real in the first place (it becomes an illusion in the course of the development of capitalistic contradictions), and by linking the 'delusion of the ideologists' to the division of labour he reasserts his view about the need for an objective practical supersession of such manifestations of consciousness.

18. *Ibid.* pp. 84-5.
19. K. Marx, *Grundrisse* London, 1973, p. 706.
20. K. Marx, *Capital* Moscow, 1957, Vol. III., p. 800.
21. F. Engels, 'Ludwig Feuerbach and the End of Classical German Philosophy', in *Marx-Engels: Selected Works* Moscow, 1951, Vol. II., p. 349.
22. *Ibid.*
23. K. Marx, F. Engels, *Collected Works* London, 1975, Vol. I, p. 17.
24. *Ibid.*
25. *Ibid.* p. 18.
26. *Ibid.* p. 19.
27. F. Engels, 'Feuerbach and the End of Classical German Philosophy', *op. cit.* pp. 330-1.
28. *Ibid.* p. 331.
29. Marx was always anxious to stress the fundamental distinction between levels of analysis—corresponding to qualitatively different types of social phenomena—to which appropriately different methods of enquiry must apply. He wrote in 1859:

    The changes in the economic foundation lead sooner or later to the transformation of the whole immense superstructure. In studying such transformations it is always *necessary to distinguish* between the *material transformation* of the economic conditions of production, which can be determined with the *precision of natural science,* and the legal, political, religious, artistic or philosophic—in short, *ideological forms* in which men become conscious of this conflict and *fight it out.* (*A Contribution to the Critique of Political Economy*, London, 1971, p. 21.)

    Clearly, there is no sign whatsoever of a 'scientistic reductionism': on the contrary, the impossibility of such reductionism is rigorously asserted. Nor is there any wavering between 'empiricist scientism' and 'romantic Hegelianism'. Instead we find the establishment of a clear line of demarcation between different forms of social praxis, pointing to a need for methods of analysis appropriate to 'material transformations', the 'ideological forms', and to the complex interactions of the two. Indeed, Marx repeatedly scorned bourgeois political economy for its attempt at reducing complex human relations into categories subsumed under claimed natural laws:

The *crude materialism* of the economists who regard as the *natural properties of things* what are *social relations* of production among people, and qualities which things obtain because they are subsumed under these relations, is at the same time *just as crude an idealism* even *fetishism*, since it imputes social relations to things as inherent characteristics, and thus mystifies them. (*Grundrisse*, p. 687).

Even when he asserted the necessary implications of socio-economic developments in England for the Continent of Europe, he hastened to add that on the Continent the consequences 'will take a form more brutal or more humane, *according to the degree of development of the working-class itself*.' (*Capital*, Vol. I, p. 9). It goes without saying that the latter cannot be determined 'with the precision of natural science', and since the development of a complex social totality always involves a multiplicity of qualitatively different factors, even the analysis of the material transformation of the economic conditions of production must be always qualified by the necessary implications of the manifold *dialectical interconnections*. Social processes, according to Marx, are inseperable from their *historical determinations*, and thus they cannot be forced into the Procrustean bed of immutable 'natural laws', conceived on the model of a schematic 'natural science'. In sharp contrast to scientism Marx identified the necessity manifest in social processes as *historical necessity (historische Notwendigkeit)* and he defined it as a *disappearing necessity ('eine verschwindende Notwendigkeit', Grundrisse*, pp. 831-2.), thanks to the active involvement of the human agency in all such processes which therefore must be opposed in principle to any form of reductionism.

30. 'Natural science has invaded and transformed human life all the more *practically* through the medium of industry; and has prepared human emancipation, however directly and much it had to consummate dehumanization. *Industry* is the actual historical relation of nature, and therefore of natural science, to man. If, therefore, industry is conceived as the *esoteric* revelation of man's *essential power* we also gain an understanding of the *human* essence of nature or the *natural* essence of man. In consequence, natural science will lose its *abstractly material*—or rather, its *idealistic*—tendency, and will become the *basis of human science*, as it has already become the *basis of actual human life*, albeit in an estranged form. One basis for life and another basis for *science* is *a priori* a lie.' (K. Marx, *Economic and Philosophic Manuscripts of 1844*, Lawrence & Wishart, London, 1959, pp.

110- 1).

31. *The German Ideology*, pp. 37-8.
32. *Ibid.* p. 38.
33. *Ibid.* p. 50.
34. *Ibid.* pp. 37-8.
35. In other words, through the reorientation of philosophy as 'real, positive science:' concerned with 'the representation of the practical activity, of the practical process of development of men.' *The German Ideology*, p. 38.
36. *Ibid.* Translation is my own. Rendering '*Betrachtung*' is particularly difficult. In addition to 'surveying' it also means 'consideration', 'contemplation', 'meditation', 'reflection', 'observation', etc. When we talk about a synthesis based on the comprehensive historical development of men, the empiricist immediacy of 'observation' is clearly out of place.
37. K. Marx. 'Difference between the Democritean and Epicurean Philosophy of Nature', Marx- Engels, *Collected Works*, Vol. I, p. 85.
38. *Ibid.*
39. See *Ibid.* p. 86.
40. *Ibid.*
41 Having defined the 'immediate realisation of philosophy' as the *objective* aspect of the problem, Marx turns to the *subjective* aspect:

    This is *the relationship of the philosophical system* which is realised *to its intellectual carriers*, to the *individual self-consciousnesses* in which its progress appears. This relationship results in what confronts the world in the realisation of philosophy itself, namely, in the fact that these individual self-consciousnesses always carry a *double-edged demand*, one edge turned against the world, the other against philosophy itself. . . . Their liberation of the world from un-philosophy is at the same time their own liberation from the philosophy that held them in fetters as a particular system. (*Ibid.*, pp. 86-6).

42. K. Marx, Preface to *A Contribution to the Critique of Political Economy*, January 1859.
43. *Collected Works*, Vol. I. p. 337.
44. Marx to Dagobert Oppenheim, 25 August 1842, *Werke*, Dietz Verlag, Berlin, 1958, Vol. 27, p. 409.
45. K. Marx, 'Introduction to the Critique of the Hegelian Philosophy of Right.'
46. The reason why this is of a capital importance is that the *same phenomena*, inasmuch as the competing classes are directly involved, appear quite different as viewed from the opposite standpoint, and thus yield *radically different* interpretations. As Marx noted in the *Grundrisse* (p. 832): 'this process of *objectification* appears in fact as a process of *alienation* from the

standpoint of labour, and as *appropriation* from the standpoint of capital.' Marx's critical adoption of the standpoint of labour meant a conception of the proletariat not simply as a sociological force diametrically opposed to the standpoint of capital—and thus remaining in the latter's orbit—but as a *self-transcending* historical force which cannot help superseding alienation (that is, the historically given form of objectification) in the process of realizing its own ends that happen to coincide with 'reappropriation'. For Marx's remarks on the proletariat as the 'universal class' in this sense, see his 'Introduction to the Critique of the Hegelian Philosophy of Right.'

47. 'Hegel's standpoint is that of modern political economy. He grasps *labour* as the *essence* of man—as man's essence in the act of proving itself: he sees only the positive, not the negative side of labour.' *Economic and Philosophic Manuscripts of 1844* (London, 1959), p. 152.
48. See in this respect Marx's letter to Engels, 2 April, 1858.
49. V. I. Lenin, *Collected Works*, Vol. 38, p. 180.
50. To Engels, 11 January 1868.
51. To Kugelmann, 27 June 1870.
52. *Economic and Philosophic Manuscripts of 1844*, p. 150.
53. *Ibid.* p. 151.
54. To Kugelmann, 6 March 1868.
55. K. Marx, F. Engels, *Werke, op. cit.*, Vol. 27, p. 417.
56. To Schweitzer, 24 January 1865.
57. K. Marx, *Critique of Hegel's Philosophy of Right* Cambridge, 1970, p. 9.
58. *Ibid.*
59. *Ibid.* p. 7.
60. *Ibid.* p. 9.
61. *Ibid*, p. 18.
62. To use Sartre's expression. See his *Critique of Dialectical Reason*, especially its Introduction.
63. *Critique of Hegel's Philosophy of Right*, p. 15.
64. In fact Marx often points to such tautologies. See for instance his *Critique of Hegel's Philosophy of Right*, p. 11, and also his Introduction to the *Grundrisse.*
65. *Critique of Hegel's Philosophy of Right* p. 16.
66. *Ibid.* p. 9.
67. *Ibid.*
68. K. Marx and F. Engels, *Collected Works*, Vol. I, p. 131.
69. No doubt, what Marx meant to stress in his aphorism was that *even* the materialistic approaches—including Feuerbach's—remained anchored to the standpoint of civil society shared also by the classical political economists.
70. Not even at the moments of the 'apocalypse': a concept which plays such a vital role in Sartre's thought, from some early works to the *Critique of Dialectical Reason.*

71. In view of this, it is amazing to find accusations of 'Millennial utopianism' and of 'bringing history to a standstill' levelled against Marx.
72. K. Marx, *Capital*, Vol. I, p. 168. (cf. also p. 293 of the *Grundrisse.*)
73. *Ibid.* Vol. I, p. 179.
74. *Ibid.* (The quote is from Hegel's *Enzyklopädie*, Part I., *Die Logik*, Berlin, 1840, p. 382).
75. *Critique of Hegel's Philosophy of Right, op cit.* p. 15.
76. *Ibid.* p. 18.
77. For lack of space, let us see only two examples. The first concerns capital in relation to circulation and exchange value:

    The first quality of capital is ... that circulation is not the movement of its disappearance, but rather the movement of its real self-positing [*Sichsetzen*] as exchange value, its self-realisation as exchange value. It cannot be said that exchange value as such is realised in simple circulation. It is always realised only in the moment of its disappearance. (*Grundrisse*, pp. 259-60).

    The second analyses the value-positing (*Wertsetzen*) function of capital:

    Capital is now posited... as not merely sustaining itself formally, but as *realising itself as value*, as value relating to itself as value in every one of the moments of its metamorphosis, in which it appears at one time as money, at another time as commodity, then again as exchange value, then again as use value. The passage from one moment to the other appears as a particular process, but each of these processes is the transition to the other. Capital is thus posited as value-in-process, which is capital in every moment. It is thus posited as *circulating capital*; in every moment capital, and circulating from one form into the next. The point of return is at the same time the point of departure and vice versa— namely the *capitalist.* All capital is originally circulating capital, product of circulation, as well as producing circulation, *tracing in this way its own course. (Ibid.* p. 536).
78. They are far too numerous even to be mentioned, ranging from '*Fürsichsein*' and '*Sein für andres*' to '*Aufhebung*', 'negation of the negation', etc. Let us see, instead, an unexpected but important distinction between 'boundary' and 'barrier' which Marx adopted with reference to the Hegelian *Logic*:

    Every boundary [*Grenze]* is and has to be a barrier [*Schranke*] for it [that is, capital]. Else it would cease to be capital—money as self-reproductive. If ever it perceived a certain boundary not as a barrier, but became comfortable within it as a boundary, it would itself have declined from exchange value to use value, from the general form of wealth to a specific, substantial mode of the same. ... The quantitative boundary of the surplus value appears to [capital] as a mere natural barrier, as a necessity which it constantly tries to violate and beyond which it constantly seeks to go.

And the relevant passages in Hegel's *Logic* read as follows: 'Something's own boundary posited by it as a negative which is at the same time essential, is not merely boundary as such but barrier.' 'The sentient creature, in the limitation of hunger, thirst, etc., is the drive to go beyond its limiting barrier, and it does overcome it.' (*Grundrisse*, pp. 334-5.)

79. See Marx's Introduction to the *Grundrisse* in particular.
80. To Engels, 25 July 1866.
81. Cf. Marx's letters to Engels, 1 February 1858 and to Schweitzer, 24 January 1865.
82. To Kugelmann, 27 June 1870.

IV Kant, Hegel, Marx: Historical Necessity and the Standpoint of Political Economy *

In his 'Critique of the Hegelian Dialectic and Philosophy as a Whole', Marx suggests that 'Hegel's standpoint is that of modern political economy'.[1] He shares this position with many others, including—on the face of it surprisingly—Kant himself, as we shall see later on.

What is important for us in this respect is to understand what kind of historical conceptions are both compatible with and positively helped along by the standpoint of political economy. For it is quite wrong to treat Kant and Hegel, as it is often done, merely as rationalistic varieties of St. Augustine's openly theological (and not in the least historical) philosophy of history. To say that 'Hegel's concept of "the cunning of Reason" is a substitute for the mysterious and inscrutable ways of God in history'[2] is to miss the point completely. For such a view obliterates without a trace the specificities and genuine historical achievements of the Hegelian position. Concentrating on superficial analogies, it generates the proverbial darkness in which 'all cows are black', so as to be able to eliminate the social substance of the Marxian dialectic by maintaining that 'the famous law of three stages, which Marx and Comte adopted, too, is a secular revision of the religious dialectic in St. Augustine and Joachim de Flore.'[3] Once such darkness descends upon us,

———

* This essay is an extended version of a paper presented at The Second 'Simposio de Filosofia Contemporánea: Kant, Hegel y las Ciencias Sociales', Universitad Autónoma Metropolitana de Mexico, 6-8 March 1985.

it becomes possible to put forward the most astonishing propositions, lumping irreconcilable thinkers together by defining 'the intellectual heritage of Marx, Comte, Burckhardt, Pareto, Sorel, and Freud' on the basis of their alleged identity in maintaining that 'emotive and irrational factors . . . permeated history and society.'[4]

In truth, it is important to draw the necessary lines of demarcation not only between figures like Vico, Kant, Herder and Hegel, on the one hand, and the pessimistic historical relativism of many thinkers in the nineteenth and twentieth centuries on the other, but even more so between Marx and the entire intellectual tradition which shares the standpoint of political economy. For the historical conceptions compatible with that standpoint are severely constrained by the inescapable limitations of the standpoint itself even in the works of its greatest representatives. What is particularly relevant in this regard is their conception of *necessity* as manifest in the unfolding historical process. To put it very briefly, they operate with an idea of 'historical necessity'—or 'necessity in history'—which, compared to Marx, is *not historical* at all, not even in the most monumental and coherent historical conception of the whole tradition: the Hegelian philosophy of history. Yet, curiously enough, it is Marx who is accused of 'historical determinism', of the 'idealization of historical necessity', of 'economic determinism', and the like.

The main purpose of this essay is to try to redress the balance in both directions. First, we have to see why the determinations inherent in the standpoint of political economy *in the end* bring a totally ahistorical conceptualization of the *given* structural necessity as *forever* insurmountable necessity, although, paradoxically, the subjective intention of the thinkers concerned is to demonstrate how freedom is progressively realized through the unfolding history of mankind. And second, the essay will focus attention on the generally ignored aim of Marx's project to challenge not only the shorter or longer term impact of capital's historical necessity but *historical necessity as such*—evidenced in the Marxian characterization of historical necessity as *'merely* historical necessity' or *'disappearing* necessity' which, under our present conditions, constitutes an outrage against the positive potentialities of the real social individual.

1. THEOLOGY, TELEOLOGY, AND PHILOSOPHY OF HISTORY

Looking back from a certain distance at actual historical development—a distance from which the *already consolidated* plateaus stand out as 'necessary stages' of the whole itinerary, while the manifold specific struggles and contradictions leading to them (which contain numerous pointers towards possible alternative configurations) fade into the background—one may have the illusion of a 'logically necessary' progression, corresponding to some hidden design. Viewed from such perspective, everything firmly established acquires its *positive* sense, and the consolidated stages by definition must appear to be positive/rational—in virtue of their actual consolidation.

The historical images conceived in this way represent a most ambiguous achievement. They are simultaneously historical and ahistorical, and in a specific sense even 'theological', in accordance with the contradictory determinations of the social ground from which they arise. For, strangely enough, by treating the historically created presuppositions of the given order as *absolutely* given—and therefore structurally untranscendable—the situation that preceded the realization of the absolutized conditions can be recognized from the latter's vantage point as subject to *necessary historical qualifications,* insofar as the rejected position is considered to be objectively opposed to the interests of the more advanced stage, as its anachronistic social adversary. Consequently, a genuine possibility is opened up for depicting the *negated* aspects and dimensions of social development as historical in the meaningful sense which envisages their *practical supersession.*

At the same time, since the newly assumed position is uncritically absolutized, from its perspective everything prior to it (or in conflict with it) must appear as strictly subordinated moments of an *a priori* self-fulfilling teleology. To take an example: both these aspects are in evidence when Kant radically dismisses the restrictive hereditary principle of *feudalism* as contrary to Reason, and simultaneously approves the new irrationality of the *alienation of land by sale,* as well as its fragmentary subdivision, as conditions which are in perfect harmony with the 'supreme reason for constituting a civic constitution'.[5]

But even so, one cannot treat the Kantian or Hegelian teleology of historical development simply as the rationalistic translation of St. Augustine's theological conception. For the 'theological' aspects of their historical teleology arise from the limitations of a determinate social horizon, and not from a consciously assumed theological framework. In other words, the theological elements display the—far from desired—*contradictions* of their approach, and not their inherent positive intent. They come into play at the point where, in accordance with the insurmountable limits of the social horizon in question, history must be *brought to an end,* instead of representing the explanatory framework of the whole theory. Thus, they constitute only a greater or smaller *part* of the whole conception—comparatively, greater in Kant, that is, than in Hegel—but not the central tenets and unifying principles of the attempted historical explanations, quite unlike the openly and deliberately theological visions of the Divine purpose and intervention in the historical world, from St. Augustine to Bossuet and Friedrich Schlegel, as well as to their twentieth-century descendants.

There is a tendency to treat teleology in general as a form of Theology. This is due to a large extent to the long prevailing conjunction of the two in an important current of the European philosophical tradition which formulated its explanations in terms of 'final causes' and identified the latter with the manifestation of the Divine purpose in the order of nature. However, the summary equation of teleology and Theology is quite unjustifiable since, as will be shown later, the objective teleology of labour is an essential part of any coherent materialistic historical explanation of social development. Such an explanation, dealing with actually unfolding causal factors and not with *a priori* preconceived schemes, has nothing whatsoever to do with *theological* assumptions, even though determinate *teleological* propositions are inseparable from it.

But even with regard to the philosophies of Kant and Hegel in which some theological elements undoubtedly reassert themselves, it is necessary to put the issue in perspective. To see nothing but theology in their teleological conceptions would be like asserting about Liberation Theology the totally unenlightening truism that it has been influenced by the teaching of Jesus Christ. For whatever the generic truth of such assertions, they fail to grasp the theoretical specificity and socio-historical determinateness of the respective views. The fact of the matter is, of course, that the Liberation Theologians have also studied Marx and tried to incorporate some of his ideas into their own conceptual framework. And it is precisely their point of contact with Marx that happens to be the decisive factor under the circumstances. For, obviously, they are not being threatened with excommunication by Pope Voytila on account of their adherence to the teaching of Jesus Christ.

Similar considerations apply to the assessment of Kant and Hegel. To be sure, no one should deny that their teleological systems are thoroughly incompatible with the Marxian teleology, in view of their *necessary* relapse into a—socially specific—theology. Indeed, this curious relapse into theology fulfils the highly revealing function of freezing history in the Kantian and Hegelian historical conceptions at an ideologically convenient point in time, thereby rationalizing the ahistorical temporality of the present, together with the idealized bourgeois social order. However, the problem that really matters is how to explain the socio-historical determinations behind such relapse, instead of merely asserting the permanence of theological teleology as an *a priori* assumed condition. For, as we shall see in a moment, in both Kant and Hegel the theology in question is the self-legitimating 'theology' of an ahistorically conceived *civil society*, brought into their systems on the ground of ideological determinations, and not for the purpose of asserting the absolute merits of the Christian religious creed.

2. THE KANTIAN CONCEPTION OF HISTORICAL DEVELOPMENT

Let us have a brief look at Kant's 'Idea for a Universal History with Cosmopolitan Intent' which is directly relevant in this respect. One of the most important aspects of Kant's conception of history is that he brings the principle of *work* to the fore, insisting that historical development happens to be so determined that everything 'should be achieved by *work* . . . as if nature intended that man should owe all to himself'.[6] The paradoxical intelligibility of the relationship between the innumerable particular individuals and the human species, and the strange but coherent development resulting from such relationship, is described by Kant in the following terms:

It is like the erratic weather the occurrence of which cannot be determined in particular instances, although it never fails in maintaining the growth of plants, the flow of streams, and other of nature's arrangments at a uniform, uninterrupted pace. Individual human beings, each pursuing his own ends according to his inclination and often one against another (and even one entire people against another) rarely intentionally promote, as if it were their guide, an end of nature which is unknown to them. They thus work to promote that which they would care little for if they knew about it.[7]

In this way, an insurmountable dichotomy is created between the individual and the species.[8] At the same time, the 'rationality' of the overall process is secured by Kant in our last quote in a way that anticipates the Hegelian 'List der Vernunft' (the 'cunning of Reason') which is said to prevail over against the conscious intentions of the particular individuals.

As to the Kantian characterization of individual human beings, it is very similar to that of all the major theoreticians of 'civil society', putting the '*antagonism of men in society*' very much into the foreground. To quote Kant again:

I mean by antagonism the *asocial sociability* of men, i.e., the propensity of men to enter into a society, which propensity is, however, linked to a *constant mutual resistance* which threatens to dissolve this society. This propensity apparently is *innate in man.*[9]

Indeed, at the plane of overall historical development Kant gives *highly positive* connotations to the negative traits and characteristics of 'human nature'. For, according to him:

Without these essentially unlovely qualities of asociability, from which springs the resistance which everyone must encounter in his egotistic pretensions, all talents would have remained hidden germs. If man lived an Arcadian shepherd's existence of harmony, modesty and mutuality, man, good-natured like the sheep he is herding, would not invest his existence with greater value than that his animals have. Man would not fill the vacuum of creation as regards his end, rational nature. Thanks are due to *nature* for his *quarrelsomeness,* his *enviously competitive vanity,* and for his *insatiable desire to possess* or to *rule,* for without them all the excellent faculties of mankind would forever remain undeveloped.[10]

Similarly, the contradiction between freedom and 'egotistic nature' is handled in much the same way as in the writings of his great predecessors who share the standpoint of civil society:

> Man is an animal who, if he lives among others of his kind, needs a master, for man certainly *misuses his freedom in regard to others* of his kind and, even though as a rational being he desires a *law* which would provide *limits for the freedom of all,* his *egotistic* animal inclination misguides him into excluding himself where he can. Man therefore *needs a master* who can break man's will and compel him to obey a *general will* under which every man could be free.[11]

As we can see, while retaining several elements of Hobbes' approach, Kant goes beyond the latter by incorporating into his system Rousseau's seminal ideas too. However, the view which historically locates him, with the greatest precision, in the company of the leading political economists of the age, is the role assigned to trade and commerce in the course of historical development towards a more advanced condition of life in 'civil society'. This is the key passage in Kant's 'Idea for a Universal History with Cosmopolitan Intent' on the subject:

> Civic freedom cannot now be interfered with without the state feeling the disadvantage of such interference in all *trades,* primarily foreign *commerce* and as a result [there is] a decline of the power of the state in its foreign relations. Therefore this *freedom is gradually being extended.* If one obstructs the citizen in seeking his welfare in any way he chooses, as long as [his way] can coexist with the freedom of others, one also hampers the vitality of all business and the strength of the whole [state]. For this reason restrictions of personal activities are being increasingly lifted and *general freedom* granted and thus *enlightenment* is gradually developing with occasional nonsense and freakishness.[12]

The 'achievement of a civil society which administers law *[Recht]* generally', on a world scale, represents in Kant's eyes 'the highest task nature has set mankind',[13] and it is brought about by the working of the complex material determinations and contradictory interactive processes which he identifies among individuals and 'even entire peoples'. Naturally, a great deal must be ascribed in this conception to the mysteries of the 'hidden plan of nature'.[14] However, the mysteries are not derived from some stated or unstated theological requirement. On the contrary, they arise from the *Kantian model of civil society* itself in which the contradictory individual interactive processes cannot be made intelligible on their own, precisely because of the inherent limitations of the individualistic standpoint which can only yield the idea of the extreme capriciousness of fluctuating weather conditions, to be set against the actuality of nature's uniformity and productive efficacy. Thus, the relapse into a 'theological teleology' here fulfils a determinate social purpose in that it fills an enormous gap in the explanatory framework of Kant's 'civil society', in accordance with the internal determinations of his system in its entirety.

As we shall see, despite its problematical character in other respects, Hegel's approach represents a significant advance over the Kantian philosophy of history. For inasmuch as it depicts an earlier and less consolidated phase in the development of 'civil society' than Hegel, the Kantian system remains tied to some abstract moral categories in its attempt to explain the motive forces of mankind's historical advancement.

It is by no means accidental that Kant insists on the *'primacy of practical reason'* as the all-important structuring principle of his system. For that principle enables him to 'resolve' the dichotomies and contradictions of social life through the postulates of the 'intelligible world' and the legislative supremacy of *formal universality* over all conceivable constraints of *matter* and *empirical existence.* The same model is applied to the assessment of the world of Right and the relationship between formal equality and substantive inequality:

Right is the limitation of every man's freedom so that it harmonizes with the freedom of every other man in so far as harmonization is possible according to a general law. Public Law is the totality of external laws which makes such a general consonance possible . . . the civic constitution is a relationship of free men who, despite their freedom for joining with others, are nevertheless placed under coercive laws. This is so because it is so willed by *pure a priori legislating reason* which has *no regard for empirical purposes* such as are comprised under the general name of happiness. . . . The *general equality* of men as subjects in a state coexists quite readily with the *greatest inequality* in degrees of the *possessions* men have, whether the possessions consist of corporeal or spiritual superiority or in material possession besides. Hence the general equality of men also coexists with *great inequality of specific rights* of which there may be many. Thus it follows that the welfare of one man may depend to a very great extent on the will of another man, just as the *poor are dependent on the rich* and the one who is *dependent must obey* the other as a child obeys his parents or the wife her husband or again, just as one man has command over another, as one man serves and another pays, etc. Nevertheless, all subjects are equal to each other before the law which, as a pronouncement of the general will, can only be one. This law concerns the *form* and not the *matter* of the object regarding which I may possess a right.[15]

The same orientation guides Kant in his reflections on history. Accordingly, he constructs a much more a prioristic unfolding of the historical process out of his postulates than Hegel, in conformity to the requirements of the categorical imperative.

This becomes clear if we remember that even in the last phase of his philosophical development—when, under the impact of the French Revolution and its equally turbulent aftermath, he tries to face some of the contradictions of the real world in his philosophy—Kant cannot get rid of the severe limitations of his a prioristic transcendentalism. He sets up a stark *dichotomy* between the *'moralist politician'* and the *'political moralist'*,[16] opting for the first on account of his conformity to the moral law as against the second who bends moral considerations to suit the statesman's advantage.

Thus, the abstract determinations of 'duty' and 'ought' (*Pflicht* and *Sollen*) are voluntaristically superimposed on both politics and history. Political actions, just like individual pursuits, are evaluated in accordance with the *formal* principle which directly *universalizes* one's subjective maxim as a general law.[17] The question of right is raised 'in relation to an apriori knowable politics'.[18] Freedom, equality, etc., are established as 'duties',[19] and 'moral evil' is declared to be by its very nature 'self-destructive'.[20] Similarly, it is stipulated that 'human rights must be held sacred' even if it means great sacrifices to the ruling powers.[21]

In harmony with this aprioristic determination of politics—which is also designed to establish 'the unity of practical philosophy with itself',[22] in accordance with the earlier mentioned principle of the *primacy of practical reason* in the Kantian system as a whole—the postulated 'moralist politician' is supposed to serve history's own purpose: by pursuing the aim of 'eternal peace' not as a 'physical good' but as a 'moral duty', desired for its own sake and 'arising out of the circumstance of acknowledging the duty itself'.[23]

Furthermore, the objective finality which is postulated by Kant becomes necessary in order to underpin the general moral construct, in view of its structural deficiency in attempting to derive the *objectivity* of universally valid law (an abstract formalistic substitute for the interpersonal objectivity of action in the social sphere) from the *subjective* maxims of isolated individuals. On the one hand, it is stated that parallel to the expansion of individual needs we find in history a necessary *decrease* in the possibility of their gratification (an idea very similar to the Malthusian view of socio-economic development), from which it is deduced that in an *inverse ratio* to the *empirical* satisfaction of the *individuals* grows the *moral* figure of the *whole*, thereby bringing nearer the rule of practical reason. And on the other hand, nature's original 'finality' to make men live everywhere on earth, using *war* as its 'despotic' instrument to realize this purpose,[24] is said to be progressively displaced by the teleology of *'reciprocal self-interest'* and the *'commercial spirit' (Handelsgeist*: a concept borrowed from Adam Smith) corresponding to it. Accordingly, it is postulated that *'commercial spirit*, which is *incompatible with war* [sic!!], sooner or later will bring all people under its power',[25] thus pointing in the right direction of history's inexorable march towards moral perfection and eternal peace in the framework of a global system of harmoniously co-existing states.

As we can see, Kant's horizon, too, is hopelessly constrained by the 'standpoint of political economy'. So much so, in fact, that even in the midst of ever-intensifying conflagrations in Europe—and despite the growing evidence with regard to their material determinations—he idealizes 'commercial spirit' to the point of completely disregarding the possibility that the exact opposite of his expectations (i.e., the total destruction of mankind) might come true on the basis of the extreme negative potentialities implicit in this 'spirit'.

Thus, it is the contradiction between the given historical reality and the idealized 'commercial spirit' that produces the Kantian moral construct of politics and history, resolving the striking contradictions between the benevolently embellished ideal and the cruelly prosaic reality by its abstract discourse on history as a 'progressive approximation'[26] to the state of eternal peace and the universal rule of the moral law.

3. THE RADICAL OPENNESS OF HISTORY

Conceptualizing an earlier stage of social development and identifying itself with the Englightenment's attitude to Reason as the ultimate determinant of human action on the universal scale of the species, the Kantian conception pays much less attention to the recognizable characteristics of actual history than Hegel. For the latter incorporates in a strikingly realistic fashion many details of human development into his grandiose speculative scheme.

But even so, no matter how great is Hegel's advance over Kant, he fails to conceptualize the *radical openness* of history, since the ideological determinations of his position stipulate the necessity of a reconciliation with the present and thus the arbitrary *closure* of the historical dynamic in the framework of the modern state. (Hence the necessary identification of 'rationality' and 'actuality' from which the equation of actuality and *positivity* can be derived.) Thus, the characteristic 'theological' teleology of 'civil society', in its circular reciprocity with the bourgeois state, asserts itself as the ultimate reconciliatory frame of reference—and 'point of rest'—of the Hegelian construct.

Just as in the case of Kant, his great predecessor, the final responsibility for the reconciliatory closure of Hegel's conception resides with the ideological determinations, and not simply with the idealism of the Hegelian teleology *per se.* However, the latter is a most welcome methodological complement and vehicle of the social standpoint of political economy from which the apologetic ideological determinations necessarily arise.

To be sure, human history is not intelligible without some kind of teleology. But the only teleology consistent with the materialist conception of history is the objective and open-ended teleology of labour itself. At the fundamental ontological level such teleology is concerned with the way in which the human being—this unique 'self-mediating being of nature'—creates and develops itself through its purposeful productive activity.

In this process, labour fulfils the function of active mediation in the progressively changing metabolism between men and nature. All potentialities of the socialized human being as well as all characteristics of the social intercourse and social metabolism emerge from the objective teleology of this mediation. And since the labour involved in these processes and transformations is men's own labour, the active mediation between men and nature, too, cannot be considered other than *self-mediation* which, as a framework of explanation, is radically opposed to any theological conception of teleology.

Consequently, it is obvious already at this level that history must be conceived as necessarily open-ended in virtue of the qualitative change that takes place in the natural order of determinations: the establishment of a unique framework of ontological necessity of which *self-mediating human teleology* itself is an integral part.

The *historically created* radical openness of history—human history—is, therefore, inescapable in the sense that there can be no way of theoretically or practically *predetermining* the forms and modalities of human *self*-mediation. For the complex teleological conditions of this self-mediation through productive activity can only be satisfied—since they are constantly being created and recreated—in the course of this self-mediation itself. This is why all attempts at producing neatly self-contained and closed systems of historical explanation result either in some arbitrary reduction of the complexity of human actions to the crude simplicity of mechanical determinations, or in the idealistic superimposition of one kind or another of *a priori transcendentalism* on the *immanence* of human development.

4. CRITIQUE OF THE HEGELIAN PHILOSOPHY OF HISTORY

It is well known that Marx credited idealism—in contrast to traditional materialism—with being the first to conceptualize the 'active and subjective side' of historical development. However, in view of the uncritical presuppositions of the philosophers concerned with regard to the established social order, idealism could envisage active intervention in the unfolding history only in an extremely abstract form. That is to say,it had to superimpose its preconceived 'categories' on historical events and personalities alike, substituting the 'self-development of the idea' for the objective determinations of actual social changes.

All the same, there can be no doubt that focussing attention on the subjective and active side of the multifaceted process of socio-historical interchanges constituted a major achievement on the road to making the overall dynamic of historical development intelligible in terms of *conscious*—even if, as far as the particular individuals were concerned, only paradoxically and contradictorily conscious—human intervention in the complex order of determinations.

It was due to the inner requirements of the 'standpoint of political economy' that even the peak of such conceptions of history—the Hegelian philosophy—had to remain trapped within the contradictions of its necessarily abstract and preconceived teleological categories. For although Hegel boldly asserted that 'the History of the World is nothing but the development of the Idea of Freedom',[27] this grand statement sounded utterly vacuous on account of its merely *contemplative*[28] posture. Furthermore, it also suffered from the self-contradictory character of its apologetic tendency which saw the Idea's ultimate 'self-realization' in the modern capitalist state,[29] notwithstanding the internal divisions and antagonisms of the latter. Antagonisms which, to a significant extent, the Hegelian philosophy itself could not help acknowledging.

As a result, Hegel equated the historical development that was supposed to have reached its final completion in the modern state with nothing less than the 'justification of God in History.' This is how Hegel summed up his vision of historical development:

> The inquiry into the essential *destiny of Reason*—as far as it is considered in reference to the World—is identical with the question, what is the *ultimate design* of the World? And the expression implies that that design is destined to be realized.[30]

However, despite the religious phraseology, Hegel was not expressing here a religious concern as such. On the contrary, he considered it a great historical advance—accomplished by the 'Germanic world' on behalf of the whole of mankind, as the climax of the unfolding of 'universal history'—that 'in the Protestant Church the reconciliation of Religion with Legal Right has taken place. In the Protestant world there is no sacred, no religious conscience in a state of separation from, or perhaps even hostility to Secular Right.'[31]

Thus, he put forward a secularized interpretation of history—one culminating in the rational actuality of the Germanic state—as the *true Theodicaea.* These were the final words of his *Philosophy of History:*

That the History of the World, with all the changing scenes which its annals present, is this process of development and the realization of Spirit—this is the *true Theodicaea,* the justification of God in History. Only this insight can *reconcile* Spirit with the History of the World—viz., that *what has happened, and is happening every day,* is not only not 'without God', but is essentially His Work.[32]

Others may have had their—strictly theological—view of Theodicaea, but that was of no interest to Hegel. His meaning of the *'true Theodicaea'* was made perfectly clear in his recapitulation of the climax of the historical process which preceded the lines just quoted:

Feudal obligations are abolished, for freedom of property and of person have been recognized as fundamental principles. Offices of State are open to every citizen, talent and adaptation being of course the necessary conditions. The government rests with the official world, and the personal decision of the monarch constitutes its apex; . . . Yet with firmly established laws, and a settled organization of the State, what is left to the sole arbitrament of the monarch is, in point of substance, no great matter. . . . a share in the government may be obtained by every one who has a competent knowledge, experience, and a morally regulated will. Those who know ought to govern . . . Objective Freedom—the laws of real Freedom—demand the subjugation of the mere contingent Will—for this is in its nature formal. If the Objective is in itself Rational, human insight and conviction must correspond with the Reason which it embodies, and then we have the other essential element—Subjective Freedom—also realized.[33]

In this sense, what counted in Hegel's eyes as the true Theodicaea was the realization of Objective Freedom in the actuality of the modern state. And the historical process itself was defined as the establishment of the identity of the Objective and the Rational, as well as of Subjective Freedom and the requirements of the Law, reconciling at the same time the particular individuals to the state-oriented 'rational actuality' of the present.

To be sure, in this conception the room for real historical

determinations—i.e., determinations which would acknowledge the objective weight of the past and the present without blocking off the future—had to be extremely limited. 'Activity' itself, in an idealistically respectable sense of the term, had to be made synonymous with *self-contemplation* in order to befit the definitional characterization of 'Spirit'. For, according to Hegel, 'The very essence of Spirit is activity; it realizes its potentiality—makes itself its own deed, its own work—and thus it becomes an object to itself; *contemplates itself* as an objective existence.'[34]

Such a definitional determination of the nature of historical development, in accordance with an, *a priori* assumed, *quasi*-theological finality of 'civil society' and its corresponding state, inevitably vitiated Hegel's conception of necessity and temporality alike. 'Necessity' was conjured up by a conflation of logic and actuality, superimposing the abstractly preconceived categories of the *'Science of Logic'* on real historical movements and transformations, at times in the most grotesque form.[35] 'Temporality', on the other hand, had to be turned in the end from a three-dimensional determination of past, present and future into an essentially *one-dimensional present,* partly for apologetic reasons and partly as a result of the internal conceptual requirements of the Hegelian system dominated by the Logic.[36]

We can see this through the fact that, despite defining History as 'the Ideal necessity of transition',[37] Hegel could simultaneously also maintain that 'The History of the World travels from East to West, for *Europe is absolutely the end of History',*[38] in keeping with the key position of the glorified modern (Germanic) state in his overall system as the 'final aim' of actual historical development. The 'necessitated gradations'[39] of this far from open-ended 'transition' were all modelled on the Logic[40] which conveniently also lent itself to the apologetic requirements of compressing the dynamic three-dimensionality of actual historical time into a mythically inflated and metaphorically embellished present:

Spirit is essentially the result of its own activity: its activity is the transcending of immediate, simple, unreflected existence—the negation of that existence, and the *returning into itself.* We may compare it with the seed; for with this the plant *begins,* yet it is also the *result* of the plant's entire life.... We have already discussed the *final aim* of this progression. The *principles* of the successive phases of Spirit that animate the Nations in a *necessitated gradation,* are themselves only steps in the development of the one universal Spirit, which through them elevates and completes itself to a self-comprehending totality. While we are thus concerned exclusively with the Idea of Spirit, and in the History of the World regard everything as only its manifestation, we have, in traversing the past—however extensive its periods—only to do with what is *present;* for philosophy, as occupying itself with the True, has to do with the *eternally present.* Nothing in the past is lost for it, for the Idea is *ever present;* Spirit is immortal; with it there is *no past, no future,* but an *essentially now.* This necessarily implies that the present form of Spirit comprehends within it all earlier steps. These have indeed unfolded themselves in succession independently: but what Spirit is it has *always been* essentially; distinctions are only the development of this essential nature. The life of the ever present Spirit is a *circle* of progressive embodiments, which looked at from another point of view *appear* as past. The grades which Spirit *seems* to have left behind it, it still possesses in the *depths of its present.*[41]

However, no amount of metaphorical flourish, not even the one arising from the soil of Hegel's philosophical and linguistic genius, could turn the abstract 'self-activity' of Spirit—'returning into itself' through its *a priori* conformity to the timeless 'principles' and categorial requirements of a speculative Logic—into real history. For the seed does not simply fall out of the sky, but comes into being through the actual processes of inorganic and organic matter, before it can reproduce itself as a *new* beginning, and not as an abstract logical coincidence of the *categories* of end and beginning. Real historical determinations have to *account for* the *genesis* and subsequent *transformations* of social/historical structures, in all three dimensions of actual historical time, instead of conveniently assuming them through the self-referential circularity of 'Spirit returning into itself' in accordance with the logically stipulated 'essential nature' of its 'eternal presentness' and 'self-comprehending totality'.

Comparably to the role of the 'primacy of Practical Reason' in Kant's system in general and in his philosophy of history in particular, it was because of the internal hierarchy of the Hegelian system as a whole—with the *Philosophy of Right* and its corresponding state formation at its apex—that the 'eternal present' and its manifold circles had to come into dominance in Hegel's conception of historical determination. This is why the *Philosophy of History* had to reach its climax in its apotheosis of the modern state, just as the *Philosophy of Right* had to culminate in an identically circular account of world history as the 'self-realization of Reason' in the form of the state. History, according to Hegel, could exist in the past—though even then only *'in the depths of Spirit's present'*, thus anticipating the given structures of the *'essentially now'*—but not in the future: and especially not at the level of 'civil society' eternally locked into the pseudo-universal politics of the modern state. Thus, despite Hegel's boundless admiration for the Greek world—particularly pronounced with regard to art which he could locate in his scheme of things at an earlier stage of Spirit's 'self-activity'—he could find nothing positive to say about the political dimension of that civilization. He had to maintain that in politics 'the Ancient and the Modern have not their essential principle in common',[42] for if they did, the process of sociopolitical development would have had to be admitted to be inherently contradictory, hence necessarily open-ended, instead of being terminated in its 'Germanic form', in a 'civilizing' (i.e., imperialistically dominant) Europe defined as 'absolutely the end of History'.

In this philosophical glorification of the established power relations—which in fact sharply contradicted the Hegelian claims with regard to the historically unstoppable realization of the 'principle of freedom'—national and colonial oppression were declared to be perfectly in accord with the inner requirements of 'Spirit returning to itself' as 'fully developed Spirit'. The dominant imperialist states received their philosophical legitimation *vis-à-vis* the 'minor states' which they oppressed—and through such legitimation could in principle forever *rightfully* oppress—by saying that:

> *Minor states* have their existence and *tranquillity* secured to them more or less by their neighbours: they are therefore, properly speaking, *not independent,* and have not the *fiery trial of war* to endure.[43]

The idea of such 'fiery trial of war'—as a 'life-and-death struggle', said to be necessary because 'it is solely by risking life that freedom is obtained'[44]—appeared in Hegel's thought at a much earlier stage. However, in contrast to the *Philosophy of History* as well as to the *Philosophy of Right,* in the Hegelian *Phenomenology of Mind* it constituted only a limited and necessarily transcended *moment* of the objective dialectic of 'Master' and 'Bondsman'. Indeed, in the *Phenomenology* the Bondsman was able to assert itself against the initially dominant Master in its own way, through the *power of labour,* thereby not merely limiting but totally *reversing* the original relationship:

For just where the master has effectively achieved lordship, he really finds that something has come about quite different from an independent consciousness. It is not an independent, but rather a *dependent* consciousness that he has achieved. He is thus not assured of self-existence as his truth; he finds that his truth is rather the unessential consciousness, and the fortuitous unessential action of that consciousness. The truth of the *independent* consciousness is accordingly the consciousness of the *bondsman.* This doubtless appears in the first instance outside itself, and not as the truth of self-consciousness. But just as lordship showed its essential nature to be the *reverse* of what it wants to be, too, bondage will, when completed, pass into the *opposite* of what it immediately is: being a consciousness repressed within itself, it will enter into itself, and change round into *real and true independence.* . . . Through *work and labour* this consciousness of the bondsman comes to itself. . . . The negative relation to the object passes into the *form* of the object, into something that is *permanent* . . . . This negative mediating agency, this activity giving shape and form, is at the same time the individual existence, the pure self-existence of that consciousness, which now in the work it does is *externalized* and passes into the *condition of permanence.* The consciousness that toils and serves accordingly attains by this means the direct apprehension of that *independent being as its self.* . . . in fashioning the thing, self-existence comes to be felt explicity as *his own proper being,* and he attains the consciousness that he himself exists in its own right and on its own account *[an und für sich].*[45]

Horrified of the explosive implications of the objective dialectic of 'Master and Bondsman'—which asserted the adequately self-sustaining existence and 'an und für sich' character of labour, together with the necessary historical supersession of 'lordship': shown to be totally superfluous in terms of Hegel's own account—the author of *The Phenomenology of Mind* desperately tries to take back his conclusion already on the last half page of the chapter on 'Lordship and Bondage', with the help of linguistic juggling and conceptual sophistry.[46] By the time we reach *The Philosophy of History* (and the *Philosophy of Right),* Hegel's earlier inner doubts completely disappear, and the ideological rationalization of the materially and politically dominant social order's brutal self-assertion through the 'fiery trial of war' acquires the anti-dialectical rigidity of an arbitrary metaphysical postulate in the Hegelian conception.

As we have seen, Kant advocated and postulated the universal rule of a 'perfect constitution', the successful institution of 'eternal peace', and the harmonious co-existence of all states within the framework of a League of Nations equally beneficial to all. He formulated these postulates on the explicity stated ground that 'the commercial spirit is incompatible with war', thus elevating to the level of the so-called 'apriori principles of Reason' the wishful thinking and *universalistic illusions* of 'enlightened' capital: incorrigibly *particularistic,* in fact, in its objective constitution to the core.

Hegel, representing—with a greater sense of realism—a much more consolidated stage in the historical development of capital, had no use for the Kantian illusion of 'eternal peace' which was supposed to be established at a certain point of human advancement thanks to the enlightened dictates of the 'commercial spirit'. He did not hesitate to state quite categorically that 'The *nation state* is . . . the *absolute* power on earth', and that the '*universal* proviso of international law therefore does not go beyond an *ought-to-be*'.[47] Consequently, according to Hegel, the necessity of settling disputes by war had to assert its absolute primacy on the material ground of 'civil society'. And he insisted that the realization of the idea of peace—a mere 'ought-to-be', even though it was arbitrarily and circularly *assumed* by Kant as the necessary culmination of historical development—'*presupposes* an accord between states; this would rest on moral or religious or other grounds and considerations, but in any case would always depend on a particular sovereign will and for that reason would remain *infected with contingency.*'[48]

In this sense, Hegel was anxious to keep the dimension of 'ought' at bay in his account of historical development, and to concentrate, instead, on the dominant tendencies of 'actuality', even if in the end he always transubstantiated the latter into specific manifestations of the Idea's self-realizing 'rationality'. Not surprisingly, therefore, in his discussion of the historically most advanced embodiment of the 'commercial spirit' the pride of place had to be assigned to imperialistically expanding

England. For, according to Hegel:

> The material existence of England is based on *commerce and industry,* and the English have undertaken the weighty responsibility of being the *missionaries of civilization* to the world; for their *commercial spirit* urges them to traverse every sea and land, to form connections with barbarous peoples, to *create wants and stimulate industry,* and first and foremost to establish among them the *conditions necessary to commerce,* viz. the relinquishment of a life of lawless violence, *respect for property* and civility to strangers.[49]

And to all those who might have criticized the inherent amorality of his conception, he firmly retorted that their doctrine rested on 'superficial ideas about morality, the nature of the state, and the state's relation to the moral point of view.'[50]

Since it was Kant himself who formulated the irreconcilable opposition between the 'moralist politician' and the morally reprehensible 'political moralist', one could hardly fail to see the contradiction between these two outstanding figures of German philosophy in this respect. Indeed, Hegel was thoroughly convinced that his own philosophy represented the radical supersession of the Kantian conception as a whole.

And yet, a closer look at the Kantian and Hegelian philosophies of history reveals that the contradiction between the two concerning the ultimate perspectives of development is much more apparent than real. For both conceptions base their conclusions on the material premise of 'civil society', assumed by them in a totally uncritical manner as the absolute horizon of all conceivable social life as such.

Hegel, though an acute observer of a later phase of historical development, is not in the least more historical in this respect than Kant. It is true that he is incomparably more realistic in his characterization of the state's actual behaviour in international matters than Kant, who simply postulates the radical transcendence of the identified contradictions of 'human nature' and 'civil society' by the beneficial self-assertion of the 'commercial spirit' and the ensuing realization of an ideal system of inter-state relations. However, while the Kantian 'ought' is undoubtedly nothing more than the moralistic counter-image of a reality which he cannot conceivably criticize from the 'standpoint of political economy' (which he fully supports, nay idealizes),

Hegel has his own way of glorifying the social order of bourgeois 'civil society', in conformity to a historically more advanced—and also more obviously antagonistic—stage of development which he conceptualizes in a representative fashion.[51]

The generic moral postulates of the Kantian solution are no more telling about his uncritical acceptance of the social horizons of the 'commercial spirit' than about the—both on the internal and on the international plane—as yet far from fully articulated and consolidated character of the socioeconomic order which the standpoint of political economy expresses. By the time Hegel writes his *Philosophy of History* and *The Philosophy of Right*, well after the conclusion of the Napoleonic wars and the consolidation of the new social order, the antagonisms of 'civil society' and its state formation are too much in evidence to be able to reassert Kant's Enlightenment illusions. Thus, the contradictorily 'indeterminate' determination of the state's behaviour through the material interests of 'civil society' must be acknowledged for what it appears to be from the standpoint of political economy itself. As Hegel puts it:

> A state through its subjects has *widespread connexions and many-sided interests,* and these may be readily and considerably injured; but it remains *inherently indeterminable* which of these injuries is to be regarded as a specific breach of treaty or as an injury to the honour and autonomy of the state.[52]

As in Kant's metaphor about the 'erratic weather', the principle of *'inherent indeterminacy'* rules also in Hegel's account of the ongoing developments. And the reasons why to both Kant and Hegel the underlying law must remain the mystery of a quasi-theological teleology is because they take for granted the permanence of 'civil society', in all its contradictoriness, as the necessary premise of all further explanation. The uneasy coalescence of the multifarious constituents of the historical process is described by Hegel with graphic imagery:

> It is as particular entities that states enter into relations with one another. Hence their relations are on the largest scale a maelstrom of external contingency and the inner particularity of passions, private interests and selfish ends, abilities and virtues, vices, force, and wrong. All these whirl together, and in their vortex the ethical whole itself, the autonomy of the state, is exposed to contingency. The principles of the national minds are

wholly restricted on account of their particularity, for it is in this particularity that, as existent individuals, they have their objective actuality and their self-consciousness.[53]

At the same time, the 'world mind' is postulated as the imaginary resolution of the manifold actual contradictions without questioning, however, the social world of 'civil society' in the slightest. Particular states, nations and individuals are said to be 'the *unconscious tools* and organs of the world mind at work within them',[54] and the 'individuals as subjects' are characterized as the '*living instruments* of what is in substance the deed of the world mind and they are therefore directly at one with that deed though it is *concealed* from them and is *not their aim and object*'.[55]

In this way, again, a genuine insight is inextricably linked to an apologetic mystification. On the one hand, it is recognized that there is an inherent lawfulness in the historical process which necessarily transcends the limited and self-oriented aspirations of particular individuals. Accordingly, the objective character of historical determinations is grasped the only way feasible from the standpoint of political economy and 'civil society': as the paradoxically conscious/unconscious set of individual interactions effectively overruled by the totalizing 'cunning of Reason'. On the other hand though, the stipulated historical law must be ascribed to a force—be it Adam Smith's 'hidden hand', Kant's providential plan of 'nature', or Hegel's 'cunning of Reason'—which asserts itself and imposes its own aims *over against* the intentions, desires, ideas and conscious designs of human beings, even if it is said to act *mysteriously through them.* For envisaging the possibility of a real *collective subjectivity* as the—materially identifiable and socially efficacious—historical agent is radically incompatible with the eternalized standpoint of 'civil society'.

This has the welcome consequence from the point of view of the Hegelian conception that history—whose inner dynamism is ascribed to the design of 'Reason returning to itself'—can be brought to an end at the ideologically required juncture in actual history, whatever people might think of this solution. For any conscious rejection of the Hegelian idea of the end of history can be readily dismissed with reference to the same 'cunning of Reason' as no more than the 'unconscious' individual conceptualization of the hidden ways in which the 'world mind'—outwitting, by definition, the particular individuals—asserts its own ultimate aim of preserving the absolute finality of its now reached finality. Accordingly, the possibility of any real—i.e., comprehensive—critique of the advocated apologetic scheme is deflected and *a priori* discredited. And the radically anti-dialectical conclusions which speak of the Europe of Hegel's own times as 'absolutely the end of history' can be misrepresented as the final completion of the historical dialectic.

Thus, ironically, despite the significant advances of Hegel in detail over Kant, we end up in his philosophy of history with the fictitious finality of the 'Germanic realm', which is said to represent the *'absolute turning point'*. For it is claimed that in the Germanic realm the world mind 'grasps the principle of the unity of the divine nature and the human, the reconciliation of objective truth and freedom as the truth and freedom appearing within self-consciousness and subjectivity, a reconciliation with the fulfilment of which the principle of the north, the principle of the Germanic peoples, has been entrusted.'[56]

Hegel hails the developments under the nordic principle of the Germanic peoples—including the empire-building English, animated, as we have seen above, by the 'commercial spirit'—as the 'reconciliation and resolution of all contradiction', and he sums up his claims as to what is in the process of being accomplished in the following terms:

> The *realm of fact* has discarded its barbarity and unrighteous caprice, while the *realm of truth* has abandoned the world of beyond and its arbitrary force, so that the *true reconciliation* which discloses the *state as the image and actuality of reason* has become objective. In the state, self-consciousness finds in an organic development the actuality of its substantive knowing and willing.[57]

Hegel often protested against the intrusion of 'ought' into philosophy. In truth, though, what could be more blatantly dominated by the 'ought' of wishful thinking than his own way of making historical development culminate in the modern state identified with the image and actuality of reason?

One of the most contradictory aspects of the Hegelian conception is its far-sighted grasp of the irresistibly *global* character of the ongoing development and, at the same time, its transubstantiation into an abstract logico/philosophical category—the category of the 'world spirit's' self-anticipating 'universality'—through which the objective dynamism of the whole process can be frozen into the static finality of the established present, under the absolute hegemony of the 'Germanic peoples'. The use of the *Logic* in the service of such end is highly symptomatic. For once the anticipated categorial development is completed—in accordance with the stipulated requirements of the Hegelian 'dialectical circle'—and the logico/historical stage of 'universality' is reached, there can be no conceivable advance beyond it. From that moment on the 'principle of the north, the principle of the Germanic peoples'—declared to be the fully adequate principle of the accomplished stage of universality—acquires its representative significance and historically insurmountable validity. Thus, while the actual unfolding of history is radically incompatible with the idea of its closure, the arbitrary identification of its 'Germanic stage' with the category of universality successfully accomplishes the apologetic ideological purpose of terminating history in the present. Accordingly, the Hegelian category of 'universality' becomes the absolute legitimator of the dominant power relations, as well as the self-righteous judge of everything that fails to conform to its standard favouring itself and nothing else.

We can see the devastating intellectual consequences of the ideological determinations which produce such pseudo-universal rationalization of the most narrowly particularistic social interests in Hegel's discussions of the 'African character'. He sets out from stating that:

> The peculiarly African character is difficult to comprehend, for the very reason that in reference to it, we must quite give up the principle which naturally accompanies all our ideas—the category of Universality. In Negro life the characteristic point is the fact that consciousness has not yet attained to the realization of any substantial objective existence . . . . The Negro exhibits the natural man in his completely wild and untamed state. We must lay aside all thought of reverence and morality—all that we call feeling—if we would rightly comprehend him; there is nothing harmonious with humanity to be found in this type of character.[58]

As to the evidence required to substantiate such assertions, Hegel is not ashamed to rely on—what he would elsewhere dismiss with the greatest contempt as 'hearsay and popular prejudice', if not much worse—'the copious and cirucumstantial accounts of Missionaries'.[59] And here is an example of the 'reports' whose intellectual level is not higher than the worst kind of missionary imbecility which Hegel, nonetheless, incorporates in all seriousness into his 'philosophical evaluation' of the 'African character':

> Tradition alleges that in former times a state composed of women made itself famous by its conquest: it was a state at whose head was a woman. She is said to have pounded her own son in a mortar, to have besmeared herself with the blood, and to have had the blood of pounded children constantly at hand. She is said to have driven away or put to death all the males, and commanded the death of all male children. These furies destroyed everything in the neighbourhood, and were driven to constant plunderings, because they did not cultivate the land. Captives in war were taken as husbands: pregnant women had to betake themselves outside the encampment; and if they had born a son, put him out of the way. This infamous state, the report goes on to say, subsequently disappeared.[60]

All alleged defects and negative traits of the 'African character' are attributed to the fatal absence of any consciousness of universality. Thus, according to Hegel, 'The Negroes indulge that perfect contempt for humanity, which in its bearing on Justice and Morality is the fundamental characteristic of the race. They have moreover no knowledge of the immortality of the soul, although spectres are supposed to appear. The undervaluing of humanity among them reaches an incredible degree of intensity. Tyranny is regarded as no wrong, and cannibalism is looked upon as quite customary and proper. Among us instinct deters from it, if we can speak of instinct at all as appertaining to man. But with the Negro this is not the case, and the devouring of human flesh is altogether consonant with the general principles of the African race'.[61]

If a thinker of Hegel's stature indulges in such absurd racist fantasies, one cannot simply come to terms with that by circularly asserting that this is an 'error' of some kind on his part. For there is a great deal more to his ideological eagerness to believe the unbelievable than 'naivety' and philosophical 'error'. Indeed, the real motivation behind his assessment of the 'African race' reveals itself in Hegel's discussion of *slavery*. It is full of elementary logical contradictions for which he would not have hesitated to fail his first year high-school pupils when he taught philosophy at the Nüremberg Gymnasium.

On the one hand he states that 'Turning our attention in the next place to the *category of political constitution,* we shall see that the *entire nature* of this race is such as to *preclude* the existence of any such arrangement.'[62] And again: 'want of self-control distinguishes the character of the Negroes. This condition is *capable of no development* or culture, and as we see them at this day, *such have they always been.*'[63] Yet, while categorically insisting—as a matter of absolute, racial determinations—on the *impossibility* of improvement and advancement with regard to 'Africa, the Unhistorical',[64] at the same time, he can both 'oppose' and defend slavery in the name of the—*a priori* unfulfillable—condition of 'gradual maturation', by saying that:

> Slavery is in and for itself injustice, for the essence of humanity is Freedom; but for this man must be *matured.* The *gradual* abolition of slavery is therefore wiser and more equitable than its sudden removal.[65]

A 'logic' worthy indeed of Ian Smith of Rhodesia at his worst.

At the roots of such blatantly self-contradictory philosophy of history we find not only the arrogant 'principle of the north of the Germanic peoples'—dominating the greater part of the world even today—but, again, the glorification of the modern state. For it is in relation to the 'inherent rationality' of the latter that Hegel has the nerve to maintain that the 'Negroes' are better off in slavery within the framework of the Germanic state than under their inferior 'natural condition' among themselves:

> Negroes are enslaved by Europeans and sold to America. Bad as this may be, their lot in their own land is even worse.... The only essential connection that has existed and continued between the Negroes and the Europeans is that of slavery. In this the Negroes see nothing unbecoming them, and the English who have done most for abolishing the slave-trade and slavery, are treated by the Negroes themselves as enemies. ... viewed in the light of *such facts,* we may conclude slavery to have been the occasion of the increase of human feeling among the Negroes. ... existing *in a State,* slavery is itself a phase of *advance* from the merely isolated sensual existence—a phase of *education*—a mode of becoming *participant in a higher morality* and the culture connected with it.[66]

And that is not all. For within the frame of reference of the allegedly higher rationality of the Germanic state everything can be turned upside down, whenever the interest of ideologically justifying the unjustifiable requires this. Accordingly, we are told by Hegel that if the Europeans exterminate thousands of Africans, responsibility and blame for that must be attributed to the 'want of regard for life' of those who resist their invaders:

> In the contempt of humanity displayed by the Negroes, it is not so much a despising of death as a want of regard for life that forms the characteristic feature. To this want of regard for life must be ascribed the great courage, supported by enormous bodily strength, exhibited by the Negroes, who allow themselves to be shot down by thousands in war with Europeans. Life has a value only when it has something valuable as its object.[67]

And, of course, the 'great courage of the Negroes' is totally worthless on account of its failure to match up to the aprioristic requirements which measure the 'intrinsic worth' of everything in public life in terms of their conformity or otherwise to the uncritically assumed interests of the Germanic state. For: 'The intrinsic worth of courage as a disposition of mind is to be found in the genuine, absolute, final end, the sovereignty of the state.'[68] How could one possibly argue against the 'image and actuality of Reason' championed in such terms?

The peculiarity of the Kantian and Hegelian philosophies of history was that they could not content themselves with claiming *necessity* on the ground of natural determinations. Viewing, as they did, the object of their aspirations, the idealized world of the 'commercial spirit', from the distance of an economically as well as politically underdeveloped country—a distance that painfully underlined the fact that their 'necessity' was to a large extent a mere *desideratum* in their own country—they had to strengthen their claims through references to the 'apriori principles of reason' and to the 'absolute determinations' of the 'science of logic'. By contrast the classics of English political economy, as we shall see later on, had no need for the crutches of idealist 'logical necessity'. Contemporaries to the unfolding power of capital and of its 'industrial revolution', they could confidently elevate to the rank of unchallengeable necessity the alleged characteristics of 'human nature' and the prevailing contingencies of the capitalistic mode of production without any further ado. Nor did they need to idealize the modern state. On the contrary, what they were interested in was precisely to secure the greatest possible margin of action to the self-expanding economic forces themselves. This implied, of course, the most severe curtailment of the state's power of direct interference in the socioeconomic metabolism which was said to be in any case ideally regulated by the benevolent 'invisible hand' itself.

The Hegelian transubstantiation of the particularistic contingency of 'civil society' into 'logical necessity' and 'universality', and the stipulated identity of such universality with the 'principle of the modern world' was, thus, also the expression of weakness and a search for ideal allies under the materially and politically precarious conditions of the 'German misery' (Marx). Paradoxically, however, this precarious position turned out to be a major asset in some ways in the development of German philosophy. For the enforced distance from the immediate determinations of capital's unfolding dynamism enabled its greatest representatives—above all Hegel himself—to elaborate the fundamental principles of dialectical thought, even if in a mystified form. (We shall see in this respect the comparative superiority of Hegel over Ricardo, with regard to the dialectical relationship between content and form, in the next section.)

Nevertheless, the idealist rationalization of material contingencies—and thereby their elevation to the lofty plane of 'ideal necessity'—imposed its negative consequences at all levels of the Hegelian philosophy. Even the most obvious material processes had to be turned upside down and twisted around so as to be able to 'deduce' them from the Idea's self-determination, in accordance with the ideally stipulated 'principle' and 'category' of the historical period to which they belonged. As an example, we may think of the way in which even the technology of modern warfare was deduced by Hegel from 'thought and the universal'. For, according to him:

> The *principle of the modern world*—thought and the universal—has given courage a higher form, because its display now seems to be *more mechanical,* the act not of this particular person, but of a member of a *whole.* Moreover, it seems to be turned not against single persons, but against a hostile *group,* and hence *personal* bravery appears *impersonal.* It is *for this reason* that thought had *invented the gun,* and the invention of this weapon, which has changed the purely personal form of bravery into a more *abstract* one, is *no accident.*[69]

In this way, through its direct derivation from 'the principle of the modern world', the material contingency of ever-more powerful modern warfare, rooted in a globally expanding capitalist technology, acquired not only its 'ideal necessity' but was simultaneously also set above all conceivable criticism in virtue of its full adequacy—the 'rationality of actuality'—to that principle. And since courage as 'intrinsic worth' was itself inextricably linked to the 'absolute, final end, the sovereignty of the state', as we have seen above, the apologetic circle of history reaching its culmination in the Germanic 'civilizing' state, with its ruthlessly efficacious modern warfare 'invented by thought' for the sake of realizing in a suitable 'impersonal' form the 'image and actuality of reason', was fully closed.

Inevitably, thus, such a conception of history and the state could only produce in the Hegelian system a truncated dialectic, with 'Spirit returning into itself' as its orienting principle and *circularity* as its necessary concomitant with regard to actual historical determinations. The circular conceptualization of the established order, stipulating that 'what is rational is actual and what is actual is rational',[70] dissolved every contradiction of the 'essentially now' by escaping from the real to the 'inward freedom' of thought-activity while leaving the practical world intact, together with all its contradictions, in its necessary 'otherness': as, by definition, the realm of a permanent—but philosophically irrelevant—alienation.[71] At the same time, it had to conclude with apologetic resignation that 'to recognize reason as the rose in the cross of the present and thereby to *enjoy the present* is the *rational insight* which *reconciles us to the actual.*'[72]

If Hegel had to acknowledge that there was 'chill in the peace with the world' which he was advocating, he could always escape from this difficulty by insisting that 'there is less chill'[73] in his reconciliation of 'Reason' with actuality than otherwise would be. At a certain point, in accordance with his logico/anthropological[74] characterization of the stages of development—which suited his apologetic conclusions in other respects, indicating that there could be no conceivable advance beyond the final phase of 'Old Age' corresponding to the Germanic state formation—he had to admit that the comparison was inherently problematical. But he succeeded in extricating himself even from that corner through definitional sophistry, by saying that: 'The Old Age of Nature is *weakness;* but that of Spirit is its *perfect maturity* and *strength,* in which it returns to unity with itself, but in its fully developed character as Spirit.'[75]

However, no such ingenuity could remove *resignation* from the advocated reconciliation with the established world. For the earlier quoted assertion that 'the true *reconciliation* which discloses the state as the image and *actuality of reason*'[76] could not be separated from Hegel's pessimistic 'owl of Minerva' metaphor. This conclusion appeared in the same work which reiterated, in the strangest possible opposition to 'ought', the acceptance of the chilling imperative of a 'peace with the present' by acknowledging that it all happens only by default:

> One word more about giving instruction as to what the world ought to be. Philosophy in any case always comes on the scene too late to give it. As the thought of the world, it appears only when actuality is already there cut and dried after its process of formation has been completed. The teaching of the concept, which is also history's inescapable lesson, is that it is only when *actuality is mature* that the ideal first appears over against the real and that the ideal apprehends this same real world in its substance and builds it up for itself into the shape of an *intellectual realm.* When philosophy paints its grey in grey, then has a shape of life *grown old.* By philosophy's grey in grey it *cannot be rejuvenated* but only understood. The owl of Minerva spreads its wings only with the falling of the dusk.[77]

Thus the recognition of an inherently problematical state of affairs could not be carried any further, since it would have undermined the entire philosophical construct and its social efficacy. As so often in the Hegelian philosophy, the 'theoretical interest' of knowledge—a genuine dialectical insight into an objective contradiction—collided with the 'practical interest' of maintaining the established order as given, no matter how acute its contradictions.

This is why, ultimately, Hegel's historical conception had to founder on the rock of his own social horizon—the horizon of 'civil society' in tune with the standpoint of political economy—which could offer no solution to the perceived contradictions. For while in *labour,* for instance, he recognized, with a tremendous insight, both the foundation of history and the wretched condition of alienated individuality, he produced a pseudo-solution to this objective contradiction, preserving it in reality while transferring its phantom-image to the 'intellectual realm' of speculative philosophy, thereby totally emptying it of its actual historical dimension and explanatory power. Since he could see no way out of the contradictory condition in virtue of which 'the full-grown man [in Hegel's general logico/anthropological sense of the term] devotes his life to labour for an objective aim; which he pursues consistently, even at the *cost of his individuality*',[78] he had to end up with the chimera of 'Spirit's self-activity' fulfilling its 'historical destiny' in the totally ahistorical realm of the 'eternally present' as invented by speculative Logic.

5. NATURALISTIC AND DIALECTICAL CONCEPTIONS OF NECESSITY

The materialist conceptions which originate in the social ground of 'civil society'—idealized from the standpoint of political economy—are equally constrained by their characteristic vantage point. It is not surprising, therefore, that Marx is not less critical of the materialist conceptualizations of historical development than of their idealist counterparts. For while Marx's materialist predecessors operate with *naturalistic* models of social life, Marx consciously defines his own position as dialectical, hence irrepressibly historical.

Nowhere is the irreconcilable opposition between dialectical and naturalistic materialism more acute than in their respective conceptions of *necessity.* The dialectical conception puts into relief the *historical* dynamic and *specificity* of the processes concerned. By contrast, the naturalistic approach tends to obliterate the historical specificities and transubstantiate them into claimed *natural* characteristics and determinations.

Marx clearly illustrates this opposition in his critique of political economists, underlining the apologetic ideological function of their general approach. Thus Malthus, for instance,

> regards overpopulation as being of the same kind in all the different historic phases of economic development; he does not understand their *specific* difference, and hence stupidly reduces these very complicated and varying relations to a single relation, two equations, in which the *natural* reproduction of humanity appears on the one side, and the *natural* reproduction of edible plants (or means of subsistence) on the other, as two *natural series,* the former geometric and the latter arithmetic in progression. In this way he transforms the *historically distinct* relations into an *abstract numerical* relation, which he has fished purely out of thin air, and which rests neither on natural nor on historical laws. There is allegedly a natural difference between the

reproduction of mankind and e.g. grain. This baboon thereby implies that the increase of humanity is a *purely natural process,* which requires *external restraints,* checks, to prevent from proceeding in geometrical progression. . . . He transforms the *immanent, historically changing* limits of the human reproducton process into *outer barriers;* and the outer barriers to natural reproduction into immanent limits or *natural laws* of reproduction.[79]

As we can see, the transubstantiation of the historically specific into a timeless 'natural' determination, and the concomitant *inversion* of the relationship between immanent limits and outer barriers for the sake of inventing an alleged 'natural law', are not simply 'mistakes' or conceptual 'confusions'. On the contrary, they fulfil the obvious ideological function of 'eternalizing' the given social/economic order: by transferring its historical, and therefore changeable, characteristics to a fictitiously permanent 'natural' plane.

This happens to be the case not only with Malthus, the 'clerical baboon', but even with the outstanding figures of bourgeois political economy—including Adam Smith and Ricardo—who are often highly praised by Marx. Thus Adam Smith treats labour and the division of labour as human *natural* force in general, ahistorically linking the latter to capital and rent, and constructing out of these elements a 'vicious circle' of self-sustaining presuppositions from which there can be no escape.[80]

Similarly, Ricardo conceives the relationship of wage labour and capital

as a *natural,* not as a *historically specific* social form, for the creation of wealth as use-value; i.e. [for Ricardo] their form as such, precisely because it is *natural,* is irrelevant, and is not conceived in its *specific* relation to the form of wealth, just as wealth itself, in its *exchange-value* form, appears as a *merely formal mediation* of its *material* composition; thus the specific character of *bourgeois* wealth is not grasped—precisely because it appears there as *the adequate* form of *wealth as such,* and thus, although exchange-value is the point of departure, the specific economic forms of exchange themselves play no role at all in his economics. Instead, he always speaks about distribution of the general product of labour and of the soil among the three classes, as if the form of wealth based on *exchange-value* were concerned only with *use-value,* and as if exchange-value were merely a *ceremonial* form, which vanishes in Ricardo just as money as medium of circulation vanishes in exchange.[81]

Again, the historically specific is turned into the allegedly 'natural' and thereby that which is in reality *transient* is given the status of a *natural necessity.* The conflation of 'use-value' and 'exchange-value'—which we can witness also in Adam Smith—is by no means accidental. For thanks to such conflation, a highly problematical (indeed *contradictory* and ultimately *explosive*) form of wealth—one that necessarily subordinates the production of use-value to the, no matter how wasteful, expansion of exchange-value—can be presented as *'the adequate* form of *wealth as such'.* The method used is equally telling. It consists in the undialectical separation and opposition of content and form[82] through which the potentially critical aspect of the given value form (the *duality* of use-value and exchange-value) can be reduced to 'merely formal' irrelevance, whereas the apologetic dimension of the selfsame historical value form (exchange-value misrepresented as use-value) is elevated to being a *'material'* and *'natural'* substance so as to confer upon it the status of an absolute necessity.

The obliteration of the historical dialectic, the elimination of sociohistorical specificities for the sake of producing imaginary natural necessities—in the service of the 'eternalization' of the bourgeois relations of production—is one of the principal objects of the Marxian critique. What is implicit in this critique is the concern for the self-emancipation of the associated producers from the fetishistic 'power of things' (a constant theme of Marx's writings from his youth to his old age), opposing to capitalistic 'reification' the objectively unfolding potentialities of a genuinely autonomous mode of action. Getting to grips with the question of 'necessity'—in the sense of both drawing the line of demarcation between natural and social necessity, and determining with precision the historical, hence transitory, character of the latter—is an integral part of this concern.

Referring to Ricardo's definition of circulating and fixed capital in terms of their relative degree of perishability, Marx writes: 'According to this [view], a coffee-pot would be fixed capital, but coffee circulating capital. The *crude materialism* of the economists who regard as the *natural* properties of *things* what are *social relations* of production among people, and qualities which things obtain because they are subsumed under these relations, is at the same time just as crude an *idealism,* even *fetishism,* since it *imputes social relations to things* as inherent characteristics, and thus *mystifies* them.'[83]

The point is that things do not become capital—whether circulating or fixed—in virtue of their *natural* properties, but on account of being *subsumed* under determinate social relations. If it was really the case, as Adam Smith, Ricardo and others had claimed, that the historically given mode of production was 'the adequate' expression of the *natural* characteristics of things and of the *natural* law of social intercourse and production as such, then there could be no way out of the 'vicious circle' of *a priori* presupposing capital so as to live with it forever. The 'crude materialism' and fetishistic idealism of the political economists—their capitulation, in one way or another, to the power of things—serves precisely the apologetic ideological end of declaring their vicious circle unbreakable. This is why the task of 'demystification' is inseparable from a precise definition of the natural and the social, the absolute and the specifically historical, grasping the necessities involved within their social/historical parameters, and not as untranscendable absolutes on account of their arbitrarily imputed 'natural' ground.

6. NEED AND NECESSITY IN THE HISTORICAL DIALECTIC

One of the most important aspects of this problematic concerns the relationship between *need* and *necessity,* and indeed the inherently *historical* character of both. Nothing illustrates this more clearly than the changing ratio between natural necessities and social needs in the course of the reduction of necessary labour time and the growing adoption of 'luxuries' as social necessities. The necessity involved in such transformations:

> is itself subject to changes, because needs are produced just as are products and the different kinds of work skills. Increases and decreases do take place within the limits set by these needs and necessary labours. The greater the extent to which *historic needs*—needs created by production itself, *social needs*—needs which are themselves the offspring of social production and intercourse, are posited as *necessary,* the higher the level to which *real wealth* has become developed. Regarded materially, wealth consists only in the *manifold variety of needs.* ... This pulling away of the *natural ground* from the foundations of

every industry, and this transfer of its conditions of production outside itself, into a general context—hence the transformation of what was previously *superfluous* into what is *necessary,* as a *historically created necessity*—is the tendency of capital. The general foundation of all industries comes to be general exchange itself, the *world market,* and hence the totality of the activities, intercourse, needs etc., of which it is made up. *Luxury* is the opposite of *naturally necessary.* Necessary needs are those of the individual himself *reduced to a natural subject.* The development of industry *suspends this natural necessity* as well as this former luxury—in bourgeois society, it is true, it does so only in *antithetical form,* in that it itself only posits another specific social standard as necessary, opposite luxury.[84]

It may sound strange to hear that necessity is 'subject to changes' until we recall that the natural being to which this condition applies is a unique natural being who introduces a thoroughly new mode of causality into the order of nature through its productive activity. Hence the original natural relationships are not merely modified to a certain degree but can be radically reversed in the course of historical development. This is how that which is for a start naturally necessary becomes *historically superseded* through the production of the *new needs* themselves. Consequently, clinging to the notion of the timeless 'natural' is nothing but mystification which implies the absurd *reduction* of the human individual to an unrecognizably crude, animal-like 'natural subject'.

The other side of the same coin is that just as the original natural necessity is historically displaced and becomes a *superfluous* and intolerable constraint from the point of view both of the individual and of the social metabolism in general, likewise the formerly superfluous and generally unaffordable 'luxury' becomes vitally necessary not simply from the point of view of the separate individuals but, above all, with regard to the continued reproduction of the newly created elementary conditions of social life as such. For through the advance of the productive forces the strictly natural progressively recedes and a new set of determinations enters into its place. Consequently, the removal of the newly acquired and structurally incorporated (diffused, generalized) 'luxuries' from the existing framework of production would carry with it the collapse of the entire production system.

This is a far from unproblematical process in that the

transformation of the formerly necessary into superfluous, and vice versa, simultaneously removes all kinds of objective constraint and opens up the possibility of not only genuine historical achievements but also that of finding quite arbritrary and manipulative 'solutions' to the newly generated problems and contradictions of social/economic life. Hence the necessary distinction between the growth of wealth as the development of 'the manifold variety of needs' on the one hand, and the manipulative production and imposition of 'artificial appetites' on the other, since the latter arise from the wasteful needs of an alienated production process and not from those of the 'rich social individual'. For so long as the production process follows its own determinations in multiplying wealth as divorced from conscious human design, the products of such alienated procedure must be superimposed on the individuals as 'their appetites' in the interest of the prevailing production system, irrespective of the consequences in the longer run. As a result, the 'pulling away of the natural ground from the foundations of every industry' brings with it not a liberation from *necessity* as such but the ruthless imposition and universal diffusion of a new kind of necessity.

7. THE CONFLATION OF NATURAL AND HISTORICAL NECESSITY

From the point of view of the bourgeois social order this new kind of necessity is just as *absolute* as natural necessity was prior to being displaced by historical development. This is why the political economists cannot conceptualize the true liberating potentials of the ongoing social/economic transformations. Instead, they must conflate the prevailing historical necessity with 'natural necessity' so as to be able to defend the ultimately *unnecesssary necessity* of the capitalist labour process as the *absolute necessity* and untranscendable natural horizon of all social life.

This conflation of the 'natural' and the 'necessary' is accomplished not for the sake of paying the slightest attention to nature itself but, on the contrary, so as to be able to contradict it in the most blatant fashion: by declaring the self-propelling necessities of the prevailing mode of production to be 'natural/absolute', thereby decreeing the unquestionable 'naturalness' of even the most artificial appetites that arise from the alienated needs of self-expanding exchange-value.

If the arbitrarily stipulated, fixed 'human nature'—with its necessary 'egotism' (Hobbes, Kant, etc.) and 'propensity to exchange and barter' (Adam Smith)—cannot establish the claimed link between 'nature/necessity' and the wastefully proliferating artificial appetites, other mythical concepts and arbitrary assumptions come to the rescue. Accordingly, the myth of the 'pursuit of *diversity*'—as 'implanted by nature into all individuals'—is postulated in order to subsume under the force of yet another apriorism the specific pressures and requirements of even the most parasitic phase of development. Such *a priori* determination of 'diversity', then, conveniently functions as the universal label under which anything and everything can be explained and justified, from the self-serving platitudes and formalism of liberal political theory to putting stripes into toothpaste and shaping like fishtails the wings of motor cars: all in the name of the 'individual sovereignty' and 'consumer sovereignty' of a 'free society', in perfect harmony with nature, of course.

The point is, though, that both 'natural' and 'necessary' must be questioned as a result of historical development. At one end, *natural necessity* progressively leaves its place to historically created necessity, and at the other *historical necessity* itself becomes *potentially unnecessary necessity* through the vast expansion of society's productive capacity and real wealth. Thus, historical necessity is indeed 'a *merely historical* necessity': a necessarily disappearing or 'vanishing necessity' [eine verschwindende Notwendigkeit][85] which must be conceptualized as inherently *transient,* in opposition to the *absoluteness* of strictly natural determinations (like *gravity*).

However, natural and historical necessity are inextricably intertwined in the objective dynamic of social development itself, which makes an adequate conceptualization of their relationship extremely difficult. Since the disappearing necessity of historical necessity is visible only from a standpoint able and willing to acknowledge the ultimately *unnecessary* necessity of the given social/economic necessities, there can be no real understanding of the intricate historization of nature in the human context if the necessarily transient character of all forms of production in terms of which such historization first becomes possible is denied in order to be able to maintain the *permanent necessity* of the capitalist mode of production.

It is not possible to grasp the meaning of 'historical necessity' without simultaneously questioning in the human context 'natural necessity' as well. And vice versa: it is not possible to understand the true meaning of 'natural necessity'—i.e., the vital distinction between the *absolute* conditions of production, the *elementary* requirements of the social metabolism itself[86] and the *historically transcendable* natural conditions and determinations of social life—without radically questioning at the same time the historical limits (i.e., the strictly *relative* validity) of all historical necessity. Failing to do so, due to some prevailing social interest, carries with it in all bourgeois historical conceptions—even in the greatest of them, as we have seen in Hegel's case—the contradiction of ending up with a negation of history, despite the original intentions of the theoreticians concerned, substituting thus an idealized 'nature', or some other abstract schematism, for real history. In view of these determinations it is by no means accidental that the political economists resort to the conflation of the social and the natural, the historically necessary and the naturally necessary, the sociohistorically transient and the absolute. They cannot have a clear view of *any* of these concepts since it is inconceivable for them to see the rule of capital as an ultimately unnecessary and therefore potentially disappearing necessity.

The conflation of natural and historical necessity and the concomitant obliteration of the inherently *historical* character of all historical necessity in bourgeois conceptions corresponds to the objective processes of capital's social/economic metabolism which ruthlessly subdue everything under their 'iron determination', from the articulation of the material infrastructure to the production of art and philosophy as saleable commodities. It is possible to speak in Marxist theory of the quasi-natural law of the capitalist mode of production only because capital itself objectively asserts its inner determinations in this fashion, refusing to accept any limits and overpowering all obstacles to its own self-expansion.

Ironically, however, liberal ideologists attempt to combine their total capitulation to this 'iron necessity' of capital's quasi-natural law—the belief that *'there can be no alternative'* to the prevailing capitalistic processes—with a mythology of 'freedom' as confined either to some lofty imaginary realm, like the Hegelian 'self-understanding of Reason', or to the prosaic margins of operating in submission to capital's reified determinations while maintaining the illusion of 'consumer sovereignty' and 'individual freedom'. And since the Marxian theory openly challenges both capital's objective determinism and the corresponding ideological capitulation to its claimed 'natural necessity', it is, of course, the Marxian conception of freedom and human self-emancipation and not the targets of its critique that must appear in this upside-down world of bourgeois ideology as *'historical and economic determinism'* and the negation of freedom.

8. THE DISAPPEARING NECESSITY OF HISTORICAL NECESSITY

In reality, though, the Marxian conception of history points in the opposite direction. Far from remaining trapped within the horizon of any determinism, it indicates, in fact, a movement towards the supersession of not just the *capitalistic* economic determinations but of the preponderant role of the *material base as such.* As Marx puts it (immediately after defining historical necessity as 'a *merely* historical, a *vanishing*' necessity): 'the result and *inherent purpose* of this process is to *suspend this basis itself.*'[87]

The 'purpose' here referred to is not some hidden 'destiny', foreshadowed from time immemorial, but the *objective telos* of the unfolding historical process that itself produces such possibilities of human self-emancipation from the tyranny of the material base which are by no means anticipated from the outset. Nor is it simply a self-propelling material determination that produces the positive result of the 'suspension of the basis itself'. On the contrary, at a crucial point in the course of the historical development a *conscious break* must be made in order to alter radically the destructive course of the ongoing process.

As we have seen earlier, the historical dynamic of ever-expanding needs and correspondingly growing productive forces pulls away the natural ground from every industry and objectively transfers the conditions of production *outside* them, to the plane of ultimately *global* interchanges. This progressive displacement of natural necessity by 'historically created necessity' opens up the possibility of a universal development of the productive forces, involving the 'totality of the activities'[88] within the framework of the growing international division of labour and of the ever-expanding world market. Since, however, the conditions of production are outside the particular industrial enterprises—outside even the most gigantic multinational corporations and state monopolies—capital's 'universalizing tendency' turns out to be a very mixed blessing indeed. For while on the one hand it creates the genuine *potentiality* of human emancipation, on the other it represents the greatest possible complications—implying the danger of even totally destructive collisions—in that the conditions of production and control happen to be *outside,* thus, nightmarishly, everywhere and nowhere. As Marx argues:

> The barrier to capital is that this entire development proceeds in an entirely contradictory way, and that the working-out of the productive forces, of general wealth, knowledge etc., appears in such a way that the working individual alienates himself *[sich entäussert];* relates to the conditions brought out of him by his labour as those not of his own but of an alien wealth and of his own poverty. But this antithetical form is itself fleeting, and produces the real conditions of its own suspension. The result is the *tendentially and potentially* general development of the forces of production—of wealth as such—as a basis; likewise the universality of intercourse, hence the world market as a basis. The basis as the *possibility* of the universal development of the individual, and the real development of the individuals from this basis as a constant suspension of its barrier, which is *recognized* as a barrier, not taken for a sacred limit. Not an *ideal or imagined universality* of the individual, but the universality of his real and ideal relations. Hence also the grasping of his own history as a process, and the *recognition* of nature (equally present as practical power over nature) as his real body. The process of development itself posited and known as the presupposition of the same. For this, however, necessary above all that the *full development* of the forces of production has become the *condition of production;* and not that *specific* conditions of production are posited as a *limit* to the development of the productive forces.[89]

Thus capital's universalizing tendency can *never* come to real fruition within its own framework, since capital must declare the barriers which it cannot transcend—namely its own structural limitations—to be the 'sacred limit' of all production. At the same time, what should indeed be recognized and respected as a vitally important objective determination—nature in all its complexity as 'men's real body'—is totally disregarded in the systematic subjugation, degradation and ultimate destruction of nature. For the interests of capital's continued expansion must overrule even the most elementary conditions of human life as directly rooted in nature.[90]

Whether or not the 'possibility of the universal development of the individual' comes to fruition, therefore, depends on the conscious *recognition* of the existing barriers. Accordingly, 'the result and the inherent purpose of the process' mentioned by Marx cannot be the unproblematical outcome of some material mechanism since its realization requires both the conscious recognition of the prevailing contradictions/barriers and the ability to institute a new mode of non-alienated social intercourse on the basis of that recognition. In other words, what is at stake is a conscious intervention in the material processes so as to *break* the vicious circle of their self-asserting chaos on a global scale, instead of accommodating oneself to the course of the prevailing material mechanisms in the spirit of a naive reliance on a new kind of benevolent 'invisible hand' or 'cunning of Reason' as manifest through the world market and the fully accomplished international division of labour.

In fact Marx's description of the inherent logic of these processes culminates in indicating a mode of social intercourse whose contrast with the dominance of self-asserting material determinations could not be greater. This is how he assesses the ongoing development and its implications:

> There appears here the universalizing tendency of capital, which distinguishes it from all previous stages of production. Although limited by its very nature, it strives towards the universal development of the forces of production, and thus becomes the *presupposition of a new mode of production,* which is founded not on the development of the forces of production for the purpose of reproducing or at most expanding a given condition, but where the *free, unobstructed, progressive and universal* development of the forces of production is itself the presupposition of society and hence of its reproduction; where advance beyond the point of departure is the only presupposition.[91]

Thus just as the pulling away of the natural ground from the foundations of every industry—i.e., the ever-receding necessity of natural necessity—transfers the conditions of production outside them, in the same way the progressively disappearing necessity of historical necessity transfers the positive potentiality of capital's universalizing tendency outside it, to a radically new mode of social production and intercourse. Without a *conscious* break from the *tyranny of the material base* necessitated by this transfer, the 'universalizing tendency' we can witness in the ever-more-chaotic interlocking of the global social intercourse can only assert its *destructive* potentialities, given the impossibility of a viable overall control on the basis of capital's own 'presuppositions'. And no one could seriously describe the project of articulating the conceptions and corresponding institutions needed for a conscious global control of the conditions of human self-realization as the spontaneous unfolding of material inevitability.

The 'free, unobstructed, progressive and universal' development of social life under the conditions of the new mode of production implies the *end of one-sided material determinism* and thereby also a radically new relationship between the former base and superstructure—their effective 'fusion'—in the new 'realm of freedom'. And this is precisely the fundamental meaning of the Marxian discourse on base and superstructure. For Marx is not simply concerned with providing a realistic as well as flexible/dialectical explanation of the complex relationship between material structures and ideas, important though as such explanation might be in the context of cultural theory. His main concern is to chart the course of human emancipation and the obstacles—material, institutional, ideological—in its way. Naturally, emancipation includes the freeing of ideas, too, from the power of blind material determinations. For it would be a very strange 'realm of freedom' indeed, one in which everything could be produced freely except ideas.

Just as it is not possible to talk about individual freedom without forcefully opposing the subsumption of individuals under their own class, and not merely their domination by the ruling class, in the same way it is not possible to take the idea of the future 'realm of freedom' seriously without envisaging at the same time the emancipation of the various forms of consciousness from the preponderant constraints of the material base as such. This is why the disappearing necessity of historical necessity is so important in the dialectic of historical development.

NOTES

1. Marx, *Economic and Philosophical Manuscripts of 1844*, Lawrence & Wishart, London, 1959, p. 152.
2. Hans Meyerhoff (ed.), *The Philosphy of History in Our Time*, Doubleday Anchor Books, New York, 1959, p. 6.
3. *Ibid.*
4. *Ibid.*, p. 15.

   The scholarship behind such theoretical generalizations is extremely shaky. We find in a footnote of the same work: 'Herder's major work is the vast study called *Ideas for a Philosophical History of Mankind*, which prompted Kant's review article (1874) entitled "The idea of a Universal History from a Cosmopolitan Point of View".' (*Ibid.*, p. 5.) Naturally, the issue is not the date, which must be a printing error and should read 1784. Rather, we are misled on a substantive point, and the reversal of the actual chronology between Kant and his former pupil, Herder—besides, part two of Herder's work was only published in 1785, therefore Kant could not have reviewed it in 1784—minimizes the importance of history in the Kantian system, making it appear as if it had been only a minor afterthought to Herder. Indeed, later on we read: 'Descartes specifically excluded history from his *Discourse on Method;* and *this choice prevailed among his philosophical successors, including Kant.' (Ibid.*, p. 12.)

   Thus, we are not concerned here with an accidental slip but with a symptomatic misrepresentation of the real state of affairs which turns the actual relationship between the eighteenth century's genuine attempt at understanding historical development, and the predominance of extreme historical relativism and scepticism from the middle of the nineteenth century onwards, upside down. Accordingly, a few lines later we are offered the conclusion which asserts that the investigation of the nature of historical knowledge 'did not become of serious concern to either historian or philosopher until the great awakening of history as an empirical and/or scientific discipline in the nineteenth century.' (*Ibid.*)

In truth, Kant's preoccupation with the nature of history was not confined to an occasional review article but constitutes an integral part of his conception as a whole. As with many of his projects, the time that had elapsed between the first germs of his ideas on man and history and the final product was considerable. But even as regards the particular essay on 'The Idea for a Universal History with Cosmopolitan Intent' (*Idee zu einer allgemeinen Geschichte in weltbürgerlicher Absicht*), its preparation went back to 1783, announced in print at the beginning of 1784; i.e., a fairly long time before the publication of Herder's work and Kant's two subsequent review articles on it. To quote an Italian book which, belying its modest title, is as exemplary in its scholarship on this point as on all other aspects of Kant's work:

> The issue of 11 February 1784 of the *Gotasche Gelehrte Zeitungen* mentioned, in an unsigned article, that one of Kant's favourite ideas was that the ultimate end of human history should be the establishment of the best possible political constitution. In this respect, the writer continued, Kant hoped that there would be a historian able to offer a history of humanity from the philosophical standpoint, to show how far or near, in the various epochs, we had been to this end and how much still remained to be done to reach it. Kant had spoken in these terms in a conversation with a scholar who visited him in Königsberg. Having been drawn into the argument, Kant felt obliged to make clear his ideas on the subject in public. In the November issue of *Berlinische Monatschrift* of Biester—the Enlightenment periodical of Berlin—appeared his 'Idea of a Universal History from a Cosmopolitan Point of View', an exposition, in nine theses, of a philosophy of history founded on the principle of a progressive and universal coming of the realm of Right. (Augusto Guerra, *Introduzione a Kant*, Editori Laterza, Roma-Bari, 1980, p. 88.)

In fact Kant's review articles on Herder's work—which should not be confused with his nine theses on 'Universal History from a Cosmopolitan Point of View'—appeared in 1785, in the *Allgemeine Literaturzeitung* of Jena. However, his interest in understanding the history of mankind as a unity *sui generis* did not stop there. The same preoccupation played a vital role not only in some of his writings which directly address themselves to the subject, but in his conception of morality in general. As a matter of fact, the two so deeply interpenetrate one another that neither his view of history is understandable without his conception of morality, nor indeed the other way round.

5. Kant, 'Theory and Practice Concerning the Common Saying: This May Be True in Theory But Does Not Apply to Practice' (1793), in Carl J. Friedrich (ed.), *Immanuel Kant's Moral and Political*

Writings, Random House, New York, 1949, p. 421.

Like Rousseau, Kant, too, firmly favours the 'middle condition' and opposes the great concentration of wealth. Thus, his denunciation of feudal irrationality is linked to a rather romantic critique of that process, unable to find, however, any practical weapon against it, other than the naive expectation that 'one vote to the owner of any amount of property' might make some difference in this respect. This is how he argues his case:

In any case it would be *contrary to the principle of equality* if a *law* established the *privileged status* for those large estate owners so that their descendants would always remain large estate owners as under *feudalism,* without there being any possibility that the estates would be *sold* or *divided* by inheritance and thus made useful for more people. Nor is it proper that only certain arbitrarily selected classes acquire some of these *divided properties.* Thus the big estate owner destroys the many smaller owners and their voice [in the commonwealth] who might be occupying his place. He does not vote in their stead for he has only one vote. . . . Not the amount of property, but merely the number of those owning any property, should serve as a basis for the number of voters. (*Ibid.,* pp. 420-1.)

6. Kant, 'Idea for a Universal History with Cosmopolitan Intent', in C. J. Friedrich (ed.), *Op. cit.,* p. 119.
7. *Ibid.,* pp. 116-17.
8. Kant insists on more than one occasion that according to his scheme of things 'those natural faculties which aim at the use of reason shall be fully developed in the *species,* not in the *individual.*' (*Ibid.,* p. 118.) This leads him to further dilemmas. For he has to admit that in the rational administration of civil society the reconciliation of egotism and justice represents a practically insoluble problem. As he puts it: 'The task involved is therefore most difficult; indeed, a complete solution is *impossible.* One cannot fashion something absolutely straight from wood which is as crooked as that of which man is made. Nature has imposed upon us the task of approximating this idea.' (*Ibid.,* p. 123.)

Taking this view, together with Kant's radical exclusion of the consideration of *'happiness'* as a merely *'empirical'* matter from the field of his concerns—characterized in this way in order to be able to concentrate on the vacuous formal principle that stipulates the 'general equality of men as subjects' while accepting the permanence of the 'greatest inequality in degrees of the possessions men have', on the ground that 'material things do not concern the personality' ('Theory and Practice . . .', *Op. cit.,* pp. 417-19.)—makes a very disconsolate reading indeed. For such ideas rationalize and legitimate the structural parameters of the established social order as the unquestionable horizon of human life itself.

9. 'Idea for a Universal History . . . ', *Op. cit.*, p. 120.
10. *Ibid.*, pp. 120-1.
11. *Ibid.*, p. 122.
12. *Ibid.*, p. 128.
13. *Ibid.*, p. 121. For an analysis of the Kantian concept of 'civil society' as an essentially legal/political concept, see Norberto Bobbio, 'Sulla nozione di "società civile".', *De homine*, No. 24-5, 1968. See also 'Kant e le due libertà', in Bobbio, *Da Hobbes a Marx*, Morano editore, Napoli, 1965.
14. Kant, 'Idea for a Universal History with Cosmopolitan Intent', *Op. cit.*, p. 127.
15. Kant, 'Theory and Practice . . .', *Op. cit.*, pp. 415-18.

    As we can see, in the Kantian construct many things are turned upside down. We are told that 'the poor are dependent on the rich'—rather than the other way round—so as to confer on the historically established material power relations the permanent solidity of a natural order and the halo of its conformity to the dictates of reason. Accordingly, the ruthlessly enforced relations of dependency are justified on the 'rational' ground that 'the one who is dependent must obey the other as a child obeys his parents or the wife her husband'. Similarly, we are merely told that it is well and proper that 'one man serves and another pays', without questioning the dubious historical legitimacy of such relationship of dehumanizing material dependency, nor indeed of the source of the self-perpetuating wealth a fraction of which is used for paying the 'one who serves'. Instead, they are circularly assumed as already given, with an unchallengeable finality, on par with the relationship between the child and his parents and the wife and her husband, in the spirit of patriarchy.

    Naturally, it would be a wild overstatement to suggest that Hegel can offer a satisfactory solution to such problems. However, at least he perceives them as *problems*—see above all his discussion of the relationship between 'Lordship and Bondage' in *The Phenomenology of Mind*—even if the 'universal class of civil servants' as the watchdog over the enforcement of the 'general interest' in the Hegelian *Philosophy of Right* is devoid of any real substance.
16. Immanuel Kant, *Zum ewigen Frieden* (1795), Reclam Verlag, Leipzig, 1954, p. 80.
17. *Ibid.*, p. 88.
18. *Ibid.*, p. 89.
19. *Ibid.*, p. 90.
20. *Ibid.*, p. 91.
21. *Ibid.*, p. 94
22. *Ibid.*, p. 87.
23. *Ibid.*, p. 88.
24. *Ibid.*, p. 66.

25. *Ibid.*, p. 73.
26. *Ibid.*, p. 103.
27. Hegel, *The Philosophy of History,* Dover Publications, New York, 1956, p. 456.
28. 'Philosophy concerns itself only with the glory of the Idea mirroring itself in the History of the World. Philosophy *escapes* from the weary strife of passions that agitate the *surface* of society into the calm region of *contemplation;* that which interests it is the recognition of the process of development which the Idea has passed through in realizing itself—i.e. the *Idea* of Freedom, whose reality is the *consciousness* of Freedom and nothing short of it.' *Ibid.*, p. 457
29. 'In the history of the World, only those peoples can come under our notice which form a state. For it must be understood that this latter is the realization of Freedom, i.e. of the *absolute final aim,* and that it exists *for its own sake.* It must further be understood that all the worth which the human being possesses—all spiritual reality, he possesses only through the State. . . . For Truth is the Unity of the universal and subjective Will; and the Universal is to be found in the State, in its laws, its universal and rational arrangements. *The State is the Divine Idea as it exists on Earth.*' *Ibid.*, p. 39.

    'The State is thus the embodiment of rational freedom, realizing and recognizing itself in an objective form.' *Ibid.*, p. 47.

    'Objective or Real Freedom: to this category belong Freedom of Property and Freedom of Person. . . . Real Liberty requires moreover freedom in regard to trades and professions . . . Government has to provide for the internal weal of the State and all its classes—what is called administration: for it is not enough that the citizen is allowed to pursue a trade or calling, it must also be a source of *gain* to him; . . . nothing must be considered higher and more *sacred* than *good will towards the State.*' *Ibid.*, pp. 448-9.
30. *Ibid.*, p. 16.
31. *Ibid.*, p. 456.
32. *Ibid.*, p. 457.
33. *Ibid.*, p. 456.
34. *Ibid.*, pp. 73-4.
35. See in this respect the discussion of Hegel's analysis of the 'character of the Negroes', together with his advocacy of a strictly 'gradual abolition of slavery', below.
36. These two reasons are, of course, deeply interconnected and may be separated only for analytical purposes.
37. Hegel , *The Philosophy of History,* p. 78.
38. *Ibid.*, p. 103.
39. *Ibid.*, p. 78.
40. 'Universal history—as already demonstrated—shows the development of the consciousness of Freedom on the part of

Spirit, and of the consequent realization of that Freedom. This development implies a *gradation*—a series of increasingly adequate expressions or manifestations of Freedom, which result from its Idea. The logical, and—as still more prominent—the dialectical nature of the Idea in general, viz. that it is self-determined—that it assumes successive forms which it successively transcends; and by this very process of transcending its earlier stages, gains an affirmative, and, in fact, a richer and more concrete shape;—this *necessity* of its nature, and the *necessary series of pure abstract forms* which the Idea successively assumes—is exhibited in the department of *Logic.'* *Ibid.*, p. 63.

41. *Ibid.*, pp. 78-9.
42. See in this respect Hegel's summarily negative treatment of this problem in his *Philosophy of History*, p. 47
43. *Ibid.*, pp. 456.
44. Hegel, *The Phenomenology of Mind*, Harper Torchbooks, New York, 1967, pp. 232-3.
45. *Ibid.*, pp. 236-9. 'Form' italicized by Hegel.
46. The problem for Hegel is that:

By the fact that the form is *objectified [hinausgesetzt wird]*, it does not become something *other [ihm nicht ein Anderes als es]* than the consciousness moulding the thing through work; for just that form is his pure self-existence, which therein becomes truly realized. Thus, precisely in *labour* where there seemed to be merely some *outsider's mind* and ideas involved, the *bondsman* becomes aware, through this *re-discovery of himself* by himself, of having and being a 'mind of his own' [*sich selbst eigner Sinn*]. (*Ibid.*, p. 239.)

Thus, we are dangerously near to clearly distinguishing and opposing to one another *objectification* and *alienation*, thereby undermining the conceptual impossibility of labour's self-emancipation through the transcendence of alienation.

Hegel extricates himself from this difficulty by simply *declaring* in the next—and final—paragraph of 'Lordship and Bondage' that it is *'necessary' to have 'fear* and *service* in general', as well as 'the *discipline* of service and *obedience'* coupled with 'formative activity' in a 'universal manner'. Thus the *temporal* dimension of the historical dialectic is radically liquidated and its phases become permanent 'moments' of the externalized pseudo-universal structure of domination in which labour is 'through and through infected' by internalized, rather than external, fear.

To be sure, the Hegelian enthusiasm for 'universal formative activity' as an 'absolute notion' which ought to extend its mastery 'over the entire objective reality' (*Ibid.*, p. 240.) is historical in the sense that it rejects the historically no longer tenable claims of *feudal bondage*—and corresponding idleness—from the standpoint of political economy. However, its criticism of the past is inseparable from the 'uncritical positivism' with which the timeless 'moments' of structural domination become the defining characteristics of the Hegelian notion of 'universal formative activity'.

The problem is that while *discipline* is indeed an absolutely necessary requirement of all successful formative activity, it is quite another matter as far as 'fear' and 'service' as well as 'obedience' are concerned. Nor is there a necessary connection between disciplined formative activity and fear/service/obedience, provided that the activity in question is determined by the 'associated producers' themselves who also determine the *self-discipline* appropriate to their own aims and to the inherent nature of the activity itself which they embark upon.

Naturally Hegel, from the standpoint of political economy, cannot embrace such perspective. Nor can he find, of course, anything to prove the 'universality' of an inherently particularistic and iniquitous system of 'formative activity' which retains the domination of one class by another in 'civil society'. This is why the profound historical dialectic of 'Lordship and Bondage' is in the end liquidated partly through the transformation of its actual historical phases into timeless 'moments' and logical 'categories', and partly through arbitrary declarations (of the non-existent 'necessary connections' which we have just seen) and equally arbitrary linguistic devices. As an example of the latter it is enough to think of the use to which Hegel puts the expression 'mind of its own' [*der eigene Sinn*] in his precarious argument. For he categorically declares that if labour does not conform to the stipulated necessary connection between fear/service/obedience and formative activity, 'then it has a merely vain and futile mind of its own' [*so ist es nur ein eitler Sinn*]. Indeed, a few lines further on Hegel makes great play about the (strictly German, purely linguistic) connection between 'mind of its own' and '*stubbornness*' [*der eigne Sinn ist Eigensinn*], so as to totally discredit any departure from the idea of 'universal formative activity'—as wedded to fear, service and obedience—which reasserts labour's permanent dependency.

47. *The Philosophy of Right,* pp. 212-13. Hegel is, in fact, realistic about war almost to the point of cynicism. He writes in *The Philosophy of Right* (pp. 210-11): 'War has the higher significance that by its agency, as I have remarked elsewhere [*Über die wissenschaftlichen Behandlungsarten des Naturrechts*], the ethical health of peoples is preserved in their indifference to the stabilization of finite institutions; just as the blowing of the winds preserves the sea from the foulness which would be the result of a prolonged calm, so also corruption in nations would be the product of prolonged, let alone "perpetual" peace. . . . This

fact appears in history in various forms, e.g. *successful wars have checked domestic unrest* and consolidated the *power of the state at home.* . . . if the state as such, if its autonomy, is in jeopardy, all its citizens are duty bound to answer the summons to its defence. If in such circumstances the entire state is under arms and is torn from its domestic life at home to fight abroad, the *war of defence turns into a war of conquest.*'

48. *Ibid.*, p. 214.
49. *The Philosophy of History,* p. 455.
50. *The Philosophy of Right,* p. 215.
51. The dated historical character of the phase conceptualized by Hegel is clearly indicated when he contrasts 'civil society' and the state by suggesting that 'in civil society individuals are *reciprocally interdependent* in the most numerous respects, while *autonomous states* are principally *wholes whose needs are met within their own borders.*' (*Ibid.*, p. 213.) Today, of course, no one in his right mind could assert this.
52. *Ibid.*, p. 214.
53. *Ibid.*, p. 215
54. *Ibid.*, p. 217.
55. *Ibid.*, p. 218.
56. *Ibid.*, p. 222.
57. *Ibid.*, pp. 222-3.
58. *The Philosophy of History,* p. 93.
59. *Ibid.*
60. *Ibid.*, p. 97.
61. *Ibid.*, p. 95.
62. *Ibid.*, p. 96.
63. *Ibid.*, p. 98.
64. *Ibid.*, p. 99.
65. *Ibid.*
66. *Ibid.*, pp. 96-9.
67. *Ibid.*, p. 96.
68. *The Philosophy of Right*, p. 211.
69. *Ibid.*, p. 212.
70. *Ibid.*, p. 10.
71. 'A *practical* interest makes use of, *consumes* [mark it: not *produces*] the objects offered to it: a *theoretical* interest *calmly contemplates* them, assured that in themselves they present no alien element. Consequently, the *ne plus ultra* of Inwardness, of Subjectiveness, is thought. *Man is not free when he is not thinking;* for except when thus engaged, he sustains a relation to the world around him as to *another, an alien* form of being.' *The Philosophy of History,* p. 439.
72. *The Philosophy of Right,* p. 12.
73. *Ibid.*
74. This framework of logico/anthropological deductions is adopted not only in his Philosophy of Right and *Philosophy of History* but

also in his *Philosophy of Mind.*

75. *The Philosophy of History,* pp. 108-9.
76. Hegel's *Philosophy of Right,* p. 222. The passage continues by claiming that 'In the state, self-consciousness finds in an organic development the actuality of its substantive knowing and willing'. (*Ibid.,* pp. 222-3.)
77. *Ibid.,* pp. 12-13. It is important to notice that the concept of the 'maturity of actuality' in this passage—like the 'perfect maturity of Spirit' in Hegel's *Philosophy of Mind*—is a thoroughly apologetic concept. Indeed, these two concepts—Spirit's 'maturity' and the 'maturity of actuality'—are closely linked together and can acquire their full meaning only in relation to one another. Likewise, the organic/anthropological analogy of 'The Ages of Man' (again, in the *Philosophy of Mind)* in its linkage to Spirit's unfolding—an analogy which remains a mere externality in that it completely disregards the actual historical determinations and objective presuppositions of *real organisms*—becomes intelligible in terms of the apologetic ideological functions which it has to fulfil in the Hegelian conception.
78. *The Philosophy of History,* p. 223.
79. *Grundrisse,* pp. 605-7.
80. With Adam Smith 'labour is in principle the source of value only in so far as in the division of labour the surplus appears as just as much a *gift of nature,* a natural force of society, as the soil with the Physiocrats. Hence the weight Adam Smith lays on the *division of labour.* Capital, on the other hand, appears to him—because, although he defines labour as productive of value, he conceives it as *use-value,* as productivity for-itself, as *human natural force in general* (this distinguishes him from the Physiocrats), but not as *wage labour,* not in its *specific* character as form in *antithesis to capital*—not as that which contains wage labour as its *internal contradiction* from its *origin,* but rather in the form in which it *emerges from circulation,* as money, and is therefore *created out of circulation,* by saving. Thus capital does not originally realize itself—precisely because the *appropriation of alien labour* is not itself included in its concept. Capital appears only *afterwards,* after already having been *presupposed* as capital—a *vicious circle*—as *command over alien labour.* Thus, according to Adam Smith, labour should actually have its own product for wages, wages should be equal to the product, hence labour should not be wage labour and capital not capital. Therefore, in order to introduce *profit* and *rent* as *original* elements of the cost of production, i.e. in order to get a *surplus value* out of the capitalist production process, he *presupposes* them, in the clumsiest fashion. The capitalist *does not want* to give land and soil over to production for nothing. They want something in return. This is the way in which they are *introduced,* with their *demands,* as historical fact, but not *explained.'*

Grundrisse, pp. 329-30.

Thus, the 'clumsy' behaviour of a great thinker—the blatantly circular presupposition of what must be historically traced and explained—produces the ideologically welcome result of transforming the specific conditions of the capitalistic labour process into the timeless *natural* conditions of the production of wealth in general. At the same time, a determinate *social/historical* necessity—together with the temporality appropriate to it—is turned into a *natural* necessity and an *absolute* condition of social life as such. Furthermore, since the question of capital's *origin* is circularly avoided—i.e., its genesis from the 'appropriation of alien labour', in permanent *antithesis* to labour—the inherently *contradictory,* indeed ultimately explosive, character of this mode of producing wealth remains conveniently hidden from sight, and the bourgeois conceptualization of the capitalist labour process, predicating the absolute finality of the given 'natural' conditions, cannot be disturbed by the thought of the historical dynamic and its objective contradictions.

81. *Grundrisse,* p. 331.

82. In this respect we can clearly identify Hegel's superiority in that he produces genuine insights on the dialectical interrelationship between content and form. Significantly, however, such insights are made possible not *despite* but, on the contrary, *because* of the abstract-speculative character of the Hegelian philosophy. For the ideological determinations of the bourgeois 'standpoint of political economy' assert themselves at once with great immediacy when one has to descend from the lofty realm of abstraction to a terrain where one must confront the tangible issues of exploitation and domination as manifest in the inner contradictions of the value form. On that terrain, understanding the objective material determinations underneath the changes in form through which, for instance, living labour is transformed into capital/stored-up labour and dominates itself in a hostile fashion, in the guise of an untranscendable external power, becomes rather dangerous for the beneficiaries of the standpoint of political economy, since the *reversal* of the selfsame transformations—in the sense of living labour assuming control over its own material conditions—might be envisaged under the impact of the persistent and ever-intensifying contradictions. It is relatively easy to see the truth of certain conceptual interconnections when it does not hurt. The whole thing radically changes, however, when revealing the dialectical intricacies and objective interdeterminations of content and form tends to undermine the interests of some apologetic intent. In that case the status quo is much better served if the dynamic of dialectical transformations can be frozen by opposing the 'merely formal' to the claimed permanent 'material substance' and by making a mystery out of their stipulated *a priori* separation.

83. *Grundrisse*, p. 687.
84. *Ibid.*, pp. 527-8.
85. *Ibid.*, pp. 831-2.
86. These concepts are centrally important to all serious theory of ecology concerned with identifying the threat inherent in the ongoing economic developments with regard to the elementary conditions of the social metabolism itself. The problem is capital's *necessary* inability to make the real distinction between the safely transcendable and the absolute since it must assert—irrespective of the consequences—its own, historically specific, requirements as absolute ones, following the blind dictates of self-expanding exchange-value.
87. *Grundrisse*, p. 832.
88. This expression—from page 528 of the *Grundrisse*—refers to one of Marx's seminal insights, articulated in great detail already at the time of *The German Ideology.* In this early work Marx laid great stress on the destructive implications of the contradiction between the forces and the relations of production and concluded that 'Modern universal intercourse cannot be controlled by individuals, unless it is controlled by all.' (Marx and Engels, *Collected Works*, Vol. 5, p. 88.)
89. *Grundrisse*, pp. 541-2.
90. In this respect the same considerations apply as mentioned in Note 86.
91. *Grundrisse*, p. 540.

V Marxism and Human Rights *

The problems of legal theory and of the state's part in administering the law occupied an important part in Marx's conception from the very beginning. He studied Jurisprudence at Berlin University and he articulated his own theoretical framework in the first place in a radical criticism of the dominant legal conceptions. Indeed, his first major work, apart from the youthful doctoral dissertation, was dedicated, in 1843, to a *Critique of Hegel's Philosophy of Right.*

This interest remained with Marx for the rest of his life. The *Economic and Philosophical Manuscripts of 1844* and *The German Ideology* (1845) spelled out in a positive form his conception of human nature as well as his views on the relationship between the individual and the state. His famous 'Preface' to *A Contribution to the Critique of Political Economy* (1859) located with utmost precision the 'legal and political superstructure' in the network of dialectical inter-relations between the material base of a given society and its various institutions and forms of consciousness. And his *Critique of the Gotha Programme* (1875) defined his position on the vital role played by a socialist-oriented system of rights in the transformation of the structures and human relations inherited from capitalism into a qualitatively different society in which the communist principle of distribution—*'to each according*

---

* A paper presented at a conference held in Dublin from 30 November to 4 December 1978, on the 30th anniversary of the U.N. Declaration of Human Rights. A shorter version of this paper was published in Alan D. Falconer. (ed.) *Understanding Human Rights.* Irish School of Ecumenics. Dublin 1980. pp. 47–61.

to his need'—can be successfully operated. Marx also planned to write an entire volume on the state as an integral part of his lifelong project on *Capital* but, most regrettably, he never reached the point of its realization.

Given the manifold interconnections of the subject before us with Marx's theory as a whole, it is impossible to deal in a short paper with all its complex ramifications. Thus, I intend to survey here those aspects of Marx's theory of law which carry the most important implications for human rights.

1. CAPITALIST DEVELOPMENTS AND THE 'RIGHTS OF MAN'

The widespread idea that Marxism is a crude economic reductionism according to which the functioning of the legal system is directly and mechanically determined by the economic structures of society, represents a Liberal interpretation of Marx's radical rejection of the Liberal conception of law. To be sure, no one could deny that Marx had no use for the 'juridical illusion' which treats the sphere of rights as independent and self-regulating. However, the rejection of an illusion does not mean in the slightest that the legal sphere as a whole is considered to be illusory. Far from it, as we shall see in a moment. But first we must glance briefly at Marx's critique of Liberal theory in the context of human rights.

Marx's principal objection concerns the fundamental contradiction between the 'Rights of Man' and the reality of capitalist society in which these rights are supposed to be implemented. Marx makes it clear in his *Economic and Philosophic Manuscripts of 1844* that 'The political economist reduces everything (just as does politics in its 'rights of man') to man, i.e. to the individual whom he strips of all determinateness so as to class him as capitalist or worker.'[1] He contrasts this tendency with the conditions of feudal landed property. Under feudalism the ties between land and its proprietor are not yet reduced to the status of mere material wealth:

> The estate is individualised with its lord: it has his rank, is baronial or ducal with him, has his privileges, his jurisdiction, his political position etc. It appears as the inorganic body of its lord. Hence the proverb *nulle*

> *terre sans maitre* which expresses the fusion of nobility and landed property. Similarly the rule of landed property does not appear directly as the rule of mere capital. For those belonging to it, the estate is more like their fatherland. It is a constricted sort of nationality.[2]

Thus Marx pinpoints the illusory element in the various theories concerned with the 'Rights of Man' in their *abstraction* from the material conditions of a radical social transformation which sees a shift from *nulle terre sans maitre* to *l'argent n'a pas de maitre;* the latter corresponding to conditions in which alienation predominates in all walks and over all facets of life, from the functioning of the fundamental economic structures to the most intimate personal relations of the individuals who constitute society.

We cannot go into the details of why the bourgeois opposition to feudal ideology had to champion the rights of 'Man' in its insistence on the alienability of land and with it the equality of the right to possession and acquisition.[3] The point that directly concerns us here is that this insistence on the 'rights of man' could not be more than a formal-legalistic postulate ultimately devoid of content. It is precisely the latter characteristic which meets with Marx's sarcastic disapproval. For the application of the claimed equal right to possession culminated in a radical contradiction in that it necessarily implied the *exclusion* of everybody else from one's effective possession. Thus the only form in which land could be alienated in accordance with the 'rights of man' was one that transferred the *rights of possession*—though not in principle, as in feudal ideology, but *de facto*—to a limited number of people, excluding at the same time the rest of the population from the possession of land while maintaining the legal fiction of equality at the level of abstract rights.

As we can see, Marx's point is that the 'abstractness' we witness is not just a feature of legal theory which could in principle be remedied through an adequate theoretical solution, but an insoluble contradiction of the social structure itself. Bourgeois theories which abstractly champion the 'rights of man' are inherently suspect because they also champion the rights of universal alienability and exclusive possession, and thus they necessarily contradict and effectively nullify the selfsame 'rights of man' which they claim to establish. According to Marx the solution to this contradiction can only be envisaged at the level of social practice, where it originates. And he identifies this solution as the necessary abolition of the right to exclusive possession: the right which serves as the ultimate legal buttress to the whole network of exploitative relations which turn the 'rights of man' into an obscene mockery of its own rhetorics.

The irony is that somewhere at the beginning of the developments which produce the universal diffusion of 'contractual' relations, Hobbes can still assert with a somewhat naîve openness that

> . . . Riches, are Honourable; Poverty, Dishonourable'; 'The Value, or Worth of a man, is as of other things, his Price; that is to say, so much as would be given for the use of his Power: and therefore is not absolute; but a thing dependent on the need and judgement of another . . . 'And as in other things, so in men, not the seller, but the buyer determines the Price'.[4]

By the time we reach Locke, the idol of modern Liberalism, the main concern is the rationalization of the prevailing inequality—no matter how grotesque are the devices employed, such as the blatantly self-serving concept of a 'tacit consent'—while maintaining the fiction of an 'original compact'. The real meaning of the 'rights of man' inherent in such an attitude becomes transparent when we remind ourselves of the unequal standard which Locke wants to apply on the one hand to the strictly controlled poor (requiring special passes even for the 'privilege' of begging, with dire consequences for the infringement of the rules: 'whoever shall counterfeit a pass shall lose his ears for the forgery for the first time that he is found guilty thereof')[5] and on the other to those who are in charge of the poor ('if any person *die* for want of due relief in any parish in which he ought to be relieved, the said parish be *fined* according to the circumstances of the fact and the heinousness of the crime.'[6])—not to mention the top of the social hierarchy which assumes the right to enact such 'enlightened' measures.

Even Rousseau, the most radical of Marx's predecessors, fails to resolve the contradiction mentioned above. While he insists on the essential requirement of a genuine equality and condemns the ways in which legal systems perpetuate inequality,[7] he can only oppose an abstract moral ideal to the prevailing conditions. The reason for this deficiency in his theory is that he cannot imagine civilised life without private property as its ultimate foundation and regulatory force:

> Must *meum* and *tuum* be annihilated, and must we return again to the forests to live among bears? This is a deduction in the manner of my adversaries, which I would as soon anticipate as let them have the shame of drawing.[8] It is certain that the right of property is the most sacred of all the rights of citizenship, and even more important in some respects than liberty itself; . . . property is the true foundation of civil society, and the real guarantee of the undertakings of citizens: for if property were not answerable for the personal actions, nothing would be easier than to evade duties and to laugh at the laws.[9]

No wonder therefore, that in the end even Rousseau must content himself with an abstract advocacy of the idealized circumstances 'when all have something and none too much', without being able to define what would amount to being 'too much' and what would constitute the necessary and sufficient 'something' to the advantage of all. Nor does he show whether or not the posession of just 'something' by some and the vaguely undefined 'not too much' by others are compatible, indeed permanently tenable. He simply assumes the feasibility of his idealized Social Contract without seriously questioning its necessary implications for the rule of private property.

The human rights of 'Liberty' 'Fraternity' and 'Equality' are therefore problematical, according to Marx, not in and by themselves, but in the context in which they originate as abstract and unrealizable ideal postulates, set against the disconcerting reality of the society of self-seeking individuals. A society ruled by the inhuman forces of antagonistic competition and ruthless acquisition coupled with the concentration of wealth and power in fewer and fewer hands. There can be no *aprioristic* opposition between Marxism and human rights. Quite the contrary. In point of fact, Marx never ceases to advocate 'the *free development of individualities*'[10] in a society of *associated,* and not antagonistically opposed, individuals (the necessary condition of both 'Liberty' and 'Fraternity') simultaneously anticipating 'the artistic, scientific, etc. development of individuals in the time set free, and with the means created, for all of them'[11] (the necessary condition of a true equality). The object of Marx's criticism is not human rights as such but the use of the alleged 'rights of man' as prefabricated rationalizations of the prevailing structures of inequality and domination. He insists that the values of any given system of rights must be assessed in terms of the concrete determinations to which the individuals of the society in question are subjected, otherwise they become supporting pillars of partiality and exploitation which they are in principle supposed to oppose in the name of the interest of all.

The sore point for Liberal theory is that Marx emphatically rejects the view that the right to private property (exclusive possession) constitutes the foundation of all human rights. For self-serving Liberal theory the equation is astonishingly simple; since Marx wants to abolish the 'sacred rights' to private property, he is the enemy of all human rights. But then we happen to know the necessary implications of the axiomatic assumption of private property for human rights in general. We know that the 'rights of man' in their application to possession are destined to mean for the overwhelming majority of individuals nothing more than the mere possession of rights to possess the 'rights of man'. Thus we know only too well—and not simply as a matter of theoretical consistency but also as a matter of bitterly dehumanizing and ever-worsening historical fact in our divided world of 'haves' and 'have-nots'—that private property as the ultimate foundation of human rights deprives them of any meaningful content and transforms them, whether in the name of a 'tacit consent' or of its more sophisticated later versions, into a blatant justification of the crude reality of power, hierarchy and privilege.

2. THE LEGAL FRAMEWORK OF SOCIAL INTERACTION

Marx's rejection of the 'juridical illusion' according to which 'law is based on the will, and indeed on the will divorced from its real basis—on free will,'[12] serves the purpose of identifying the real nature of the legal system precisely in order to grasp, and ultimately to gain control over, the actual determinations which arise from the legal system itself and affect the life-activities of all individuals. There can be no question of an economic reductionism, since the various legal factors are not one-sidedly determined by the material base but simultaneously also act as powerful determinants in the overall system of complex interchanges. Thus while it is nothing more than a 'juridical illusion' to assume that the contractual relations of capitalist society simply emanate from the 'individual (free) will of the contracting parties',[13] in view of the fact that they correspond to the objective needs of functioning of the existing socio-economic structures, it would be completely foolish to deny the vitally important active role of the legal framework in the development and stabilization as well as continued reproduction of the society in question under changing circumstances and in the face of both internal and external pressures. Consequently, the radical social transformation advocated by Marx becomes feasible only if the full weight of the legal sphere is duly acknowledged, with a view to facing up to the challenge represented by the specific legal structures themselves in the overall process.

The difficulty is that 'all elements exist in *duplicate form,* as *civic* elements and those of the *State'.*[14] Hence nothing is resolved by the proclamation of rights alone, not even by the most solemn proclamation of the rights of man. The legal sphere becomes effective to the very extent to which it succeeds in penetrating deep into the body of 'civil society'. By the same token, while in principle even the totality of legal statutes could be abolished through some generic proclamation to this effect, such an act would accomplish absolutely nothing without the corresponding real tranformation of 'civil society', without which the abolished legal devices would be reproduced in some other form. When Marx refers to the 'fight for the abolition of the State and of bourgeois society'[15] in this necessary coupling of the two, he acknowledges not only the 'duplicate form' in which the civic elements and those of the State exist and co-exist in a reciprocal interpenetration, but simultaneously also the immense power which the legal structures continue to exercise until the radical tranformation of civil society is really accomplished.

This acknowledgment of the determining power of the legal forms and structures is totally unintelligible in terms of the traditional (mechanistic) view of Marxism which stipulates a relationship of direct correspondence between the 'material base' and the 'ideological superstructure'. Such a view would be not only crudely simplistic, in its direct reduction of ideas to material processes, but would become also self-contradictory the moment it tried to assert the active role of the ideological forms in the overall process of social metabolism, having condemned them to passivity in the first place through the mechanistic reduction. Thus either the interpretation of Marx as an economic reductionist is untenable or his constant references to the active role of the ideological forms are totally devoid of meaning.

There is no space here to explore this problem in detail. Let it suffice to say that the necessary condition of an active intervention of ideas in the fundamental material processes is their mediation through the agency of individuals and institutions which occupy the required intermediary position between the two in virtue of being simultaneously both material and ideal. Man is both *homo faber* and *homo sapiens,* and inseparably so. At the same time, the ideas which are not mediated to the material base of social life through the life-activities of the individuals who constitute society are in no sense active; on the contrary, they are lifeless relics of a bygone age. And since the individuals operate in determinate social contexts, they have to mediate their ideas in an institutional form appropriate to the nature of the problems involved. Kierkegaard may well be right in saying that the question of 'faith' concerns the relationship between the individual and God; but the moment the idea of faith is generalized in a human context and enters the world as a 'religion' in the form of values and actions, the institution of the Church is born as the concrete (and historically changing) framework of the religious 'idea in action' in the totality of social interchanges. The same goes, *mutatis mutandis,* for the intricate network of legal forms. The 'juridical illusion' is an illusion not because it predicates the impact of legal ideas on material processes but because it does so while ignoring the necessary *material mediations* which make such an impact possible at all. Laws do not simply emanate from 'the individuals' free will' but from the total life-processes and institutional realities of a dynamic social development of which the individuals' volitional determinations are an integral part.

3. HUMAN RIGHTS AND SECTIONAL INTERESTS

In his attempt at locating with precision the legal and political structures in the total framework of social interaction, Marx first asserts that 'the anatomy of civil society has to be sought in political economy'[16] in that the analysis of the material conditions of life makes possible the solution of problems which remained a mystery to the 'ideologists' who tried to explain the development of juridical, political, philosophical, etc. ideas as self-developing entities. In opposition to such views this is how Marx summarizes what he calls his own 'guiding principle':

In the social production of their existence, men inevitably enter into definite relations which are *independent of their will,* namely *relations of production* appropriate to a given stage in the development of their material forces of production. The totality of these relations of production constitutes the *economic structure* of society, the real foundation, on which arises a *legal and political superstructure* and to which correspond definite forms of social consciousness.[17]

As we can see, Marx's terms of reference are incomparably more complex than traditionally assumed. His primary concern is how to change the dehumanizing conditions that make men enter into relations which are 'independent of their will' so as to be able to oppose to them a social interchange in accordance with a 'general plan of freely combined individuals.'[18] Thus his dismissal of the juridical illusion is coupled with a search for the conditions under which the exercise of one's will is not nullified by the reifying power of the prevailing material and institutional conditions of existence. Far from being a 'crude determinist' and an 'enemy of human rights', Marx is very much concerned here with the conditions of personal freedom, defined as a meaningful control by the individuals themselves of the relations into which they enter, as sharply opposed to their given conditions of existence which escape their will. This analysis of 1859 is conceived in the same spirit as his earlier discussion of freedom in another context where Marx writes:

in imagination, individuals seem freer under the dominance of the bourgeoisie than before, because their conditions of life seem accidental; in reality, of course, they are less free, because they are more subjected to the violence of things.[19]

At the same time, it is important to notice that even Marx's concept of the 'economic structure of society' is very different from the distorting technological-reductionist interpretation. The economic structure of society for Marx is not a brute material existent but a set of determinate *human relations* which precisely as such are subject to change, and indeed even to the most radical change arising out of a socially conscious (socialist) human deliberation. Furthermore, we should also notice that Marx's set of concepts does not define the forms of social consciousness (let alone the individuals' ideas) in a direct relationship to the economic structure or material base but through the *intermediary link* of the 'legal and political superstructure' to which they 'correspond' at the level of ideas, without, however, being *identical* with it. Asserting the simple identity of the legal and political superstructure and the forms of social consciousness would in fact undermine the whole conception and make a mockery out of the idea of the active role of the superstructure. For the autonomy of ideas vis-à-vis the legal and political superstructure is a necessary pre-condition of the latter. The production of ideas beyond the immediate institutional constraints of the legal and political superstructure acts as a powerful propellent on this superstructure which in its turn dynamically affects the material functions of social life. Without it, the class realities would automatically assert themselves as an iron determination, destroying the very concepts of law and politics in any meaningful sense of these terms. Their place would be taken by the crudest form of legal dictates—which would be in fact identical with the determination of the most elementary production functions—devoid not only of any system of justification, appeal and adjustment (with dire implication for the destruction of this framework of 'law') but also of the possibility of a proper legislature whose function would be taken over by the frightful mechanism of the totally dehumanized material dictates. And since this sham 'law' as strictly determined by the immediate material dictates could not possibly regulate itself, nor indeed the vital material functions of the given economic structure, the contradictions of the latter would run riot and totally disrupt the social metabolism in no time at all. Similarly with a 'politics' of direct material determinations, it would exhibit the same structure and contradictions as its legal counterpart, with the most devastating implications for social life as a whole.

Accordingly, the elementary condition of a successful functioning of the social metabolism in a society in which the economic structure is not free from contradictions is the active role of the legal and political superstructure made possible by its relative autonomy from the material base—which in its turn necessarily implies the relative autonomy of ideas and forms of social consciousness from the legal and political superstructure itself, as we have seen. It is in this framework of complex dialectical interactions that the idea of human rights becomes intelligible and truly meaningful. For whatever the material determinations of a class society, its contradictions are tolerable only up to the point when they start endangering the fundamental social metabolism itself. When this happens, the self-legitimation of this society is radically undermined and its class character is sharply pushed into relief through its failure to sustain itself as a system corresponding to the requirements of elementary human rights. Thus, paradoxically, the conditions of its erstwhile legitimation—the ideologically successful appeal to human rights—turn against it, in that at the time of a devastating crisis of the social metabolism itself it is no longer able to claim to represent the most adequate realization of human aspirations.

The point is that the 'interest of the social metabolism' is not an arbitrary or rhetorical notion, but a most vital reality, since it refers to the ultimate conditions of human existence itself. In this sense, the legitimation of a socialist alternative to the capitalist mode of social interchange cannot bypass the issue of human rights. Socialism must prove its superiority to capitalism precisely in overcoming the contradictions of partiality by releasing the suppressed energies of human fulfilment for *all* individuals. This is why Marx—'young' and 'old' alike—insists on the 'free development of individualities'[20] anticipating a framework of social interaction in which men live 'under conditions most favourable to, and worthy of, their human nature.'[21] Equally, his way of pointing to the dramatic alternative of 'socialism or barbarism' indicates the same appeal to the higher interest of human self-realization, as opposed to the threatening perspectives of self-destruction: this ultimate, categorical, and final negation of all human rights.

Admittedly, human rights—i.e. the most comprehensive category in which legal relations can be articulated—concerns the whole of humanity. Yet, the idea of human rights would be meaningless if they did not apply directly to the individuals. Offenders against human rights are individuals or groups of individuals, and their offence does not affect some impersonal collective entity but the conditions of existence of particular individuals, including in the last analysis the offenders themselves. Socio-economic systems which ultimately threaten us with the destruction of mankind are operated by individuals who carry on their activities on a limited time scale and under determinations (e.g. the danger of bankruptcy) which make it difficult for them to see the destructive implications of their line of conduct in the longer run. This circumstance, however, does not alter the fact that what we see at work here is an objective contradiction between a sectional interest and the interest of humanity at large in which the offenders themselves participate.

Enforcing the conditions of a genuine exercise of human rights, therefore, necessarily involves the application of an equal standard to the totality of individuals. For 'right by its very nature can consist only in the application of an equal standard'.[22] If the application of this equal standard simultaneously requires the denial of another right—in that the destructive functioning of the partial interest must be restricted—this is not a contradiction of the system of human rights but of the given socio-economic structure which produces such contradictory determinations. And while there is no conceptual difficulty in suggesting that the right expressing the higher interest of humanity overrules the sectional interest, in reality the exercise of human rights remains a mere postulate and an ideological rhetoric so long as the sectional interests of a divided society prevail and paralyse the realization of the interest of all. In such a society 'the interest of all' is defined as the undisturbed functioning of a social order which leaves the prevailing sectional interests intact and circumscribes the possibilities of an admissible social change from that perspective. Seeing how things work in such a society, it is tempting to conclude that 'the interest of all' is an empty ideological concept whose function is the legitimation and perpetuation of the given system of domination. However, to agree with this view would mean to be trapped by the contradiction which sets permanently one sectional interest against another and denies the possibility of escaping from the vicious circle of sectional determinations.

4. RIGHTS AND THE EMANCIPATION OF INDIVIDUALS

In sharp contrast to such views Marx formulates his strategy of a social transformation as embracing the interest of the whole of society. He insists that the proletariat is fit to accomplish the task of 'universal emancipation' precisely because it constitutes the 'universal class'[23] which cannot impose itself on society as a new form of exploitative and parasitic sectional interest since it represents the condition of labour. Marx is, therefore, not concerned with establishing a social order simply on the basis of the *de facto* effective power of the majority to subdue the sectional interest of the formerly ruling minority, but with the superiority *de jure* of socialism over capitalism, defined as the ability to release the energies of self-realization in all individuals, as against capitalism which must deny to them the possibility of self-realization in the interest of the unhampered 'self-expansion of capital',[24] no matter how destructive its consequences.

Marx describes the conditions of liberation as the emancipation of all individuals from the overpowering forces and determinations to which they are subjected. In this respect he repeatedly stresses not only that the exploited class must be emancipated from the domination of the ruling class but also that the individuals must be emancipated from their subjection to their own class and to the corresponding social division of labour:

> The class in its turn achieves an independent existence over against the individuals, so that the latter find their conditions of existence predestined, and hence have their position in life and their personal development assigned to them by their class, become subsumed under it. This is the same phenomenon as the subjections of the separate individuals to the division of labour and can only be removed by the abolition of private property and of labour itself.[25]

The defeat of the exploiting class is therefore a hollow triumph if it does not carry with it the emancipation of individuals as individuals. The real issue at stake is personal freedom, in the fullest sense of the term. It necessarily implies the abolition of the division of labour in that the latter sharply contradicts the conditions of self-realization of individuals as individuals:

> The transformation, through the division of labour of *personal* powers (relationships) into *material* powers, cannot be dispelled by dismissing the general idea of it from one's mind, but can only be abolished by the *individuals* again subjecting these material powers to themselves and abolishing the division of labour. This is not possible without the community. Only in community with others has each individual the means of cultivating his gifts in all directions; only in the community, therefore, is *personal freedom* possible. In the previous substitutes for the community, in the State, etc., *personal freedom* has existed only for the individuals who developed within the relationships of the ruling class, and only insofar as they were individuals of this class. The illusory community, in which individuals have up till now combined, always took on an *independent* existence in relation to them, and was at the same time, since it was the combination of one class over against another, not only a completely illusory community, but a new fetter as well. In the real community the *individuals* obtain their *freedom* in and through their *association.*[26]

Marx lays great stress on the point that so long as the individuals are subsumed under a class they do not possess a true individuality: they can only assert themselves as '*average* individuals',[27] but not as unique individuals who realize to the full their potentialities. This is why in Marx's view the realization of true individuality necessarily implies not only the abolition of the division of labour but simultaneously also the abolition of the State, which can only deal with average individuals,[28] and thus even in its most enlightened possible form it imprisons them in the conditions of abstract individuality.

Thus, Marx distinguishes three very different phases of social development to which human rights apply in significantly different form:

(1) Under the conditions of a capitalist society the appeal to human rights involves the rejection of the ruling sectional interests and the advocacy of personal freedom and individual

self-realization, in opposition to the forces of dehumanization and increasingly more destructive material domination or reification.

(2) In a society of transition, human rights provide the standard which stipulates that in the interest of true equality 'right instead of being equal would have to be unequal,'[29] so as to be able to discriminate positively in favour of needy individuals, in order to redress the inherited contradictions and inequalities.

(3) In a 'higher phase of communist society', when—on the premise of the highest development commensurate with them—society gets 'from each according to his ability' and gives 'to each according to his needs,'[30] the need for the application of an equal standard is no longer present, since the full development of one individual in no way interferes with the self-realization of others as true individuals. Under such circumstances—when both the division of labour and the State are effectively superseded—the question of enforcing rights (be they human rights) cannot and need not arise in that the 'free development of individualities' (which in previous forms of social development, including the transitional society, could only be postulated in a more or less abstract form) is integral to the social metabolism and acts as its fundamental regulating principle.

But so long as we are where we are, and so long as the 'free development of individualities' lies as far ahead of us as it does, the realization of human rights is and remains a concern of paramount importance for all socialists.

NOTES

1. Marx, *Economic and Philosophic Manuscripts of 1844,* p. 129.
2. *Ibid.,* p. 61.
3. I discussed these problems in Chapters 4 and 5 of my book on *Marx's Theory of Alienation,* London, 1970.
4. Hobbes, *Leviathan,* Chapter 10.
5. Locke, *Project for the Reform of the Poor Law in England.*
6. *Ibid.*
7. 'Under bad governments, this equality is only apparent and illusory; it serves only to keep the pauper in his poverty and the rich man in the position he has usurped. In fact, laws are always of use to those who possess and harmful to those who have

nothing: from which it follows that the social state is advantageous to men only *when all have something and none too much.'* Rousseau, *The Social Contract.*

8. Rousseau, *A Discourse on the Origin of Inequality: Appendix.*
9. Rousseau, *A Discourse on Political Economy.*
10. Marx, *Grundrisse,* Penguin edn., p. 706.
11. *Ibid.*
12. Marx/Engels, *The German Ideology,* Op. Cit., p. 80.
13. *Ibid.,* p. 81.
14. Marx, *Draft Plan for a Work on the Modern State* (1845).
15. *Ibid.*
16. Marx, 'Preface' to *A Contribution to the Critique of Political Economy.*
17. *Ibid.*
18. *The German Ideology,* p. 90.
19. *Ibid.,* p. 95.
20. *Grundrisse,* p. 706.
21. Marx, *Capital,* Vol. III., p. 800.
22. Marx, *Critique of the Gotha Programme.*
23. Marx, 'Introduction' to the *Critique of Hegel's Philosophy of Right.*
24. *Capital,* Vol. I., p. 621.
25. *The German Ideology,* pp. 69–70.
26. *Ibid.,* p. 93.
27. *Ibid.,* pp. 85 and 93.
28. *Ibid.,* p. 96.
29. *Critique of the Gotha Programme.*
30. *Ibid.*

VI A Critique of Analytical Philosophy*

A few years ago a philosophical conference was held at Royaumont. Its proceedings were published under the title *La Philosophie Analytique*,[1] and a reviewer wrote about the volume:

> This is the record of a dialogue that didn't come off, a *dialogue de sourds*. . . . . The will to dialogue seemed to be absent with some of the 'Oxonians'. This may well have been due to the contempt in which 'Continental' philosophers are often held at Oxford, which hardly accords them the status of worthy interlocutors. But, except for one case, this cannot really provide the explanation. The root of this reluctance seems to lie more in the fact that the Continental questioners wished to discuss matters which are rarely discussed in Oxford and usually thought to be a waste of time. . . . The questioners naturally wanted to bring the discussion to matters of *methodology*, to the philosophical justification of the procedures of the school. And this is not a popular subject of discussion at Oxford. Indeed, it rarely needs to be raised, since Oxford has lived for so long in a state of cultural solipsism, out of communication with rival schools, that it rarely meets a challenge which would require clarification.[2]

Are the chances of a successful dialogue any better today than at the time of the Royaumont conference? If the answer is yes, we cannot leave the question at simply asserting the existence of a more optimistic attitude to philosophical problems, as is done in the introduction of a fairly recent collection of essays on political philosophy from which we learn that '*the mood is very different and very much more favourable than it was six years ago*'.[3] Changes of

---

* First published in Bernard Williams and Alan Montefiore (eds.) *British Analytical Philosophy*, Routledge & Kegan Paul, London, 1966, pp. 312-30.

this kind need explanation, and the explanation is certainly not given by stating that 'we do not believe any more that political philosophy is dead' because it remains to be answered: 'why did you believe it in the first place?'

On the following pages I'll try to review those problems which confronted me in the course of teaching philosophy in Britain as I came into close contact with contemporary British philosophy. For these problems are likely to cause headache to all those who were not brought up in the school which dominated British philosophical thinking during the past two decades.

1. UNRECOGNIZED PREFERENCES

The first questions the outsiders are likely to ask may sound something like this: what are the main characteristics and the origins of contemporary British philosophy? They will find, no doubt with disappointment, that the number of writings dealing directly with these questions is rather small. Most often they will be advised by British philosophers to read the originals and find out for themselves what these characteristics are.

The relative justification for such advice is that on the Continent there are too many textbook-like generalizations which enable the student to avoid reading the originals and to acquire a rather superficial knowledge of names and skeleton systems without grasping the spirit of the various philosophical schools he is forced to race through.

But why should one assume that there can be no other way between these two extremes? After all, one is not necessarily hindered by a map if one wants to find places of importance in an unknown land. No one could dispute that by learning all the names on a map one would hardly know anything about the land itself. But from this it does not follow that maps are to be discarded.

As far as the history of philosophy is concerned, British analytical philosophy is mainly centred upon the less systematic heritage of Plato, Hume, John Stuart Mill, G. E. Moore and Wittgenstein. This set of preferences is, however, presented as the *natural choice* which needs no justification whatsoever. That Aristotle as a systematizer is neglected, that great philosophers like Diderot are completely ignored, that Hegel only appears as a kind of evil spirit, that there is little inclination to deal with or even to recognize problems raised by Marx, and that existentialism is hardly taken notice of, all this cannot matter if you believe that your orientation is so natural and unbiassed that it should not even be called a choice. Thus, rival claims must be dismissed not with concrete arguments but *en bloc* as manifestations of the 'metaphysical muddle' that keeps one from recognizing the natural choice.

In this way, if you ask for the justification of a set of preferences, the answer is that your demand itself is the proof of how muddled you are. Needless to say, there can be no dialogue on such a basis. Arguing in this manner is circular because it takes as evidence for its own wisdom the dismissal of alternative approaches, while both self-approval and the rejection of alternatives would need separate justification.

The elementary condition of a fruitful dialogue is, naturally, not the readiness to give up existing preferences, but the sober recognition that these preferences *are preferences*, however justified they might be. In this context one should recognize that one of the main characteristics of British analytical philosophy, the refusal to discuss issues of a comprehensive character, is one of the possible approaches to the contemporary world, but not '*the* revolution in philosophy' as the partisans of this approach called it a few years ago.[4]

It would be an important task to investigate why British philosophy took the turn which it did. Here we may refer to Gilbert Ryle's attempt at explaining the analytic character of British philosophy. He writes in the Introduction to *The Revolution in Philosophy*:

> Philosophy developed into a *separate academic subject*, partly detached from classical scholarship, from theology, from economics, and last of all from psychology. The teachers of philosophy of a university came to constitute a faculty, and they organized their own discussion-groups. From 1876 there existed the quarterly journal *Mind*, and not very much later there was formed the Aristotelian Society, at the meetings of which were read and discussed papers that were subsequently printed in the Society's annual proceedings. . . . *This new professional practice of submitting problems and arguments to the expert criticism of fellow craftsmen led to a growing concern with questions of philosophical technique and a growing passion for ratiocinative rigour.*

... *Philosophers had now to be philosophers' philosophers.*[5]

This analysis is revealing in more than one respect. First of all because, to borrow a comparison, it tries to explain the origin of evil by the fall of man. Ryle here undertakes to find an explanation for the highly professionalized analytic character (what he optimistically calls 'the sophistication of the virtuoso') of British philosophy. He does, of course, stress the influence of the natural sciences on the general temper of British philosophy. Nevertheless, he finds an important part of his explanation in that philosophy has become 'a separate academic subject'. He undertakes to find out why British philosophers have become 'more technical in their discourse', i.e., philosophers' philosophers, and finds that it was because 'Philosophers had now to be philosophers' philosophers.' Thus, his explanation is given in a circular reference to facts which themselves badly need explanation.

Or do they? Obviously not, if you are convinced that the present state of philosophy is the *ideal* one. In this case, everything that preceded *the* revolution in philosophy will appear as a subordinate moment of this ultimate climax. And the implicit rejection of the possibility that it *could* be (now and tomorrow) otherwise carries with it the extremely problematical tendency of treating historical facts with the greatest liberality, one-sidedly emphasizing in the past, quite out of proportion, practices which seem to resemble current ones, neglecting all contrasting features, in order to be able to reach the well-known uncritical conclusions.

The attitude of those who are not very happy with the state of affairs optimistically described by Ryle—and there are quite a few of them among British philosophers—will be quite different. As soon as they realizc that, for instance, 'One of the consequences of treating ethics as the analysis of ethical language is that it leads to the increasing triviality of the subject',[6] they will be prepared to state their preferences as preferences and enter on this basis into a dialogue with other trends.

Ryle's approach not only fails to give an explanation to the problems at issue but also neglects or obscures important facts which are essential to a plausible explanation. It lays too much emphasis on all this being a specifically British phenomenon. Yet the truth is that:

(1) Analytic philosophy did not originate in Britain, but on the Continent. Frege deeply influenced not only Wittgenstein but also Bertrand Russell and, mainly in its Russellian version, G. E. Moore as well. Even in the later development of British analytic philosophy the vital stimulus came essentially from Austria (the 'Viennese School', Wittgenstein), although at this stage one can detect of course a certain amount of reciprocal influence in the affinity between G. E. Moore and the later Wittgenstein.

(2) It is characteristic of the culture of our century to concentrate on the straightforward description and analysis of different types of experience. ('The Age of Analysis!') This tendency embraces the majority of social sciences and a variety of artistic trends, and it is by no means confined to philosophy, let alone to British philosophy.

Set against this background, the attempted explanation in the form of the reference to the fact that British philosophers had to publish short articles in *Mind* and in the *Proceedings of the Aristotelian Society* must seem trivial and utterly irrelevant. For even if it were true that 'the span of an article or a discussion paper is not broad enough to admit of a crusade against, or a crusade on behalf of, any massive "Ism",'[7] this could not be said about the numerous long books which British philosophers went on publishing just as much as their Continental colleagues. Here one needs first to try and explain a European phenomenon, in its broadest context, in its proper framework and on a European scale.

The most important questions to explore are why these analytic trends could not become *dominating* in their place of origin, on the Continent, and why they were able to conquer the British philosophical stage. Also, why British philosophy became almost exclusively analytic in character *after the Second World War*. For, despite the impression one might get from reading *The Revolution in Philosophy*, before and also during the Second World War 'analytic philosophy' was only one of several trends in Britain, and Gilbert Ryle himself wrote in the early 1930s in an idiom very different indeed from that of *The Concept of Mind*.

These questions are important because unless one can point to phenomena which indicate the weakening of the factors that resulted after the Second World War in the domination of an *exclusivistic* attitude to philosophy, either stigmatizing all other approaches as 'metaphysical nonsense' or 'conceptual confusion' or at best giving them the polite cold shoulder of effective non-recognition, there can be no hope whatsoever for fruitful discussions on the basis of mutual understanding. The Royaumont conference was bound to fail because the participants showed no sign of being prepared to reconsider the foundations of these exclusivistic attitudes. As R. P. Van Breda put it:

> Quite often, one was given to understand: 'You are doing, no doubt, something different; go on, if it interests you. Well and good.' I believe, for my part, that there is an implicit value judgement here. When we meet you, we are sometimes too polite and not honest enough. It is the pure and simple truth, I believe, to say that *there are many continental philosophers who are not in the least interested in your philosophy. And I dare say that it is the same with you so far as continental philosophers are concerned.*[8]

Such attitudes cannot but lead to a *'dialogue de sourds'*. This is why the first step towards a fruitful communication of ideas must be the recognition of existing preferences and, by implication, a change in attitude from exclusivism to mutual understanding.

2. INCONSISTENCIES

At the Joint Session of the Aristotelian Society and The Mind Association, in 1957, A. E. Teale complained in his inaugural address about:

> the many *prohibitions* issued by philosophers who first tell us that it lies beyond the province of a philosopher to determine empirical facts, and then proceed to inform us that, e.g., 'remorse does not differ in any morally significant way from embarrassment', or that 'our consciences are the product of the principles which our early training has indelibly planted in us'.[9]

The prohibitions castigated by Teale are, of course, closely linked with a general conception of philosophy which we shall have to discuss later on. Now we are concerned with the bewildering experience of seeing a principle contradicted often in the same article and sometimes only a few lines away from the generalization in question.

A case in point may be the very influential late J. L. Austin's discussion of *Truth.* He states his opinion that 'We become obsessed with "truth" when discussing statements, just as we become obsessed with "freedom" when discussing conduct.' then he proposes to do away with the discussion of problems like freedom and truth—and of something being done freely or not freely—and to concentrate, in their stead, on adverbs like 'accidentally', 'unwillingly', 'inadvertently', because in this way, according to Austin, '*no concluding inference is required*'. But curiously enough, in the next sentence he says: '*Like freedom, truth is a bare minimum or an illusory ideal*'.[10] and nothing could have the character of a more concluding statement than this, whatever it might mean.

Of course, Austin's statement is not a 'concluding *inference*': nothing has warranted it to be drawn from what has been previously said. It is a categorical assertion without the slightest attempt at finding supporting arguments. But what is more important, the author advises us to get away from the problems of truth and freedom, not to make generalizations about them but to stick to adverbial cases of a far more particularized character, then dogmatically makes a generalization of the highest order, expressing his own highly sceptical preferences.

There are many who would deny that we become obsessed with truth when discussing statements, and with freedom when discussing conduct. These 'obsessions' are, in fact, far more ancient than philosophical discussions of this kind or, for that matter, of any other kind.

If there is anything obvious about the sources of what Austin calls 'philosophical mistakes', it is that they are manifold and far more persistent than one might wish. Therefore it is misleading to reduce this complexity of causes to alleged 'linguistic confusions'. One of the major difficulties of philosophical discussions is that what one trend refers to as mistakes the other might praise as achievements, and vice versa. In such a situation it is extremely doubtful whether the emotional use of adjectives like 'obvious' and 'notorious', etc., or indeed the peculiar use of inverted commas with which Austin's writings are so full, could help at all.[11] And when the unsupported, categorical statements are coupled with inconsistencies, or when prohibitions are violated by those who issued them, one cannot reasonably expect anything but a hardening of the other side's position. After all, it is a basic condition of any dialogue that the same criteria of judgement should be applied by the participants to the assessment of the arguments of *both* sides.

3. THE ANALOGY OF NATURAL SCIENCE

At the Royaumont conference when Austin, Ayer and Ryle were pressed to define their philosophical methodology, in one way or in another they all referred to Natural Science.[12] Austin, for instance, emphasized that the way in which one ought to proceed in philosophy is '*Comme en Physique ou en sciences naturelles*', and even said that: '*Il n'y a pas d'autre manière de procéder*'.[13]

The reason behind this attitude was clearly expressed by Austin in the same discussion, and for its importance we have to quote it at greater length. He was asked the question: what are the criteria of a good analysis? Austin answered in this way:

> Pour moi la chose essentielle au départ est d'arriver à un accord sur la question 'Qu'est-ce qu'on dirait quand? ['What we should say when']. A mon sens, l'expérience prouve amplement que l'on arrive à se mettre d'accord sur le 'Qu'est-ce qu'on dirait quand?' (sur telle ou telle chose), bien que je vous concède que ce soit souvent long et difficile. Si longtemps que cela prenne, on peut y arriver néanmoins; et sur la base de cet accord, sur ce donné, sur cet acquis, nous pouvons commencer à défricher notre petit coin de jardin. J'ajoute que *trop souvent c'est ce qui manque en philosophie: un 'datum' préalable sur lequel l'accord puisse se faire au départ.* Je ne dis pas qu'on puisse espérer partir, dans tous les cas, d'une donnée considérée comme acquise. Nous sommes tous d'accord pour penser au moins que c'est souhaitable. Et j'irai jusqu'à dire que *quelques-unes des sciences expérimentales ont découvert leur point de départ initial et la bonne direction à suivre, précisément de cette manière*: en se mettant d'accord sur la façon de déterminer une certaine donnée. Dans le cas de la physique, par l'utilisation de la méthode expérimentale; dans notre cas, par *la recherche impartiale* d'un 'Qu'est-ce qu'on dirait quand?'. Cela nous donne un point de départ, parce que, comme je l'ai déjà souligné, *un accord sur le 'Qu'est-ce qu'on dirait quand?' entraine, constitue déjà, un accord sur une certaine manière, une, de décrire et de saisir les faits.*[14]

As we can see, Austin, like some of his predecessors, advocates proceedings on the lines of experimental science in order to find a basis of departure about which everyone concerned could agree. The ideal is what he calls 'la recherche impartiale', i.e. the elimination of ideological bias. But is this programme realistic? Isn't 'la recherche impartiale' in philosophy 'a bare minimum or an illusory ideal'?

The first difficulty which arises in this context is that the datum of departure is necessarily *selective* (as indeed is everything wherever human knowledge is involved) and therefore disagreements may always arise, if the basic philosophical positions differ. The analogy with natural science does not seem to exist here, since selectiveness is just as much present in experimental sciences as in philosophy and yet it does not result there in irreconcilable oppositions concerning the point of departure and the criteria of selection. (Presumably because alternatives can be tested and the outcome of testing is an unassailable practical judgement.) In physics, for instance, the point of departure is generally agreed because a certain type of limitation imposed upon its enquiries through centuries resulted in practical conclusions that simply were bound to be incorporated in the formulations of successive generations of physicists if they wanted to advance their science. If physicists always started from nothing they would inevitably end up with nothing, and therefore if someone sets out to question the practically established point of departure and the criteria of selection of this particular science, he would put himself outside the framework of physics. In philosophy, however, questioning the alternative points of departure as well as the criteria of selection in view of finding *justification* for the one a particular philosopher proposes to adopt, is not only legitimate but also necessary. Consequently, if one aims at producing a general agreement with regard to the points of departure, one either has to do away with selectiveness (which is impossible) or to face up to the factors that result in those antagonistic oppositions which are absent from natural science.

Obviously, Austin cannot take the second alternative because this would amount to admitting that the analogy with natural science does not hold (as we have seen the situation in philosophy is not analogous but sharply contrasting with that of

Natural Science), and thus the illusions connected with the conception modelling itself on the natural sciences ought to be given up. Therefore, he must try to do away with *selectiveness*. The result is an inconsistent wavering between claims of *completeness* and the admission that what he puts forward is a *choice*. First he says that one must '*s'assurer que l'inventaire est bien complet*' and therefore one must prepare 'une liste de *tout* ce qui se rapporte, dans le langage, au sujet que nous examinons: *de tous les mots* que nous emploierions, de *toutes les expressions* dans lesquelles ces mots rentreraient' (which is not only an empirical but also a logical impossibility). But in the next sentence he says that 'il est essentiel que *ce choix* soit assez *représentatif*.' Austin sees that the programme of completeness would only sound plausible if one could 'prendre un problème qui porte sur un point suffisemment limité.'[15] But how could one even hope for a general agreement—the aim of the whole exercise—when both representativeness and 'sufficient limitation' are involved?

And this brings us to the second, far more important difficulty. The question arises how limited a problem should be to qualify as 'sufficiently limited' and thus enable us to achieve completeness and general agreement. Suppose we obtained general agreement about a sufficiently limited subject, the question that really matters is whether the subject so limited is *philosophically important* or not. If one limits and restricts problems to the extent that is deemed necessary for achieving completeness and general agreement, doesn't one also confine oneself to trivialities? (such as we are not asking for 'the truth, the whole truth and nothing but the truth' when enquiring 'about, say, the battle of Waterloo'[16]—but who on earth thought we were?). It is highly significant that Bertrand Russell, who in many ways shares the goals of a philosophy aiming at a general agreement to be reached through procedures similar to Natural Science, rejects the linguistic approach of 'Qu'est-ce qu'on dirait quand?' If disagreements are so strong between philosophers who, however differently, yet share this overall aim, how can one realistically hope for a *general agreement* on anything of philosophical importance?

In fact, all the evidence Austin puts forward in the Royaumont discussion for his thesis is the categorical '*l'expérience prouve amplement* que l'on arrive à se mettre d'accord', etc. One might ask: *whose experience*? What we are expected to accept is not only the very doubtful statement according to which on the basis of impartial linguistic research—the supposed philosophical equivalent of experimental methodology—it is possible to achieve general agreement, but also that this kind of approach is a necessary requisite of all philosophy that wants to emancipate itself from 'daydreaming' (Austin's expression).

No one would dispute that 'un accord sur le "Qu'est-ce qu'on dirait quand?" [i.e., what Austin puts forward as a *necessary condition* of fruitful philosophical proceedings] entraine, constitue déjà, un accord sur une certaine manière, *une,* de décrire et de saisir les faits'. But precisely for this reason, only those who are *already* committed to the position of linguistic philosophy can insist on the philosophical importance of agreements of this linguistic kind. Others will go on saying what T. M. Knox wrote: 'Much that these linguistic writers say seems to me to be true, but even so, it does not *matter*.'[17]

Wouldn't it be far more fruitful if instead of pursuing the frustrated aims of scientifically modelled 'unbiassed philosophy' one admitted the existing difficulties. The desire to do away with all bias in philosophy in a way which 'entraine, constitue déjà un accord', i.e. the acceptance of the *linguistic philosophical bias*, can only result in inconsistencies because aims of this kind are self-contradictory.

The neopositivistic-linguistic bias also means that all approaches that are not 'sufficiently limited' are dismissed—again, not with argument, but with the authority of a presumed analogy with science. This can be illustrated with another quotation from J. L. Austin who said in the same discussion:

Nous devons aller chercher nos sujets dans les régions moins septiques, moins âprement disputées. J'y vois pour ma part trois bonnes raisons: en premier lieu, nous nous y ferons la main, sans trop nous échauffer; en second lieu, les grands problèmes qui ont résisté à tous les assauts de front, peuvent céder si nous les attaquons par un biais; en troisième lieu, et ceci me paraît de beaucoup le plus important, n'y a-t-il pas quelque risque à *prétendre à savoir à l'avance quels sont les problèmes les plus importants*, à supposer même, ce qui est encoure à voir, que nous puissions *prétendre connaître la meilleure méthode d'approche pour les attaquer*? Je crois qu'en prenant du recul, nous aurons plus de chance de voir se profiler les sommets, et de trouver la bonne voie, chemin faisant. L'example de la physique est ici encore, instructif. En bricolant, de droite et de gauche, avec ses instruments, comme le faisait Faraday, on a plus de *chance de tomber sur quelque chose de vraiment important* qu'en se disant un beau jour: '*Attaquons-nous à quelque grand problème: demandons-nous, par example, de quoi est fait notre univers*'[18]

As we can see, Austin puts his faith into the pure '*chance* of stumbling' on something 'truly important'. In the second place he also contradicts himself by first saying that it is idle to pretend to know 'the best method of approach', and then by declaring that the best thing to do is to adopt the instructive method of physics. And we can detect a significant bias as well which consists in this: that when he wanted to justify the linguistic approach he appealed to the fact that certain linguistic distinctions are perpetuated in the written and spoken language throughout history,[19] now he is determined not to apply the same considerations to deciding which are the important philosophical problems. On the contrary, in this latter regard the fact that certain philosophical problems were perpetuated throughout history counts as an evidence for the denial that they are important and for the assertion that they only demonstrate that until recently philosophy was in a *cul de sac*. Thus, when it suits the linguistic philosophical bias, history does exist, when it would go against this bias, it does not.

The bias is present not only in the sarcastic rejection of enquiries of a *comprehensive* character, at the end of our quotation, but also in the *misleading description* (in Austin's vocabulary: 'impartial research') of science as being confined to little things and advancing *by chance*. Chance, of course, plays an important part in the development of science, just as much as in life in general. But if we are to have an important scientific achievement, there must be more to it than just 'bricoler, de droite et de gauche, avec des instruments', in the hope of 'stumbling' on something that by chance will prove to be fruitful. And this something more is: relating the *limited* problems of detail to the most *comprehensive* ones. Without wishing to minimize in the least the importance of Faraday's results one must emphasize that the Faradays operate in a general framework created by the Galileos, Newtons and Einsteins.

These great *scientists* are abundantly concerned with those comprehensive issues that are eagerly dismissed by Austin, with misplaced irony, *in the name of science*, and such a concern is an integral part—in fact, synthesizing force—of their epoch-making achievements.

Here we can see that even the scientific myth is imposed upon philosophy only by means of a misrepresentation of science, because actual scientific proceedings do not exclude comprehensive generalisations but, on the contrary, are based upon them. What lies at the root of approaches of this kind is the desire to escape from comprehensive issues, to minimize their importance, to deny their philosophical legitimacy and often[20] even their existence. It is this desire to escape from comprehensive issues that results in unsustained sceptical declarations of the kind 'Like freedom, truth is a bare minimum or an illusory ideal' just as much as in the idealization of a non-existing Natural Science.

4. THE STUMBLING-BLOCK OF AESTHETICS

The Continental reader interested in the position of linguistic philosophy on aesthetic issues will find with great disappointment that British philosophical periodicals dedicate extremely little space to the discussion of such topics. And he will find with even greater disappointment that most of what appears on aesthetic problems is highly irrelevant, because it hardly ever asks the question: how will the solution of these problems help in a better evaluation of artistic creations? Linguistic philosophers would in fact deny that such questions are philosophically relevant.

To a certain extent it is understandable that British philosophers should feel aversion towards often uncritically accepted aesthetic formulations. William Elton, editor of the volume entitled *Aesthetics and Language,* quotes in his Introduction with justifiable indignation this passage: 'the music of Lourié is an ontological music; in the Kierkegaardian style, one would also say "existential". It is born in the singular roots of being, the nearest possible juncture of the soul and the spirit';[21] and there are undoubtedly many similar generalizations, i.e. empty word-clouds, in aesthetic writings.

However, the existence of nonsensical aesthetic articles is no reason for turning one's back on the *problems themselves.* For what could be more unrewarding than an alternative of this kind, which we can read in *Aesthetics and Language* as a summing up of the essay entitled *The Expression Theory of Art:*

> Some music has some of the characteristics of people who are sad. It will be slow, not tripping: it will be low, not tinkling. People who are sad move more slowly, and when they speak, they speak softly and low. Associations of this sort may, of course, be multiplied indefinitely. And this now is the kitten in whose interest we made so much fuss about the bag. The kitten has, I think, turned out to be a scrawny little creature, not worth much. But the bag was worth it.[22]

What is not utterly trivial in all this is just plain nonsense, the result of ignoring the great varieties of musical expression. But what is even more disturbing in this quotation is the implicit suggestion that problems do not matter, only the form in which they are presented, i.e. the display of cleverness designed to create the impression that the issues with which the expression theory of art is struggling do not really exist.

If linguistic philosophers want to be true to their own programme of taking into account all the expressions (or more realistically all types of expressions) in which the problem-word of their enquiries occurs, they cannot leave out, as they have so far, the problems connected with *artistic language.* In fact, Austin was prepared to admit this when he said at Royaumont: 'Loin de moi le désir de les exclure du champ de nos recherches. *Leur heure viendra.* Je ne me sens pas de taille à les attaquer pour l'instant, voilà tout. Je sais tout ce que cette réponse peut avoir d'insatisfaisant.'[23]

It is a fact that the problems of artistic language were completely ignored during the whole history of linguistic philosophy. And considering the self-imposed limitations of linguistic philosophy one must doubt whether it makes it *possible* to tackle these problems. It is, indeed, very unsatisfactory to answer a criticism formulated on these lines by simply saying that their time *will* come. If the neglect of certain types of problem is as complete as this, there is usually more to it than just lack of time, or personal failure.

In this sense the state of these problems is revealing about linguistic philosophy in general. As a matter of fact I would not hesitate to say that their time will never come within the methods of linguistic philosophy. Let us take three examples—three different types of use of artistic language—to see why not.

(1) 'Beauty is truth, truth beauty'.
(2) 'C'est la chaude loi des hommes', 'C'est la dure loi des hommes', 'C'est la douce loi des hommes'.
(3) 'Sul ramo del nulla siede il mio cuore'.

What could the linguistic philosopher say about the first example, provided he is prepared to say anything other than what I have heard in discussions, that 'it does not make sense at all'? Considering his utterances about truth, etc., elsewhere, he might perhaps suggest that it is more profitable to dispose of abstract nouns and to take the adverbial form. But the trouble with this kind of approach is that it completely misses the point: that in poetry—because of the unity of content and form—one cannot change anything at all, without changing the poetical content itself. One can more often than not reformulate, or 'translate' as it were, the expressions of common language. But one can *never* do this to poetry, because the change that has been introduced would mean that the analyst was talking about his own version and not about the poem he intended to talk about. Adverbial translation or anything of the kind is therefore quite out of the question as far as the problems of artistic language are concerned. Thus, if Keats writes:

Beauty is truth, truth beauty—that is all
Ye know on earth, and all ye need to know,

the philosopher must talk about *beauty* and *truth* as they are represented in this particular poem.

Taking the second example, the situation is even worse. Referring to the measuring rod of common language, expressions like 'warm law of men', 'hard law of men' and 'tender law of men' appear as most peculiar. And in any case, taken by themselves, it is not clear at all what they mean (if anything). Therefore, if our philosopher is prepared to give the benefit of doubt to the poet, he will not readily dismiss them as a 'collection of words devoid of meaning' but will say that they are 'idiosyncratic expressions' and of no philosophical interest. But *all* truly poetic expressions are, by definition, 'idiosyncratic'. And the solution of the problems connected with the specific character of poetry (or more broadly speaking of art in general)—the problems of artistic idiosyncrasy—is of the highest philosophical importance. (For instance, in relation to epistemology.)

About the third example, of course, there can be no doubt that it is the worst kind of 'conceptual confusion'. For how could my heart be sitting 'on the branch of nothingness'? If it is nothingness, it surely cannot have branches, and even if hearts could be imagined in a sitting position, they could not possibly sit on a non-existing branch of nothingness! But objections of this kind, again, completely miss the point. The poet, fortunately, is not in the least worried about safeguarding himself against the possibility of similar objections at the price of communicating poetically worthless commonplaces. He wants to convey, in a poem entitled *Without Hope,* the feelings of someone who is desperately isolated, and how powerfully he achieves this through these images.

> Sul ramo del nulla siede il mio cuore
> il suo piccolo corpo, muto, rabbrividisce,
> gli si raccolgono intorno teneramente
> e lo guardano, guardano le stelle.[24]

Linguistic philosophy was always concerned with the meaning of expressions that can be reformulated or 'translated'.[25] Consequently, it could not possibly take any notice of *literary* meaning. This is why in aesthetic matters only those questions were discussed which could be formulated within the limitations imposed by an exclusive concern with *literal* meaning: i.e., questions about what the *critic* means when he uses terms like beautiful, original, etc.

Artistic language eluded linguistic philosophy, because its problems cannot be tackled with the method of listing *atomistic units,* however numerous they might be. We cannot possibly become wiser as to the meaning of the expression 'tender law of men', even by a *complete* list (a practical impossibility) of the sentences in which the words 'tender' and 'law' occur—as Austin advises us—but only by considering the poem as an *organic whole* where we read:

> C'est la douce loi des hommes
> De changer l'eau en lumière
> Le rève en réalité
> Et les ennemies en frères[26]

In a poem no word (or expression) has an *isolated meaning,* but only a meaning interrelated with all the other constitutive parts (words, expressions) of the given poem. Insofar as words or expressions can be isolated from the poem (having a meaning of their own), they do not possess the meaning they carry in the poem—through this manifold interrelation with all the other parts of the poem as a whole—but only a meaning they have in the *common language* from which they have been taken (then adapted and tranformed) by the poet.

If we are interested in the *poetic meaning*—as we must be in the analysis of artistic language—we must preserve the specific character of this part/whole relation, instead of destroying it by dissolving the manifold varieties of poetic expressions into their aesthetically irrelevant atomistic elements. When we talk about these isolated elements, we are no longer talking about parts of a work of art, and it is an illusion to think that in the end this talk may add up to an aesthetically relevant picture. This is like expecting that the separate examination of every single tessera of a mosaic will add up to an aesthetic assessment of that mosaic as a work of art. Tesserae of a mosaic taken by themselves are only coloured stones and not constitutive parts of a work of art, in the same way as isolated expressions taken from poems are just sentences (more often than not apparently quite meaningless sentences) which acquire their poetic meaning only by virtue of being in an unchangeable interrelation with all the other parts of the poem as an organic whole.

It is a well-known fact that analytic philosophy, despite a growing interest in the contextual features of language, retains many of the atomistic presuppositions which were most conspicuous in positivism. This is why it is safe to say that one cannot expect a change in the situation, as far as the analysis of artisitic language is concerned, without changes deeply involving the particular atomistic presuppositions of linguistic philosophy. If, however, these changes occur, linguistic philosophy will be very different indeed from the form in which we know it at present.

NOTES

1. 'Cahiers de Royaumont', *Philosophie No. IV: La Philosophie Analytique.* Henceforth abbreviated as *CRP IV.*
2. Charles Taylor, 'Review of *CRP IV*', *Philosophical Review,* LXXIII (1964), pp. 132–5.
3. P. Laslett and W.G. Runciman (eds.), *Philosophy, Politics and Society,* Second Series, Blackwell, Oxford, 1962, p. vii.
4. Gilbert Ryle, (Ed. and Introduction), *The Revolution in Philosophy,* Macmillan, London, 1957.
5. *Ibid.,* pp. 3–4.
6. H.M. Warnock, *Ethics Since 1900,* Oxford University Press, 1960, p. 202.
7. Ryle, *Op. cit.,* p. 4.
8. *CRP IV,* p. 344.
9. A.E. Teale , 'Moral Assurance', *Proceedings of the Aristotelian Society,* Supplementary Volume, XXXI (1957), pp. 1–42.
10. J.L. Austin, *Philosophical Papers,* Clarendon Press, Oxford, 1961, p. 98.
11. 'Mistakes in philosophy notoriously arise through thinking that what holds of "ordinary" words like "red" or "growls" must also hold of extraordinary words like "real" or "exists". But that "true" is just such another extraordinary word is obvious'. (*Ibid.,* pp. 95–6.)

    One should note here not only the absence of any attempt at substantiating these, far from obvious, assertions but also the peculiar use of inverted commas in contrasting 'ordinary' (i.e., not quite ordinary) with the allegedly extraordinary (without inverted commas). To establish that there is a philosophically useful class of what Austin calls *extraordinary words,* and that the quite commonly used word *true* belongs to it, more would be needed than the inconsistent omission of the inverted commas in one of the two contrasted classes and the dismissal of doubts that might arise by means of the peremptorily used adjective: *'obvious'.*
12. *CRP IV,* pp. 330–80.
13. To avoid misunderstanding I quote Austin's text in the French original and give the English translation in the notes. *'As in Physics or in Natural Sciences', 'There is no other way to proceed'. Ibid.,* p. 350.
14. 'For me the essential thing in the first place is to reach an agreement on the question "what we should say when". In my view, experience amply proves that one reaches agreement about the question "what we should say when" (on this or that), although I concede that to reach such an agreement is often difficult and takes a long time. No matter how long it takes, one can succeed all the same; and on the basis of this agreement, this datum, this acquisition, we can start to clean up our small corner of the garden. I add that *too often what is lacking in philosophy*

is a preliminary "datum" on the basis of which one could reach an agreement to start with. I don't say that in all cases one could hope to set out from a datum considered by all as established. We all concur in thinking at least that such an agreement is desirable. And I would go as far as to say that *some of the experimental sciences have discovered their initial point of departure and the right direction to follow precisely in this way:* by reaching an agreement on the manner of determining a particular datum. In the case of physics by utilizing the experimental method; in our case, by means of *impartial research* as to "what we should say when". This gives us a point of departure, because, as I have already underlined, *an agreement on the "what we should say when" entails, constitutes already, an agreement on a certain way, one particular way, of describing and grasping the facts'.* (*Ibid.*, p. 334.)

15. *'Make sure that the inventory is quite complete';* 'a list of *everything* that is in connection, in the language, with the subject we are examining: of *all the words* that we would employ, of *all the expressions* these words would go in'; 'It is essential that *this choice be representative enough';* 'take a problem that bears on a *sufficiently limited* point'. (*Ibid.*, p. 332.)
16. J.L. Austin *Philosophical Papers,* p. 98.
17. T.M. Knox, 'Two Conceptions of Philosophy', *Philosophy,* XXXVI (1961), p. 291. (Knox's italics.)
18. *'We have to look for our subject in the less septic regions, those that are less bitterly disputed.* For this I see three good reasons: in the first place we can try our hand without getting too heated; in the second place, the big problems that have resisted all assaults from the front might yield if we attack them from the side; in the third place, and this seems to me by far the most important, isn't it risky *to claim to know in advance which are the most important problems,* or even to suppose, what remains to be seen, that we could *claim to know the best method of approach for attacking them?* I believe that by falling back we shall have a better chance of seeing the peaks standing out, and of finding a good route, as we go along. The example of physics is again instructive. By pottering on one side and another with one's instruments as Faraday did, one has *a better chance of stumbling on something really important* than by saying one fine day: *let's attack some great problem; let's ask, for instance, what our universe is made of*'. (*CRP IV,* p. 350.)
19. 'si une langue s'est perpétuée sur les lèvres et sous la plume d'hommes civilisés, si elle a pu servir dans toutes les circonstances de leur vie, au cours des âges, il est probable que les distinctions qu'elle marque, comme les rapproachments qu'elle fait, dans ses multiples tournures, ne sont pas tout à fait sans valeur.' ('if a language has perpetuated itself on the lips and under the pen of civilized men, if it could serve them in all the circumstances of

their life, throughout ages, it is likely that the distinctions it marks, as well as the assimilation it makes, in its manifold turns of phrase, aren't altogether without value.' (*Ibid.*, p. 335.)

20. Whenever they are summarily disposed of as 'conceptual confusions'. Significantly enough, the achievements of British philosophy which followed the phase of *The Revolution in Philosophy*—Hampshire's *Thought and Action*, Strawson's *Essay in Descriptive Metaphysics*, etc.—are concerned with more comprehensive issues.
21. O.K. Bouwsma, 'The Expression Theory of Art', in W. Elton (ed.), *Aesthetics and Language*, Blackwell, Oxford, 1954, p. 2.
22. *Ibid.*, p. 99.
23. 'It is far from me to wish to exclude them from the field of our researches. *Their time will come.* I don't feel quite able to tackle them for the moment, that's all. I fully realize that this answer may sound unsatisfactory.' (*CRP IV*, p. 350.)

    In this context one can see again the inconsistency when Austin first says that in tackling the problems of artistic language one ought to proceed *'Comme en Physique, ou en Sciences naturelles . . . Il n'y a pas d'autre manière de procéder.' ('As in Physics or in Natural sciences . . . There is no other way to proceed.')* Then, apparently forgetting about this, in the next sentence he goes on to say: *'Je suis sûr, en tout cas, qu'on ne peut rien en dire à l'avance.' ('I am sure, in any case, that one can say nothing in advance.')* But he has just said something 'in advance', something quite categorical too.
24. My heart is sitting on the branch of nothingness,
    his little body numbly shivers,
    the stars gather around him
    and watch him, watch him with tenderness.
25. See on these problems *'Metaphor and Simile'*, pp. 232–52 of the present volume.
26. It is the sweet law of men
    To change water into light
    Dreams into reality
    And enemies into brothers.

VII Metaphor and Simile*

Metaphors are often used and abused in theoretical discussions. As John Philpot Curran wittily put it: 'When I can't talk sense, I talk metaphor',[1] and this seems to be a fair description of what is going on in numerous cases. One might however argue that when philosophers, like Heidegger, talk metaphor, it is not because they cannot talk sense but because they do not want to. In fact Heidegger looks down with contempt upon 'talking sense' by the 'average man' and, as we shall see later, metaphors are vital for conveying his philosophical message concerning the values he advocates.

A central point of this paper is that such a use of metaphors is extremely problematical. At the same time it is emphasized that a closer study of the logical structure of both metaphor and simile can make an important contribution to a better understanding of the *normative discourse*. But in order to make these points, it is first of all necessary to do some disentangling (in sections 1 and 2).

1. METAPHORICAL PREDICATION AND METAPHORICAL FALLACY

As a preliminary, it is important to recognize that in everyday language the term '*metaphor*' is used, as a rule, to indicate a *figurative comparison*. In other words, colloquial language uses 'metaphor' and 'metaphorical' to stand essentially for *simile*.

---

* This essay was presented to a meeting of the Aristotelian Society in London on 27 February 1967. It was first published in the *Proceedings of the Aristotelian Society*, 1966—1967, pp. 127—44.

This it must do for two very good practical reasons. First, because 'simile' is a *technical* term, and second—which explains perhaps why it remained a technical term—because, unlike 'metaphor', the word 'simile' has no adjectival form. However, unless we want to make a fetish out of 'common language', as some philosophers do, we must realize that such usage, while perfectly legitimate in its proper place, tends to obliterate the *specificities* of metaphor as such, which can be found in comparison and *contrast* to simile, rather than by assimilating one to the other.

The present essay is primarily concerned with the task of locating these specificities. In pursuit of them, we have to begin by rejecting three widespread assumptions. This will enable us to say what the metaphor is *not*:

(1) A metaphor is not simply an instance of the 'figurative use of language'.

(2) A metaphor is much more than just a sentence that contains some 'metaphorical elements' (which is a tautology anyway). One cannot understand the nature of metaphors by analysing isolated words or expressions even if they are charged with figurative meaning. The introduction of figurative metaphorical elements into propositions (e.g. 'the chairman *ploughed* through the discussion') is not sufficient to transform the proposition into a *metaphor*.

(3) Metaphors are neither *similes* nor *symbols*. They have a logical syntax very much of their own, and blurring the distinction between metaphors, similes and symbols prevents one from seeing the characteristic features of the logical structure of each.

The first two of these points are closely connected and therefore it is best to discuss them together.

The *figurative* use of language can, of course, be very important in theoretical writings. Not simply for didactic reasons, nor as embellishments of the author's style, although in both these respects the merits of the figurative use of language are fairly obvious. The philosophically important point is that figurative expressions can reflect the process of intuition itself. In this process conclusions are reached when suddenly things seem to 'click together' even though the problem in question cannot be considered *discursively* solved because some 'links' that would connect the available data or the given premises with the conclusion are 'still missing'. It is logically impossible to grasp and convey this state of affairs—this particular stage of the reasoning process—without the help of some figurative element that enables the thinker to produce a *temporary* synthesis. This synthesis—in order to be adequate as an intuitive or 'pre-discursive' synthesis—must also reflect the 'gap (or indeed gaps) in the picture'. The discursive synthesis only becomes possible once the 'gaps are filled' and thus the stage of *intuitive, anticipatory synthesis* is left behind.

This figurative use of language in theoretical writings is thus fully justified because it does not appear as a rival to discursive synthesis but rather as a necessary and transitory stage towards it. The figurative expression can never constitute an adequate conclusion to an argument, though it may well be a vitally important stepping-stone towards it. Only that kind of anticipatory intuitive synthesis is theoretically fertile which can be *elaborated* in a discursive way. If this condition is not satisfied, the 'intuitive synthesis' remains a never fulfilled anticipation, a mere figure of speech, however attractive it might be on the surface on account of its imagery.

Here the criterion of validity seems to be whether or not the figurative element fits into the discursive pattern of the theoretical discourse. To put it more simply: the question is whether or not the figurative element is 'translatable', or explicable in the form of discursive generalizations. (That such a translation or explication will leave out some 'residual meaning' need not unduly worry us. For all translation is approximate and the success of rendering in another language even a strictly discursive philosophical text is always a relative one.) This is an important contrast to the metaphor because the latter is inherently *untranslatable*.

Let us consider, for instance, Garcia Lorca's illuminating definition of metaphor: 'La metáfora une dos mundos antagónicos por medio de un *salto ecuestre* que da la imaginación'. That is to say: 'The metaphor unites two antagonistic worlds by means of an equestrian jump of the imagination'.[2]

This definition may seem at first glance an example of the untranslatable metaphor. However, it is not difficult to find a discursive approximation to 'salto ecuestre', especially if one considers the definition in the context in which it appears. For the next sentence reads as follows: 'El cinematográfico Jean Epstein dice que "es un teorema en que se salta sin intermediario desde la hipótesis a la conclusión". Exactamente'. ('The cinematographer Jean Epstein says that "it is a theorem in which one jumps, without an intermediary, from the hypothesis to the conclusion." Precisely'[3]).

In both Lorca's and Epstein's definitions we find figurative elements, and their role is by no means simply didactic or decorative. On the contrary: it clearly reflects certain limitations in the conceptual grasp of the problem (what I called 'anticipatory intuitive synthesis'). Consequently these definitions can only be accepted as temporary, transitory, that is: as points of departure of a discursive explication. At the same time it should not be forgotten that Epstein makes the discursively valid and highly important point that the metaphor is a *direct synthesis*. To this Garcia Lorca adds an equally valid and important point: namely that this direct synthesis forcibly unites in the imagination elements of reality which in our everyday experience appear as antagonistically opposed to each other. Thus in both cases the anticipatory synthesis is discursively valid and capable of further elaboration. (The fact that Garcia Lorca, by speaking of the unification of antagonistic oppositions, exaggerates the contrast, in favour of a certain kind of metaphor in which he as a poet was deeply interested, does not diminish in the least the value of his insight).

One cannot understand the nature of metaphor by analysing isolated figurative or metaphorical *elements* of a sentence. But this is precisely what is attempted by Max Black when he asserts:

> In general when we speak of a relatively simple metaphor, we are referring to a sentence or another expression, in which *some* words are used metaphorically, while the remainder are used non-metaphorically. An attempt to construct an entire sentence of words that are used metaphorically results in a proverb, an allegory or a riddle... 'The

chairman ploughed through the discussion'. In calling this sentence a case of metaphor, we are implying that at least one word (here, the word 'ploughed') is being used metaphorically in the sentence, and that at least one of the remaining words is being used literally.[4]

The author gives at the beginning of his paper *seven* examples of what he considers 'unmistakable instances of metaphor'[5] of which, however, the first *five* are either *figurative elements* or *similes*. Only the last two are genuine metaphors, but precisely these are the ones which are discarded by Black because in his view they present certain complexities that in his paper had to be neglected. Unfortunately, however, the failure to differentiate between metaphor on the one hand and simile and figurative elements on the other results in an astonishing conclusion:

If to call a man a wolf is to put him in a special light, we must not forget that the metaphor ['Man is a wolf'] makes the wolf seem more human than he otherwise would.[6]

Black seems to have forgotten that more of nothing ('otherwise would') is still nothing.

It is, of course, acceptable to use 'metaphorical' colloquially as a synonym of 'figurative', provided that we bear in mind that this is a rather loose, colloquial usage. What makes a metaphor a metaphor is by no means that it is 'figurative'. Furthermore, one must distinguish between '*figurative*' and '*non-literal*'. Treating metaphors as cases of the figurative use of language fails to make this distinction and thereby thoroughly confuses the issues. For while it is true that all metaphors are *non-literal*, it is far from being true that all metaphors are also *figurative*. Some of them are, others are not. There are in poetry innumerable instances of metaphor in which *not a single word* is used *figuratively* (i.e. 'metaphorically' in Black's sense, as clearly distinguishable from other words in the sentence), and yet *every single word* is used metaphorically, i.e. *non-literally*. Thus there are two senses of 'metaphorical' and 'metaphorically':

(1.) figurative and figuratively;

(2.) non-literal and non-literally.

All metaphors are metaphorical in sense two, but only some of them are metaphorical in both senses two *and* one.

The reason why we cannot understand the nature of metaphors

by analysing isolated metaphorical elements is because we can only assert a *tautology* about them. That is, considering them in isolation, we cannot go beyond stating that these elements are metaphorical or non-literal in relation to other, literally used, words in the same sentence. Even the distinction between figurative/metaphorical/non-literal, and non-figurative/metaphorical/non-literal, presupposes a reference to two different *types of metaphor* (one that contains figurative elements, the other that does not contain them), and not simply to different *elements* of sentences or expressions.

What makes a metaphor a metaphor is the whole structure of its predication. To introduce a figurative element into a sentence like 'The chairman *ploughed* through the discussion' does not substantially modify its structure of predication.[7] For if in a literal version—i.e. one in which we replace the figurative element by a literal expression—its pattern of predication is represented as:

S —— P

the alleged metaphor about the chairman should be represented as:

S —— Pf

'Pf' here simply indicates that there is some figurative element in the predicate.

However, *some* figurative element in the predicate does not demolish at all the discursive pattern of predication. It does not make the predicate a 'metaphorical predicate', nor does it in any way affect the subject. (Not unless one wants to maintain that the chairman is put in some 'special rural light', like Black's wolf in a 'human light'.) This is why sentences of this kind are '*translatable*', whereas metaphorical predicates are not.

If, therefore, someone defends the use of *figurative elements* in the philosophical discourse, there can be no objection to it. On similar grounds, there can be no objection to the use of *similes*. But the use of *metaphors* is an entirely different matter. *Metaphorical predication* is substantially different from discursive predication. To anticipate a main characteristic of metaphors that will be discussed in the next section, metaphorical predication is *self-referential*; that is, it has an application to the given subject only insofar as it is considered as a *metaphorical subject.* Whatever is 'established' in the metaphorical predication, it is only *metaphorically* established. To draw philosophical (or in general theoretical) conclusions from something that is only metaphorically established must be, therefore, fallacious. This kind of fallacy—much more frequently committed than one realizes—might be called the *metaphorical fallacy.*

2. THE LOGICAL SYNTAX OF METAPHORS AND SIMILES

To turn now to the third point raised at the beginning of the preceding section—the difference between metaphor and simile—let us consider the following song:

Youth's the season made for joys.
Love is then our duty;
She alone who that employs,
Well deserves her beauty.
Let's be gay,
While we may.
Beauty's a flower, despised in decay
Let us drink and sport to-day,
Ours is not to-morrow.
Love with youth flies swift away,
Age is nought but sorrow.
Dance and sing,
Time's on the wing;
Life never knows the return of Spring

If we have a closer look at the two lines set in italics, it becomes clear that '*Youth's the season made for joys*' is a very special sort of predication. An attempt at introducing into it the word 'like' is bound to fail, whereas it would work perfectly well with '*Beauty's [like] a flower, despised in decay*'. This is because there is no such thing as 'the season made for joys' independently of the metaphor in which it appears, while it is a fact of everyday life that 'flower [is] despised in decay'. The metaphorical predicate thus refers to an '*unreal object*'. By contrast, the simile refers to an object independent of the subject of the simile.

As a partial analogy one might also say that metaphors are 'analytic' whereas similes are genuinely synthetic. Metaphorical predication only *appears* to supply information about, and independent of, the subject; in fact, however, the predicate merely gives a kind of 'synonym' of the subject. Just like 'Bachelors are unmarried men' and 'unmarried men are bachelors', so 'Youth is the season made for joys' and 'The season made for joys is youth'. In this sense both analytic and metaphorical predication could be represented as:

Sp —— Ps

However, the analogy breaks down in a crucially important respect. This can be seen if we remind ourselves that bachelors really *are* unmarried men, and therefore both subject and predicate are real in the analytic predication (real at least in the sense in which 'equilateral triangles' are real). But the metaphorical 'Youth' does not become more real by predicating about it that it is 'the season made for joys'. And how could it? The predicate here is not less metaphorical than the subject. If, therefore, both S and P are *metaphorical*—i.e., *M (Sp)* and *M (Ps)*—the reciprocal pattern of metaphorical predication would be correctly represented as:

M (Sp) <——> M (Ps)

and not as:

Sp —— Ps

This brings out the fact that the metaphor is *self-referential.* A statement made in terms of *metaphorical subject* and *metaphorical predicate* can only refer to *itself.* In other words: in such statements no reference is made to contingent facts and empirical objects, but to *metaphorical objects* that can only be found in the metaphorical world of the given poem. Whatever 'truth' is established in the course of the metaphorical predication, has therefore no validity outside the metaphorical world and independently of it. (The assertion 'Love is then our duty'—in which, clearly, "love" is not used in its Christian sense—can only sound plausible in relation to the metaphorical world of 'Youth's the season made for joys').

Thus metaphorical predication is reciprocal and self-referential. The simile is radically different in both respects.

(1.) The simile's subject and predicate do not have an equivalent semantic status. There is *no reciprocity* in 'Beauty's a flower, despised in decay', nor in 'Man is a wolf'. In both cases the predicate does throw light on the subject, but *not vice versa.* In this sense predication in similes is functionally hierarchical.

(2.) Similes are by no means *self-referential.* Not even when there is some figurative ('metaphorical') element in the predicate. Indeed, not even when what we assert about the subject is a genuine metaphor, if considered on its own (e.g., 'To be a pauper is like *living from hand to mouth*'). Self-referentiality is prevented by the presence—whether explicit or implicit—of the 'like' clause (L).

The varieties of the pattern of predication in similes could be schematized as follows:

S ——— LP (explicit simile);
S ——— (L)P (implicit simile—e.g., 'Man is (like) wolf');
S ——— LPf or
S ——— (L) Pf (with figurative element in predicate);
S ——— LPm or
S ——— (L)Pm (with metaphor in predicate).

It is true, of course, that:

> *Similes* are like songs in love:
> *They much describe*; they *nothing prove.*[8]

Nevertheless in this 'describing' they make a point about something that is under assessment on its own. Some comparisons prove more illuminating than others. This is why one can improve on a simile. But *never* on a metaphor. Since the metaphor's subject derives a substantial part of its meaning from its predicate—i.e., it is not an independent subject but a 'made-up' one—any modification of the predicate calls into being a new subject. Such a modification can therefore create a *new* metaphor, but not a *better* one. Metaphors are incommensurable. So the aim of improving on a metaphor is self-contradictory. (This aim, however, should not be confused with attempts at creating a metaphor that *better fits* into a context or poetic situation. Poets do this all the time. Yet in this they do not improve on the metaphor—they replace it by some other metaphor—but on the *poem* as a whole. In fact in many cases the once *discarded* metaphors appear in later poems, and often in key positions). These contrasting characteristics make the simile suitable for being incorporated into the philosophical discourse, whereas they render the use of metaphors extremely problematical.

In the last section of this essay we shall see that a stronger claim can be put forward about the simile in positive terms: namely that the simile is a most important element of the normative discourse.

3. THE CONTEXT-BOUND VALIDITY OF METAPHORS

As we have seen above, the pattern of metaphorical predication was represented as:

M (Sp) <———> *M (Ps)*

This can be accepted as a valid depiction of the individual metaphor. Metaphors, however, appear in contexts, and their '*natural milieu*' is poetry. In poetry we find an intricate web of predication in which metaphors appear closely intertwined with similies—with or without figurative elements in their predicates—and with apparently literal statements. The individual parts—whether metaphors, similes, or apparently literal statements—are organized into a whole, and affect each other. This means that the individual metaphor—(Sp) <———> *M (Ps)*—is further affected by the links it has with the other parts of the whole. 'Life never knows the return of Spring' has an important bearing on 'Youth's the season made for joys', and *vice versa.* This is one more reason why the metaphor cannot be lifted out of its own setting and transposed into a discursive context.

The validity of the metaphor is a *metaphorical validity* and it is *context-bound.* It also creates its own context the way in which the succession of poetic elements is organized into a whole. Sometimes the changing metaphorical charge of the poetic elements that follow each other in the course of the composition requires a drastic modification of the original project.

A characteristic example is Paul Eluard's 'Liberté'. In an article the poet confessed that in 1942 he embarked on writing a love poem, with the *refrain:* 'J'écris ton nom', intending to put the name of the woman he loved at the end of the poem. To his own astonishment, however, as the poet progresssed with the writing, the metaphors themselves took charge of the situation, bringing into his love song poetic images which broke the original framework of the poem. And this is how Eluard's poem had to be brought to its conclusion:

Sur l'absence sans désirs
Sur la solitude nue
Sur les marches de la mort
J'écris ton nom

Sur la santé revenue
Sur le risque disparu
Sur l'espoir sans souvenirs
J'écris ton nom

Et par le pouvoir d'un mot
Je recommence ma vie
Je suis né pour te connaitre
Pour te nommer

Liberté.

Eluard felt that remaining faithful to the original plan would have been artificial, forced and inadequate to the overriding passion that animated the succession of the poem's closely intertwined metaphors. He himself only realized the full meaning and impact of these metaphors in the course of their complex interplay from which they simply could not be divorced. This is why in the end he had to opt for the final line of the poem—*Liberté*—which brought into a synthesizing common focus all its intricate elements and images that could no longer be contained by the original poetic intention.

As this example shows, metaphors are non-transferable because one cannot grasp the full meaning of a single poetic metaphor without elucidating those shades and aspects of its meaning which come from the structural interplay of the manifold elements of the overall complex. In other words, metaphorical meaning is strictly contextual, though not in a narrow sense but in one that takes into account even the most indirect contextual ramifications.

There is another problem we have to discuss briefly in this connexion: the case of the apparently literal predication in certain types of poetic description. As an example, let us have a look at Pope's 'Ode on Solitude':

Happy the man, whose wish and care
  A few paternal acres bound,
Content to breathe his native air
    In his own ground.

Whose herds with milk, whose fields with bread,
  Whose flocks supply him with attire;
Whose trees in summer yield him shade,
    In winter fire.

Blest, who can unconcern'dly find
  Hours, days, and years slide soft away
In health of body, peace of mind,
    Quiet by day.

Sound sleep by night; study and ease
  Together mixed; sweet recreation,
And innocence, which most does please
    With meditation.

Thus let me live, unseen, unknown;
  Thus unlamented let me die;
Steal from the world, and not a stone
    Tell where I lie.

As we can see, here we have virtually no *figurative* elements in the whole poem. Yet, it would be a great mistake to treat these lines as *literal* sentences. Their meaning is by no means literal. The instances of life—which, taken in isolation, are trivial and boringly insignificant—stand for a great deal more than just literally themselves: they are metaphorical expressions of a typical conception of life—that of a romanticized and sentimentally inflated 'possessive individualism'—however remote such a conception may appear to us now. Taken one by one, and disregarding the others, Pope's illustrative instances are bound to appear literal expressions. The metaphorical meaning is conferred upon them by their *structural interplay.* To grasp this metaphorical meaning, it is necessary to be aware of the place the individual instances occupy in relation to the whole. Thus the *non-figurative metaphor* is no less context-bound than the figurative metaphor. It is equally self-referential too.

The context-bound and self-referential character of metaphors means not only that they are *untranslatable* and *non-transferable,* but also that *nothing follows* directly from metaphors. If the validity of metaphors is a metaphorical validity, the 'truth' they contain is also *metaphorical truth.* If the mode of representation is metaphorical—self-referential—the objects thus represented are necessarily 'unreal', *metaphorical objects.*

From these considerations several problems arise which are important in the context of aesthetic, and aesthetically relevant moral, value judgements. Of these I can only mention here a few.[9]

(1) Given their structure of predication, works of art cannot be properly described as 'representing actual objects'. They represent *themselves,* i.e., a world of their own in which the *mode* of representation is much more important than the instances of reality that appear in them. (What we are interested in is not a chair, a sunflower etc., but Van Gogh's chair, his sunflower, i.e., the objects of *his vision.*) This problem represents a great difficulty for the *reflection* theory of art, and I know of no satisfactory solution to it.

(2) In view of the self-referential character of the metaphorical world, it would seem that the aims of *naturalism*—the creation

of an *illusion* of reality—are self-contradictory. In discussing these phenomena shouldn't we, however, link such aims with the unquestionable *evocative power* of the work of art? This evocative power in fact makes the work of art very much *real* as an *experience,* despite the unreal character of the *objects presented* in it. At the same time this difficulty ought to be investigated: how is it possible for an unreal object to 'appear real', i.e., to have this evocative power, to produce such a unique gripping effect?

(3) The metaphor *directly* refers to itself, that is, to the world of unreal objects that constitute it. *Indirectly,* however, it refers to a poetic (or artistic) *situation* that called it into being. One must, therefore, in a sense 'transcend' the given set of metaphors in the direction of the original poetic situation, because the latter is an important dimension of the metaphorical meaning. (Without this 'transcendence' one can only *describe,* in terms of 'how'—even that rather badly—but never *explain,* in terms of 'why'.) The major difficulty is that the original situation is not available to the critic as an experience, apart from experiencing the work itself. This is why it is so difficult to agree about 'the meaning of a poem'. The critic's interpretation of the original situation is bound to be given in the light of *his own* situation. Aesthetic norms and values thus appear to be hopelessly *subjective.* One can therefore *a priori* rule out the possibility of *the* correct interpretation of a work of art. And yet, the relevant question is: should this induce us to adopt sceptic claims and attitudes in these matters? Wouldn't it be more rewarding to aim at a relatively more accurate *approximation* of the complex and intricate metaphorical meaning? After all the sceptics's approach relies on two arbitrary assumptions: (a) that the original situation is 'dead and gone' (while in fact it lives in the work itself as well as in the dynamic social network of 'continuity in discontinuity' between the past and the present); and (b) that the critic's situation, values etc., are in no way relevant to the elucidation of the poet's and the artist's situation.

(4) In this context it would be necessary to analyse in detail the whole structure of metaphorical interplay, in its various forms and manifestations. What are the main characteristics of this structure? What kind of 'ought' sentences do we find in poetry? (There can be no doubt about the frequency of poetic oughts!)

What is the function of metaphors in relation to poetically-expressed commands, recommendations or invitations to action? What kind of power do metaphorical structures have on attitudes; how far and in what way can they affect existing attitudes and form new ones? In what way and to what extent can a metaphorical structure render 'public' the poet's 'private' experience?

(5) As we have seen, nothing follows *directly* from a metaphorical truth. Not even if it had been established by Shakespeare or Milton. This is, however, often ignored by the moralizing and directly political types of criticism (and their extreme manifestations in censorship) which try misconceivedly to impose certain norms and values on writers and public alike. A criticism of these approaches would be helpful also in showing through what *mediations* it is possible to absorb the moral message of a given work.

These and similar questions are at present greatly neglected, although answers to them would undoubtedly throw new light also on a number of issues which are constantly debated outside aesthetics.

4. HEIDEGGER'S USE OF METAPHORICAL PREDICATION

To discuss the role of metaphors in philosophical writings, I have chosen some passages from Heidegger's *Introduction to Metaphysics.* Unfortunately it is necessary to give a long quotation, even though the Heideggerian metaphor is a relatively simple one. However simple though, it branches out in various directions, and we must follow its ramifications, otherwise the overall picture will be distorted. Also, owing to the particular character of metaphor—its non-translatability—a condensed version is simply not feasible. The metaphor in question is that of being in the 'centre' of things, 'squeezed in pincers' by extremist forces—such as opposing nations.

This Europe, in its ruinous blindness forever on the point of cutting its own throat, lies today in a *great pincers,* squeezed between Russia on one side and America on the other. From a metaphysical point of view,

Russia and America are the same; the same dreary technological frenzy, the same unrestricted organization of the average man. [In this situation] such childish categories as pessimism and optimism have long since become absurd. . . .

We are *caught in a pincers.* Situated in the centre, our nation incurs the severest pressure. It is the nation with the most neighbours and hence *the most endangered.* With all this, it is *the most metaphysical of nations.* . . . All this implies that this nation, as a historical nation, must move itself and *thereby* the history of the West *beyond the centre* of their future 'happening' and *into the primordial realm of the powers of being* [sic]. If the great decision regarding Europe is not to bring annihilation, that decision must be made in terms of new spiritual energies unfolding historically *from out of the centre* . . . The beginning must be begun again, with all the *strangeness, darkness, insecurity* that attend a true beginning. . . . Here the preliminary question ['How does it stand with being?' in relation to the basic question of metaphysics: 'Why are there essents rather than nothing'?] is not by any means outside of the main question; rather it is the *flame which burns* as it were in the asking of the fundamental question; it is the *flaming centre of all questioning.* That is to say: it is crucial for the first asking of the fundamental question that in asking its preliminary question we *derive the decisive fundamental attitude* that is here essential. That is why we have related the question of being to the *destiny of Europe,* where the *destiny of the earth* is being decided—while our own historic being-there proves to be *the centre for Europe itself.*[10]

Here we have a succession of philosophical *non-sequiturs* 'deduced' from a trivial geographical metaphor. (Even as a geographical metaphor its validity is highly dubious. After all, it is a matter of arbitrary decision what is considered to be the planetary 'centre': Greenwich or the Congo, Mongolia or Bolivia; and Russia or America, despite the Heideggerian mystification, could be equally good candidates, depending on the assumed criteria.) Heidegger's philosophical conclusions are not established by the force of an argument but by inflating this trivial geographical metaphor to cosmic proportions.

It is not philosophically *proved* that the categories of pessimism and optimism are 'childish and absurd', but by bombastic rhetorical references to a metaphorically stipulated world-centredness of the German nation. The presumptive superiority of Heideggerian metaphysics, over against the common-sense of the curtly dismissed average man who is supposed to be engaged in a 'technological frenzy', is not sustained by analysis and demonstration but by a metaphorical claim that the crucial question of all authentic—i.e. Heideggerian—metaphysics is 'the flaming centre of all questioning'. The distinguishing feature of Germany's position is described in terms of being a centrally situated nation with many neighbours. But from this it is 'deduced' that Germany is 'the most metaphysical of all nations' (whatever that may mean), with a 'destiny' to rescue Europe, and the earth, from annihilation—through the 'strangeness, darkness and insecurity of a radically begun new beginning'. Image upon image running on one track, and claim upon claim running on the other. And the former is supposed to establish philosophically the soundness of the latter. Indeed an obvious case of the metaphorical fallacy.

As it happens, Heidegger himself spells out, though quite involuntarily, the philosophically revealing secret of the whole venture. Talking about 'the flaming centre of all questioning' he admits that its function is not *conceptual* but *emotive.* It is said to be required in order to 'derive the *decisive fundamental attitude* that is here essential'—a statement which is followed by Heidegger's references to German destiny as decisive for the destiny of Europe and of the earth.

The metaphorical track thus serves to induce the reader to accept the attitudes characterized as 'essential' by the philosopher. Metaphors are eminently suitable to this purpose. This is why their 'natural milieu' is literature in which the artist's fundamental aim is to *compel* us to imaginatively identify ourselves with the predicament of the various characters. But what is appropriate in this respect as far as literature is concerned is thoroughly objectionable in philosophy. For literature does not want to draw discursive conclusions from metaphorical premises: the whole structure of its predication remains metaphorical and self-referential. In philosophy, however, self-referentiality is completely out of place. The metaphorically established attitudes in the framework of the philosophical discourse are inevitably transferred to the literal plane, but without the slightest justification. While in literature the attitudes with which we imaginatively identify ourselves simply *cannot* be taken *literally* (because of the artistic medium of communication and its structure of metaphorical predication)—except, perhaps, by very small children—in philosophy they *must* be taken literally. The acceptance of 'strangeness, darkness, insecurity' which Heidegger advocates is not a metaphorical attitude but a real one. The recommendation to accept such an attitude is indeed consciously reinforced by the normative declaration that strangeness, darkness and insecurity are necessary attributes of a 'true beginning'.

Thus the main function of the metaphorical fallacy is to *exempt* the advocated attitudes from a *rational scrutiny.* Our objections, therefore, cannot be merely formal, because they are directed against one of the potentially most *dangerous* philosophical fallacies. Lending itself to establishing and reinforcing attitudes, however irrational they might be, this fallacy is eminently suitable to produce mystifications, with all their unforeseeable consequences. One should not forget the fate of 'Superman', nor the sinister implications of any programme that aims at arrogantly reshaping the 'destiny of the world' out of the self-serving 'centre' of a 'metaphysical nation', irrespective of how severely one judges Heidegger's own personal involvement as an ideological legitimator of such ventures.

5. METAPHORS, SIMILES AND MODELS

The final point I want to discuss briefly concerns the simile. As we have already seen, the simile can easily fit into the framework of theoretical discourse. What remains to be discussed is how one can sustain the stronger claim: that the simile is particularly relevant in some *normative* contexts.

Heidegger's method is revealing also in this respect. In the passage quoted above, at one point he introduces a simile when he talks about 'the flame which burns *as it were* in the asking of the fundamental question'. However, he immediately turns this *simile* into a *metaphor* when he adds that this question *'is the flaming centre of all questioning'.* Thus the 'as it were' of the simile becomes the 'is' of the metaphor to which our earlier objections apply.

What is legitimate and necessary in philosophy is to proceed in exactly the opposite way. That is to say: to turn the metaphor into a simile, and not the simile into a metaphor. To proceed in this way would be to remove the mystifying semblance of literalness of the philosophical metaphor. By contrast, the Heideggerian approach eliminates the relative openness of 'as it were'—i.e., the possibility of giving a better articulation of the problem at stake in another simile—and replaces it by a misleadingly conclusive metaphorical 'is'. (It must be added, of course, that not all metaphors can be turned into philosophically acceptable similes. But this is no argument in favour of their preservation. For those which cannot be turned into adequate similes are better discarded. The notion of 'superman' is not less problematical as a simile than as a metaphor.)

An outstanding example of the tranformation of a metaphor into a simile in the history of philosophy is the development of the theory of 'social contract'. A contract without actually contracting parties is nothing but a metaphor. Taken literally in philosophical context it is very naîve and carries no weight whatsoever. Attempts that aim to eliminate the conceptual difficulties caused by treating this metaphor literally, lead to conceptual oddities (such as Locke's 'tacit consent', for instance): this is because they themselves retain the metaphorical fiction of a (non-consensual) contract.

The situation radically changes when the *'as if'* clause is introduced into the contract theory. As soon as this is done, the contract theory ceases to be a *metaphor* and becomes a *simile.* The conceptual function of this simile is clearly *normative.* To say that a country ought to be ruled 'as if' authority were derived from a social contract is to set up certain *norms* of conduct as related to some fundamental human *values* (freedom, equality, justice, etc.). The simile functions as a *model* of action linked to a set of values. It occupies, thus, the place of a *normative intermediary* between the types of action which it advocates (e.g., legislation of a certain kind and behaviour on both sides bound by the contract in accordance with it), and the values themselves on which these actions are supposed to be based. As a model of action the normative simile reaches back to the values whose practical implications it renders more or less explicit, and forward to the particular actions, establishing their overall framework of orientation as well as indicating their range of compatibility, in accordance with the assumed values.

These considerations apply to the normative discourse in general, not only to the contract theory. In ethics much that is brushed aside by neopositivist philosophers as totally meaningless turns out to be highly meaningful if set in the light of 'as if'. To take an extreme example—extreme in that it is the worst possible offender from the point of view of neopositivism,—the idea of a 'sense of life' (or 'meaning of life') is categorically dismissed as 'unintelligible'. Such a dismissal, however, is rather hasty. For this idea may be unintelligible as a preconceived value or metaphysical ideal, but it is by no means meaningless as a *model:* as a normative intermediary between a set of values and the particular actions corresponding to and compatible with them. 'Behave as if life had a meaning'—is obviously a normative model very different from 'Live as if life had no meaning whatsoever'. (Naturally, both of them are very different from those normative models which dogmatically assert the absolute validity of some *a priori* system of values, with the exclusion of the 'as if' clause; e.g., 'The meaning of life is *X* and therefore you ought to pursue the specified course of action'.)

Such models should not be confused, though, with the values themselves on which they are based. One should not forget that they are only the intermediary link between values and action. It goes without saying that very different actions follow from adopting one model as opposed to another. And since the actions themselves take place in the world at large, the impact of the rival models is subject to empirical assessment. Consequently these *normative models,* far from being unintelligible, can be subjected to practical tests. To insist that they are meaningless or unintelligible amounts to denying the meaningfulness of models as such.

To be sure, these models can only be formulated on the basis of certain *assumptions.* This raises several difficult questions. Above all, perhaps, this: how can one justify one set of assumptions as opposed to its potential rivals? It would be a line well worth investigating: what are the practical implications of one set of norms, of one particular model, as compared to its alternatives? To put it in another way: how far can one avoid, in acting on one particular model, the various 'taboos' that, to a greater or lesser extent, are inherent in every given—and indeed every possible—set of assumptions? But this line of enquiry must be left for some future occasion.

NOTES

1. Cf. T. Moore, *Memoirs of the Life of Sheridan.* Vol. II., p. 29.
2. Federico Garcia Lorca, 'La imagen poética en Don Louis de Góngora', *Obras Completas,* Aguilar, Madrid 1957, p. 72.
3. *Ibid.*
4. Max Black, 'Metaphor', *Proceedings of the Aristotelian Society,* 1954/1955, p. 275 (Italics of M. Black).
5. *Ibid.,* p. 274.
6. *Ibid.,* p. 291.
7. In fact, Black himself finds it difficult to call the sentence about the ploughing chairman a metaphor. He has to resort to the strange and extremely vague formula which we have seen above when he talks about 'calling this sentence a case of metaphor'.
8. Matthew Prior, *Alma,* Canto III, 1. 324.
9. I have discussed in some detail a number of related problems in my book on *Attila József e l'arte moderna,* Lerici, Milano, 1964, especially in Chapters 2 and 3.
10. Heidegger, *An Introduction to Metaphysics,* Doubleday Anchor Books, New York, 1961, pp. 31–5.

VIII Alienation in European Literature*

Concern with alienation has been steadily growing over a long period of time, and in virtually every field of activity. Not surprisingly, therefore, it would be very difficult to find a modern European writer of importance who does not show at least some awareness of its bewilderingly varied manifestations.

1. FROM *EMILE* TO *THE SORROWS OF YOUNG WERTHER*

To understand this complex phenomenon we have to recall that protest against alienation and dehumanization surfaced in a striking way in the second half of the eighteenth century, with particular intensity in the writings of Jean-Jacques Rousseau. His influence was instantaneous and lasting, against a background of increasing social contradictions and of an economic development which turned the promise of the industrial revolution into the nightmare of 'the dark Satanic mills'. Thus the themes of alienation so early and forcefully taken up by Rousseau were really 'in the air'—as if bellowing straight out of the chimneys of those Satanic mills—and through whatever metamorphoses remained with us ever since.

Rousseau's great battle-cry advocated a return to nature, though by no means in the absurdly simplistic form attributed to him by his detractors and enemies. His passionate denunciation

* First published in *Studio International*, Vol. 195, No. 993-4, 1982, pp. 10-15.

of the 'evils of society' did not imply in the least a return to some primitive pre-social existence. On the contrary, it was coupled with singing the virtues of an idealized set of social relations in *Emile or Education* and in *Julie or the New Heloise.* Indeed, he dismissed in no uncertain fashion the idea of abolishing 'mine' and 'yours' in an Appendix to his *Discourse on the Origin of Inequality*: 'Must *meum* and *tuum* be annihilated, and must we return to the forests to live among bears? This is a deduction in the manner of my adversaries, which I would as soon anticipate as let them have the shame of drawing.'

Rousseau was protesting against bad laws and bad governments, stressing with great consistency in his philosophical essays the same principles which he exemplified in a graphic way in his utopian novels. His point of departure was that the inherent freedom and equality of men is alienated and destroyed by perverse social institutions, and he indicated the road to recovery in *The Social Contract* like this:

> Under bad governments, this equality is only apparent and illusory: it serves only to keep the pauper in his poverty and the rich man in the position he has usurped. In fact, laws are always of use to those who possess and harmful to those who have nothing: from which it follows that *the social state is advantageous to men only when all have something and none too much.*

Accordingly, Rousseau tried to demonstrate through the example of his utopian communities that qualitatively different human relations flourish in the absence of such iniquitous social institutions. He identified the destructive power of alienation and denounced it with passionate radicalism. He insisted that liberty and sovereignty are absolutely inalienable from the individuals of any community, and yet they are alienated from them through abuse, usurpation and social perversion. Similarly, he condemned man's alienation from nature, from his 'original constitution', and indicated this alienation as the root cause of all evil. 'Everything is good when it leaves the hands of the Creator of things; everything degenerates in the hands of man'—he thundered in the opening sentence of *Emile*, repeatedly stressing in the same work that the 'slavery' in which civilized man finds himself is secured by 'the chains of our *institutions*'. According to him, the growth of 'artificial needs' and 'useless desires' is the hallmark of such alienated development, resulting in the '*artificial being*' who populates our planet in 'this century of *calculators*' (*Emile*). Both *Emile* and *The New Heloise* condemned with great contempt the practice of alienation which turns men into 'mercenaries' interested only in the 'profit they can derive from one another', thus impoverishing all their personal relations beyond recognition.

Rousseau's great dilemma was that while he pinpointed the social contradictions as the roots of alienation he could not suggest any realistic remedies to them. His great educational utopias—put forward in the name and with the force of a categorical moral *ought*—were meant as counter-examples to a reality whose contradictions he could not help retaining and idealizing. For he was forced to admit that within the framework of his vision the sacredness of private property was the ultimate foundation of civilized life itself:

> It is certain that *the right of property is the most sacred of all the rights* of citizenship, and even more important in some respects than liberty itself: property is the true foundation of civil society, and the real guarantee of the undertakings of citizens: for if property were not answerable for personal actions, nothing would be easier than to evade duties and laugh at the laws. (*A Discourse on Political Economy*)

Thus in the end even in the utopian counter-examples the remedy to alienation was restricted to pruning the 'excesses' of the prevailing trends, in the name of an idealized 'middle condition' which, set against the dynamic power of the unfolding capitalist development, had to remain a *moral postulate.*

And yet, the vitality of Rousseau's influence was inseparable from the contradictory nature of his perspectives. For almost a century had to pass from the conception of *Emile* and *The New Heloise* before the rejection of alienation could be coupled with the practical strategy of a social movement. In Rousseau's time, given the increasing power of alienated social processes and institutions, the writer's ability to capture the tormenting complexity of alienation in its contradictoriness was a major achievement. No matter how problematical it must sound to us in hindsight, the appeal to the ideality of nature—as against the evils of social and economic perversion—in the second half of the eighteenth century served the dual function of both protesting against the historical anachronism of the feudal limitations of human relations and, simultaneously, also of sounding a passionate word of warning about the deeply problematical nature of the emerging new forms of social interaction. The contradictions, therefore, were part and parcel of the objective conditions themselves, and not simply a feature of the writer's subjective perception of the world.

Understandably, then, the pursuit of 'nature' in opposition to alienation and dehumanization marked the ideal horizon of many a great literary work in this epoch. As Goethe put it in a work deeply indebted to Rousseau, *The Sorrows of Young Werther*: '*Nature* alone is infinitely rich, and it alone forms the great artist. One can say much in favour of the *rules*, almost what one can say in praise of *bourgeois society*.' The dilemma of reconciling rules with nature invariably proved insurmountable, making the ideal itself tragically elusive. No wonder, therefore, that Werther's defence of the 'natural rights' of individual love against the cold conventions of the prevailing order had to suffer a tragic shipwreck through its collision with the requirements of bourgeois marriage. This again puts into relief the contradictions involved in that bourgeois marriage is founded on the claimed right to individual love—against feudal restrictions—only to negate its own foundations ever after: for the sake of the continuity of property, an 'orderly' transfer of society from one generation to the next, etc.,—in one word, in the name of Rousseau's 'sacred private property'. Thus the new-found ideal of nature appeared in modern European literature with its dark, often tragic, shadow. Another great work inspired by Rousseau, Schiller's *Kabale und Liebe* (Intrigue and Love)—one of the outstanding dramas of the eighteenth century—depicted with supreme mastery the collision of 'nature' and 'rules' and the inescapable tragic outcome of this collision.

2. ALIENATION AND SOLITUDE

Perhaps nothing illustrates better the contradictory character of these developments than the paradoxical response of writers to *solitude*, from Rousseau to our own days. The advancing disintegration of social ties, the growing atomization of society, the ever-increasing isolation of individuals from one another and the solitude necessarily inherent in such tendencies of fragmentation and privatization was itself the product of alienation. And yet, protest against alienation and dehumanization by modern writers often assumes the form of insisting on the individual's claimed 'sovereignty', making a virtue out of the alienating predicament of solitude and thus affirming what they originally intended to negate. Rousseau's cult of solitude in a sense provided the model—the rejection of the world at large as 'a vast desert', coupled with moralizing inwardness—and the writers of the nineteenth and twentieth centuries produced their bitter-sweet variations on the same theme.

Some, like Aldous Huxley, tried to turn the alienating social-historical reality of isolation into a romantic ideality by means of a timeless, elitist psychological mystification, claiming that 'the more powerful and original a mind, the more it will incline towards the religion of solitude'. (*Proper Studies*) Others admitted in a tone of resignation: 'Solitude is impracticable, and society is fatal.' (Emerson, *Society and Solitude*) Others still went on saying with Thackeray: 'You and I are but a pair of infinite isolations, with some fellow-islands a little more or less near to us.' (*Pendennis*), or with Matthew Arnold's words 'To Marguerite':

> Yes: in the sea of life enisl'd,
>   with echoing straits between us thrown,
> Dotting the shoreless watery wild,
>   We mortal millions live *alone.*

Views and attitudes of this kind appeared in every field of European literature, from Scandinavian drama to French poetry and to the German novel. As one of Ibsen's heroes, Dr Stockman, in *An Enemy of the People* put it, with a touch of irony: 'the strongest man in the world is he who stands most alone', accepting a doubtful predicament since there did not seem to be any alternative to it. And even when the poet A. E. Housman expressed in a most forceful way his complete alienation from the 'foreign laws of God and man', he could only do this in the form of bitter irony and resignation:

The laws of God, the laws of man,
He may keep that will and can;
Not I: let God and man decree
Laws for themselves and not for me;
And if my ways are not as theirs
Let them mind their own affairs.
Their deeds I judge and much condemn,
Yet when did I make laws for them?
Please yourselves, say I, and they
Need only look the other way.
But no, they will not; they must still
Wrest their neighbour to their will,
And make me dance as they desire
With jail and gallows and hell-fire.
And how am I to face the odds
Of man's bedevilment and God's?
I, a stranger and afraid
In a world I never made.
They will be master, right or wrong;
Though both are foolish, both are strong.
And since, my soul, we cannot fly
to Saturn nor to Mercury,
Keep we must, if keep we can,
These foreign laws of God and man.
(*Last Poems*: *XII*)

The poet, exiled to the realm of his own resources, appeared in Pierre Reverdy's words as someone who is forced to 'probe the mystery of his interior existence' (*Le gant de crin*), and he was described in Max Jacob's *Art Poètique* like this: 'The world within one man: that is the modern poet.' But what a world, if its perception is refracted through the prism of probing one's 'Inner mysteries'? Mihály Babits spelled out with stark openness the uncomforting truth of this 'world' of self-oriented alienation in *The Poet's Epilogue*:

I alone can be hero of my verse,
first and last in all my songs;
I wish to sing of the universe
but never succeed in getting beyond myself.

And now I believe: there is nothing beside me,
or if there is, God only knows where.
To be a blind walnut locked into its shell,
waiting to be broken open: how nauseating.

> There is no way out of my magic circle,
> only my arrow breaks through: my desire
> but I know well: it's just an illusion.
>
> I remain: jail for myself, because
> I am the subject and the object,
> alas, I am the alfa and the omega.

The cult of the individual and the assertion of solitude could only enhance the condition of alienation, to the point of declaring it to be '*the human condition*', whatever the original intention may have been. The astonishing popularity of existentialism, notwithstanding the impenetrable obscurity of some of its principal tenets, finds its explanation in the social development to which this philosophy responded well in tune with the mainstream of the literary depiction of solitude.

3. ALIENATION IN THE MODERN NOVEL

The development of the novel tells a similar story. Rousseau's educational novels opposed the first utopian counter-examples to the emerging forces of alienation, and the following century and a half produced many a direct or indirect rejoinder. While Schiller, in his *Letters on the Aesthetic Education of Man*, insisted that it was vitally necessary to devise a sensuous mediation for Rousseau's and Kant's 'moral education', his great contemporary, Goethe, graphically represented in his novels—especially in *Wilhelm Meister*—how the ideal of the rich human being could triumph over the crippling tendencies of fragmentation and alienation.

To be sure, the more powerfully the social trends themselves advanced, the more problematical the educational novel turned out to be, from Stendhal's *Red and Black* and Balzac's *Lost Illusions* to Flaubert's *Sentimental Education*—not to mention Dostoyevsky's novels. But even so, the development of characters in nineteenth century novels was, on the whole, structured in the spirit of 'growth' on the ground of cumulative and enriching experience, even if the personal strategies of the individuals concerned often tragically failed in the course of collisions with rival strategies and with the prevailing social forces. However, their strategies were well identifiable, unfolding through the development of the characters themselves, and the story was also unmistakably there in the novel, to be simply told from its embryonic beginnings to its ultimate climax.

The openness—one might almost say 'obviousness'—and transparency of nineteenth century novels resulted from their structural framework: the *family* as both the ground and the horizon of individual aspirations, and the *relative stability* of the overall social structure, both as regards its major social classes and, more importantly for the novel, the way in which the constitutive cell of modern bourgeois society, the nuclear family itself, was in a meaningful sense *representative* of the *whole* of society as its *microcosm*. Thus the aim of *epic totalization* in the nineteenth century novel could be successfully realized only because this 'microcosm' of bourgeois society in its representativeness was an '*intensive totality*' which, through the dynamic variety and multiplicity of its interrelations with other structures, and through the complex interconnections of partial strategies and aspirations in the general framework of a relatively stable social whole, functioned as the focal point of an *'extensive totality'*. Without the prevalence of such objective conditions Balzac's monumental enterprise of representatively embracing the social totality through the inexorably unfolding individual destinies of the *Comédie humaine* would have turned out to be a preposterous design as well as a pathetic failure, instead of being one of the truly incomparable achievements of world literature.

The contrast with the mainstream of the twentieth century novel could not be greater, from Proust to the French 'new novel', from Kafka to Joyce, and from Thomas Mann to Musil. (Needless to say, the point at issue here is simply the identification of certain structural characteristics, and not some artificial classification of these in a hierarchical order.) To say that the earlier prevailing social stability totally and irrevocably disintegrated in the twentieth century in the turmoil of revolutions and counter-revolutions, in the global collisions of two devastating World Wars, in the unimaginable horrors of the holocaust and of the sample-apocalypse at Hiroshima and Nagasaki, is no more than a modest understatement. Nor is it difficult to see what an insuperable inhibition all this represents to any attempt at an 'epic totalization' with reference to a world whose parts are deeply intertwined, and yet, at many important levels do not communicate with one another even to the most superficial degree. What is much less obvious, however, although equally important for literary developments, is the profound structural crisis of the 'microcosm' itself. For it is after all the latter that constitutes the necessary human context and point of mediation of personal aims and social objectives which appear in the forefront of literary representations.

Considered from this point of view, the strikingly contrasting development of the twentieth century novel becomes less of a literary mystery. For if the structural crisis of the family disrupts the representative significance of the nuclear 'microcosm' for the whole of society—thus rendering extremely problematical the categorial relationship between intensive and extensive totality in the new framework of epic representation—in that case the *partiality* of depicting *individual* destinies (an unavoidable feature of graphic representation) falls under the threat of being smashed against the opposing rocks of naturalistic *immediacy* and abstract *symbolism*: the latter as soon as the writer tries to overcome partiality and immediacy, and the former when he tries to extricate a more elevated and generalized literary discourse of characterization from the pressure of symbolism. And since the transparency of the 'story to be told'—or, indeed, of the 'story telling itself'—in the classical novel resulted from the self-explanatory and self-justifying movement from 'intensive totality' to 'extensive totality' and *vice versa*, the absence of such a movement produces not only the impression of an all-pervasive immobility—together with the necessity of constant interventions by the writer to create some kind of a movement: to push the *book* towards a conclusion, even if not the '*story*'—but also, and again with unavoidable necessity, it is bound to result in more or less extreme complications and obscurity in structural and stylistic terms.

There is no 'story to be told' in Proust or Joyce, and even less in Kafka. There are stories, or moments and episodes to be recalled, situations and fragments of a never fully revealed large canvas to be illuminated for a fleeting moment. No matter how long the narrative goes on, it tends to stay where it is, and it could go on forever: which amounts to the same thing. Similarly, characterization—in Kafka's *Castle* and *Trial*, for instance—is not the growth of the characters through living out their destinies in relation to others and to the broader social world, but simply the presentation of facets of something already *given* which suddenly becomes relevant in conformity with the atmosphere of the situation. Likewise, the temporal-historical dimension is rendered relative or altogether pushed into the background in the modern novel, and psychological determinations take its place, or even quasi-mythical ones, as with Kafka. Even Thomas Mann, who in several ways consciously reaches back to the nineteenth century tradition, shows a greater structural affinity with his contemporaries than with his greatly admired predecessors. He acknowledges that the heroes of his novels are not really heroes in the traditional sense but problematical 'heroes of our time'. And after quoting Harry Levin's *James Joyce* according to which '*Ulysses* is a novel to end all novels', he adds that the same goes for his own novels, for 'in the field of the novel the only thing valid today is that which is no longer a novel' (*Novel of a Novel*).

The way the novel has depicted ever since the turn of the century the structural crisis of our social microcosm is nothing short of prophetic. In this it provided a striking counterpart to Freudian psychoanalysis which perceived and handled the same phenomenon from a thoroughly apologetic standpoint, obliterating its vital social dimensions and attempting the uncritical reconciliation of the 'reconditioned' individual with his alienated predicament by idealizing as psychologically eternal a historically anachronistic form of interpersonal relations. The pressure of noticing with predilection the psychological manifestations of complex social determinations—of which the psychological aspects were, of course, an extremely important *part*—was in great affinity with the practice of 'probing the mysteries of one's inner existence'. In this sense the twentieth century novel displayed the marks of alienation, just as the cult of solitude did in literature in general, no matter for how understandable reasons. But the novel achieved a great deal more than that, even in its most problematical aspects. For through the often forbidding complexity of the structural characteristics mentioned above, it prophetically depicted the continuing disintegration of the nuclear 'microcosm', in contrast to which the apologetics of conservative psychoanalysis amounted to no more than 'whistling down the wind'.

It was because of this continuing disintegration and its valid artistic depiction that in Musil's *Man Without Qualities* 'What the story that makes up this novel amounts to is that the story that was supposed to be told in it is not told'—as Musil himself so paradoxically put it in a *Notebook* of 1932. For it was no longer possible to put in order the world on the basis of the antiquated structures that ceased to be the ground and the horizon of individual aspirations, losing simultaneously their power of cementing together the social whole. 'If mankind could dream collectively, it would dream Moosbrugger' (namely the sex maniac murderer, represented as a larger-than-life-size monster)—exclaims Ulrich, *The Man Without Qualities*. At one level one can read this as timeless 'depth psychology'. But that would be a hopelessly one-sided reading. For its essential complementary—without which Musil's work could not have reached its stature as one of the truly outstanding novels of our century—points an accusing finger at all those socially tangible horrors which this century has witnessed throughout its history with alarming frequency and intensity. Hence the larger-than life-size characterization of the denounced evil as the 'demonic' manifestation of alienation.

4. FROM THE FAUSTIAN QUEST FOR HUMANITY TO SARTRE'S 'HELL AMONG OTHER PEOPLE'

This takes us to the last point to consider, however briefly: the Faust theme and the experience of 'hell' in modern European literature.

It was Paracelsus, a real-life model of Goethe's *Faust*, who insisted at the dawn of capitalist developments: 'What else could fortune be than living in conformity to nature's wisdom? If nature goes well, that is fortune; if it does not, that is misfortune.For our essence is ordained in nature.' (*Leben und Lebensweisheit in Selbstzeugnissen*). With this view of man and nature Paracelsus introduced one of the ideal points of reference for later conceptions of non-alienated existence. And he eulogized dedication to work as the realization of the human essence, providing thus another seminal theme of modern concern with alienation:

> Happiness does not consist in laziness, or sensual pleasure, or riches, or chattering, or gluttony. In labour and in sweat must each man use the gifts that God conferred upon him on earth, either as a peasant in the fields, as a workman in the smithy, in the mines, on the seas, in medicine, or as one who proclaims the word of God. *The proper way resides in work and action, in doing and producing*; the perverse man does nothing, but talks a great deal. We must not judge a man by his words, but by his heart. The heart speaks through words only when they are confirmed by deeds. . . . No one sees what is hidden in man, but only what his works reveal.

The liberation of man through nature and the realization of the rich human potentials through productive work and action were also the ideals of capitalism until things started to go sour in the course of actual developments. By the middle of the eighteenth century, when writers began to voice a growing concern about alienation, it was no longer possible to appeal to such ideals in an unproblematical fashion. It is by no means accidental, therefore, that *Prometheus* had to remain a fragment not only for Shelley, who died very young, but also for Goethe. Nor is it surprising that when Goethe tackled these problems in *Faust*—a work with which he continued to wrestle throughout a long and prodigiously active life—his final answer had to be a deeply ironical one, as we shall see in a moment.

The theme of alienation in its earliest form appeared in the Bible, both as man's 'alienation from God' and as the well-deserved punishment for it. Needless to say, in the secularization of modern literature the religious connotations were pushed into the background and the impersonal forces of reification, fragmentation, isolation and depersonalization were identified as the targets to aim at. And yet the mystifying character and 'demonic' magnitude of the powers involved conferred a quasi-mythological dimension on the literary attempts that confronted comprehensively the human quest for meaning under the shadow of alienation, which seemed to possess the magic force of turning everything into its opposite. In this sense mythology—the figurative condensation and elliptic consciousness of deep-seated collective experience across the boundaries of many historic periods—continued to haunt modern literature even in its most secular form. The Faust theme and its more or less distant cousins—from Marlowe to Goethe, from Ibsen's *Peer Gynt* to Madách's *Tragedy of Man*, from *Don Juan* (who never ceased to fascinate Kierkegaard) to *Dr Jekyll and Mr Hyde*, from Balzac's *Melmoth* to Sartre's *No Exit* and *Lucifer and the Lord*, and from *Tonio Kröger* and *Death in Venice* to *Doctor Faustus*—acquired a very special place in literature in virtue of its particular suitability to provide this figurative condensation of some of the most burning dilemmas of modern development.

Under the conditions of alienation, *irony*—a striking characteristic of modern literature—is infinitely more than a mere literary device. For alienation itself is a condition of irony *par excellence* in that man brings it upon himself and thus cannot blame anyone or anything, not even 'destiny' or 'fate' for it. As Sartre spells it out in the words of his hero in *Lucifer and the Lord*:

> Hatred, weakness, violence, death, displeasure, all that proceeds from man alone; it is my only empire, and I am alone within it; what happens within me is attributable to me alone. . . God does not see me, God does not hear me, God does not know me. You see this emptiness over our heads? That is God. You see this breach in the wall? It is God. You see that hole in the ground? That is God again. The silence is God. The absence is God. God is the loneliness of man. There was no one but myself; I alone decided on Evil; and I alone invented God. It was I who cheated, I who worked miracles, I who accuse myself today, I alone who can absolve myself; I the man. . . . No way of escaping man. Farewell monsters, farewell saints. Farewell pride. There is nothing left but men.

The secularization of modern literature thus carries with it a growing awareness of reality and responsibility arising from the loss of former justifications, coupled, however, with the paralysing feeling of one's inability to *do* something about the diagnosed predicament. Thus consciousness recoils into itself and cries out for escape, after proving to itself that there can be no escape. Again, a situation of irony *par excellence* which assumes the form of the secularized demon: an evil force incomparably more powerful than man and yet totally indistinguishable from man himself. Irony enters modern literature via this avenue, as an *existential* condition, and has remained its salient feature ever since. The fact that the founder of existentialism, Kierkegaard, dedicated his doctoral dissertation to *The Concept of Irony* and went on using irony heavily in all his subsequent writings, finds its explanation in the same objective determinations.

Balzac's *Melmoth*, with bitter irony, allows the hero—a 'Faust' cut down to the size of an embezzling accountant so as to suit the prosaic conditions of life under the rule of capital—to escape the consequences of his pact with the devil. Balzac shows that through alienation the demon rules the *whole* of society: even the 'Holy Ghost' has its quotation on the Stock Exchange; set against this universal condition, one single man's destiny pales into insignificance: hence the bitter irony. Similarly—although with features ranging from the playful to the tragic, in accordance with the specificity of the depicted situations and characters—irony predominates in every single variation on the Faust theme, from Goethe to Mann's *Doctor Faustus* and Sartre's plays.

The fateful gap between awareness and action and the tragic inadequacy of even the most heroic solitary individual effort against the power of alienation cast this shadow of irony on the Faust theme. For what could be more ironical than the lonely figure of Faust—or for that matter Goetz in *Lucifer and the Lord*—working for mankind when the dominant conditions themselves pronounce the life sentence of isolation, with no possibility of appeal?

It was Thomas Mann, the master of irony, who noted the connection between loneliness and the Faust theme. Indeed, it is loneliness magnified to demonic proportions of inescapability that explains the character and actions not only of men like Faust and Adrian Leverkühn but also of such figures as Don Juan, who act out with desperate intensity the strategy of 'heroic escape' as their life project, only to find out in the end that it cannot be accomplished. The alienated condition of loneliness in the midst of others is the way in which the demonic ultimately seems to triumph. As Sartre puts it in *No Exit*:

Yes, now's the moment; I'm looking at this thing on the mantelpiece, and I understand that I am in hell. I tell you, everything's been thought out beforehand. They knew I'd stand at the fireplace stroking this thing of bronze, with all those eyes intent on me. Devouring me. *He swings round abruptly.* What? Only two of you? I thought there were more; many more. *Laughs.* So this is hell. I'd never have believed it. You remember all we were told about the torture-chambers, the fire and brimstone, the 'burning marl'. Old wives' tales! There's no need for red-hot pokers. Hell is other people!

Is there really 'No Exit'?

At the beginning of the developments surveyed here, Goethe gave a rather different answer, indicating work with others and for others as the only hope to secure victory over the forces of alienation. But even at that point in history he could offer this hopc only through the wonderfully subtle irony with which he depicts the final moments of Faust's life. In this scene his hero—blinded by *Sorge* (Anguish) for refusing to yield to her—greets the noise of the Lemurs who in fact dig his grave as the welcome noise of canal-digging, in realization of his great project:

A swamp along the mountains' flank
Makes all my previous gains contaminate;
My deeds, if I could drain this sink,
Would culminate as well as terminate:
To open to the millions living space,
Not danger-proof but free to run their race.
Green fields and fruitful; men and cattle hiving
Upon this newest earth at once and thriving,
Settled at once beneath this sheltering hill
Heaped by the masses' brave and busy skill
With such a heavenly land behind this hedge,
The sea beyond may bluster to its edge
And, as it gnaws to swamp the work of masons,
To stop the gap one common impulse hastens.
Aye! Wedded to this concept like a wife,
I find this wisdom's final form:
He only earns his freedom and his life
Who takes them every day by storm.
And so a man, beset by dangers here,
As child, man, old man, spends his manly year.
Oh to see such activity,
Treading free ground with people that are free!
Then could I bid the passing moment:

> 'Linger a while, thou art so fair!'
> The traces of my earthly days can never
> Sink in the aeons unaware.
> And I, who feel ahead such heights of bliss,
> At last enjoy my highest moment—this.

Thus the tormenting dilemma is resolved by Goethe in a form that asserts the validity of the Faustian ideal while indirectly acknowledging its unattainability within the perspectives of the prevailing social horizon.

It is to the 'demonic' difficulties confronting all attempts to remove the social roots of this dilemma that modern European literature, in its preoccupation with alienation, bears such an uncomforting witness.

Bibliography

Abendroth, W., *Sozialgeschichte der Europäischen Arbeiterbewegung,* 3rd edn., Frankfurt/M., 1966.

Antagonistische Gesellschaft und politische Demokratie, Neuwied, 1967.

Adorno, T.W., *Negative Dialektik,* Frankfurt/M., 1966.

Prisms, London, 1967.

and Horkheimer, M., *Dialectic of Enlightenment,* New York, 1972.

et al., The Positivist Dispute in German Sociology, London, 1976.

Alavi, H., 'State and Class under Peripheral Capitalism', in Alavi, H., and Shanin, T. *Introduction to the Sociology of 'Developing Societies',* London, 1982.

Althusser, L., *For Marx,* London, 1969.

Lenin and Philosophy and Other Essays, London, 1971.

and Balibar, E., *Reading Capital,* London, 1970.

Anderson, P., *In the Tracks of Historical Materialism,* London, 1983.

Aristotle, *Ethics. Politics.*

Aron, R., *The Opium of the Intellectuals,* London, 1957.

La lutte des classes, Paris, 1964.

18 Lectures on Industrial Society, London, 1969.

History and the Dialectic of Violence, Oxford, 1975.

Arthur C., 'Dialectic and Labour', in Mepham, J., and Ruben, D.H. (eds.), *Issues in Marxist Philosophy,* Vol. 1, Brighton, 1979.

Austin, J.L., *Philosophical Papers,* Oxford, 1961.

How to Do Things with Words, Oxford, 1962.

Avineri, S., *The Social and Political Thought of Karl Marx,* Cambridge, 1968.

Hegel's Theory of the Modern State, Cambridge, 1972.

Ayer, A.J., *Language, Truth and Logic,* London, 1936.

Babbage, C., *On the Economy of Machinery and Manufacture,* London, 1832.
Baran, P.A. and Sweezy, P.M., *Monopoly Capital,* New York, 1966.
Barber, B., *Social Stratification: a Comparative Analysis of Structure and Process,* New York, 1957.
Barthes, R., *Selected Writings,* London, 1982.
Bell, D., *The End of Ideology,* New York, 1961.
'Unstable America', *Encounter,* June 1970.
Belleville, P., *Une nouvelle classe ouvrière,* Paris, 1963.
Bendix, R., and Lipset, S.M. (eds.), *Class, Status and Power,* 2nd edn., London, 1967.
Benjamin, W., *Illuminations,* London, 1970.
Benseler, F. (ed.), *Georg Lukàcs: Festschrift zum 80 Geburtstag.,* Neuwied, 1965.
Berger, P.L. and Luckmann, T., *The Social Construction of Reality,* Harmondsworth, 1966.
Berle, A.A. and Means, G.C., *The Modern Corporation and Private Property,* New York, 1933.
Berlin, I., *Four Essays on Liberty,* Oxford, 1969.
Bettelheim, C., *Studies in the Theory of Planning,* London, 1967.
Beveridge, Lord, *Full Employment in a Free Society,* 2nd edn., London, 1960.
Bhaskar, R., *The Possibility of Naturalism,* Brighton, 1979.
Birnbaum, N., *The Crisis of Industrial Society,* London, 1969.
Black, M., 'Metaphor', *Proceedings of the Aristotelian Society,* 1954–5.
Blackburn, R. (ed.), *Ideology in Social Science: Readings in Critical Social Theory,* London, 1972.
and Cockburn, A. (eds.), *The Incompatibles: Trade Union Militancy and the Consensus,* London, 1967.
Blau, P.M., *Bureaucracy in Modern Society,* New York, 1956.
Blauner, R., *Alienation and Freedom: the Factory Worker and His Industry,* Chicago, 1964.
Bloch, E., *Subjekt-Objekt,* I–III, Berlin, 1952–9.
Das Prinzip Hoffnung, Berlin, 1954.
'Aktualität und Utopie. Zu Lukàcs: Geschichte und Klassenbewusstsein' (1923), in *Philosophische Aufsätze*, Frankfurt/M, 1969.
Bloch, M., *Feudal Society,* London, 1961.
Blumberg, P., *Industrial Democracy: the Sociology of participation,* London, 1968.

Bobbio, N., *Da Hobbes a Marx,* Napoli, 1965.
'Sulla nozione di "società civile"', *De homine,* No. 24–5, 1968.
Quale Socialismo? Torino, 1976.
Dalla struttura alla funzione, Milano, 1977.
Boden, M.A., *Piaget,* London, 1979.
Bollhagen, P., *Soziologie und Geschichte,* Berlin, 1966.
Borkenau, F., *Übergang von Feudalen zum bürgerlichen Weltbild,* Paris, 1934.
Bottomore, T.B., *Classes in Modern Society,* London, 1955.
Elites and Society, London, 1964.
Sociology and Socialism, Brighton, 1984.
(ed.), *A Dictionary of Marxist Thought,* Oxford, 1983.
Brown, M.B., *After Imperialism,* London, 1963.
Bukharin, N., *Historical Materialism,* New York, 1925.
Imperialism and World Economy, London, 1930.
Bukharin, N. and Preobrazhensky, E., *The ABC of Communism,* London 1922.
Burnham, J., *The Managerial Revolution,* London, 1943.

Campbell, T., *The Left and Rights: A Conceptual Analysis of the Idea of Socialist Rights,* London, 1983.
Cases, C., *Marxismo e neopositivismo,* Torino, 1958.
Saggi e note di letteratura tedesca, Torino, 1963.
Centers, R., *The Psychology of Social Classes: a Study of Class Consciousness,* Princeton, 1949.
Chomsky, N., *American Power and the New Mandarins,* New York 1969.
Cerutti, F., *Totalità, bisogni, organizzazione: ridiscutendo 'Storia e Coscienza di Classe',* Firenze, 1980.
Clegg, S. and Dunkerley, D., *Organization, Class and Control,* London, 1980.
Coates, K. (ed.), *Can the Workers Run Industry?,* London, 1968.
and Topham, T. (eds.), *Workers' Control,* London, 1968.
Cole, G.D.H., *Studies in Class Structure,* London, 1955.
Commons, J.R., *Legal Foundations of Capitalism,* New York, 1924.
Constantino, R., *Neocolonial Identity and Counter-consciousness,* London, 1978.
Cooper, D. (ed.), *The Dialectic of Liberation,* London, 1968.
Coser, L.A., *The Functions of Social Conflict,* London, 1956.

Dahrendorf, R., *Class and Class Conflict in Industrial Society,* London, 1959.

Davidson, A., *Antonio Gramsci: Towards an Intellectual Biography,* London, 1977.
Deborin, A., 'Lukàcs und seine Kritik des Marxismus', *Arbeiterliteratur,* 1924, No. X.
Della Volpe, G., *Critique of Taste,* London, 1978.
Logic as a Positive Science, London, 1980.
Deutscher, I., *The Prophet Armed: Trotsky 1879–1921,* Oxford, 1954.
The Prophet Unarmed: Trotsky 1921–1929, Oxford, 1959.
The Prophet Outcast: Trotsky 1929–1940, Oxford, 1963.
The Unfinished Revolution, Oxford, 1967.
Dobb, M., *Studies in the Development of Capitalism,* London, 1946.
Soviet Economic Development Since 1917, London, 1948.
On Economic Theory and Socialism: Collected Papers, London, 1955.
Draper, T., *The Roots of American Communism,* New York, 1957.
Drucker, P., *The New Society,* New York, 1949.
Durkheim, E., *The Division of Labor in Society,* Chicago, 1947.
Professional Ethics and Civic Morals, London, 1958.
The Rules of Sociological Method, New York, 1938.
Sociology and Philosophy, London, 1965.

Edgley, R., 'Marx's Revolutionary Science', in Mepham, J., and Ruben, D.H. (eds.), *Issues in Marxist Philosophy,* Vol. 3, Brighton, 1979.
Elton, W. (ed.), *Aesthetics and Language,* Oxford, 1954.
Engels, F., *Outlines of a Critique of Political Economy,* 1843.
The Condition of the Working Class in England, 1844–5.
Socialism: Utopian and Scientific, 1877.
Anti-Dühring, 1878.
Dialectics of Nature, 1875-82.
The Origin of the Family, Private Property and the State, 1874.

Falconer, A.D. (ed.), *Understanding Human Rights,* Dublin, 1980.
Fiori, G., *Antonio Gramsci: Life of a Revolutionary,* London, 1970.
Fortini, F., *Questioni di frontiera: scritti di politica e di letteratura 1965–1977,* Torino, 1977.
Friedmann, G., *Industrial Society: the Emergence of the Human Problem of Automation,* Glencoe, 1955.

Sept études sur l'homme et la technique, Paris, 1966.
Friedrich, C.J. (ed.), *Immanuel Kant's Moral and Political Writings,* New York, 1949.
Fromm, E., *The Fear of Freedom,* London, 1942.
(ed.), *Socialist Humanism,* New York, 1965.

Galbraith, J.K., *American Capitalism: the Concept of Countervailing Power,* New York, 1952.
The New Industrial State, London, 1976.
Geiger, T., *Ideologie und Wahrheit,* Neuwied, 1968.
Gellner, E., *Spectacles and Predicaments: Essays in Social Theory,* Cambridge, 1979.
Gibbs, B., *Freedom and Liberation,* London, 1976.
Giddens, A., *Central Problems in Social Theory,* London, 1979.
Glass, D.V., (ed.), *Social Mobility in Britain,* London, 1954.
Gloversmith, F. (ed.), *Class, Culture and Social Change,* Brighton, 1980.
Goldmann, L., *Recherches dialectiques,* Paris, 1959.
The Hidden God, London, 1964.
The Human Sciences and Philosophy, London, 1969.
Method in the Sociology of Literature, Oxford, 1980.
Goldthorpe, J.H. (*et al.*), *The Affluent Worker in the Class Structure,* Cambridge, 1969.
Gorz, A., *Strategy for Labour,* Boston, 1967.
Le socialisme difficile, Paris, 1967.
Gramsci, A., *The Modern Prince and Other Writings,* London, 1957.
La formazione dell'uomo (ed. G. Urbani), Rome, 1967.
Selections from the Prison Notebooks, London, 1971.
Selections from Political Writings: 1910–1920, London, 1977.
Grant, A., *Socialism and the Middle Classes,* London, 1958.
Guérin, D., *L'anarchisme,* Paris, 1965.
Guerra, A., *Introductione a Kant,* Roma & Bari, 1980.
Gurvitch, G., *Le concept de classe social, de Marx à nos jours,* Paris, 1954.

Habermas, J., *Theorie und Praxis,* Neuwied, 1963.
Hampshire, S.N., *Thought and Action,* London, 1959.
Hare, R.M., *The Language of Morals,* Oxford, 1952.
Harrington, M., *Towards a Democratic Left,* New York 1968.
Hauser, A., *The Social History of Art,* London, 1951.
The Philosophy of Art History, London, 1958.
Hegel, G.W.F., *The Science of Logic,* London, 1929.
Encyclopaedia of the Philosophical Sciences (1830), Part One:

Logic, London, 1873.
The Phenomenology of Mind, London, 1910.
The Philosophy of Right, Oxford, 1942.
The Philosophy of History, New York, 1956.
The Philosophy of Mind, Oxford, 1971.
Natural Law, University of Pennsylvania Press, 1975.

Heidegger, M., *Being and Time*, Oxford, 1967.
An Introduction to Metaphysics, New York, 1961.

Heilbroner, R.L., *The Limits of Amercan Capitalism*, New York, 1966.

Heller, C.S. (ed.), *Structured Social Inequality*, New York, 1969.

Hilferding, R., *Das Finanzkapital*, Vienna, 1910.

Hobbes, T., *Leviathan*, 1651.

Hoggart, R. *The Uses of Literacy: Aspects of Working Class Life*, London, 1957.

Holz, H.H., *Herr und Knecht bei Leibniz und Hegel. Zur Interpretation der Klassengesellschaft*, Neuwied, 1968.

Homans, G.C., *The Nature of Social Science*, New York, 1967.

Horkheimer, M., *Kritische Theorie*, Frankfurt/M., 1968.
and Adorno, T.W., *Dialektik der Aufklärung*, Amsterdam, 1947.

Hughes, G.S., *Consciousness and Society*, New York, 1958.
The Obstructed Path: French Social Thought 1930–1960, New York, 1966.

Jacobs, P. and Landau, S., *The New Radicals*, New York, 1966.

Jakubowski, F., *Ideology and Superstructure*, London, 1976.

Kaegi, P., *Genesis des historischen Materialismus*, Vienna, 1965.

Kahl, J.A., *The American Class Structure*, New York 1957.

Kant, *Idea for a Universal History with Cosmopolitan Intent*, 1784.
Theory and Practice, 1793.
Zum ewigen Frieden, 1795.

Kautsky, K., Recension of 'Geschichte und Klassenbewusstsein', *Die Gesellschaft*, 1924.

Keynes, J.M., *Essays in Persuasion*, London, 1932.

Kilminster, R., *Praxis and Method*, London, 1979.

Knox, T.M., 'Two Conceptions of Philosophy', *Philosophy*, XXXVI (1961).

Kofler, L., *Geschichte und Dialektik*, Hamburg, 1955.
Staat, Gesellschaft und Elite, Ulm, 1960.

Kornhauser, W., *The Politics of Mass Society,* Glencoe, 1959.
Korsch, K., *Karl Marx,* London, 1938.
Marxism and Philosophy, London, 1970.
Kuczynski, J., *A Short History of Labour Conditions under Industrial Capitalism*, London, 1942-7.
Kuhn, T.S., *The Structure of Scientific Revolutions,* Chicago, 1962.

Labriola, A., *Essays on the Materialistic Conception of History,* Chicago, 1908.
Saggi sul materialismo storico (ed. V. Geratana and A. Guerra), Rome, 1964.
Larrain, J., *The Concept of Ideology,* London, 1979.
Marxism and Ideology, London, 1983.
Laslett, P. and Runciman, W.G., (eds.), *Philosophy, Politics and Society,* Second Series, Oxford, 1962.
Lenin, V.I., *What Is To Be Done?,* 1902.
Marxism and Revisionism, 1908.
Controversial questions, 1913.
The Collapse of the Second International, 1915.
Imperialism, the Highest Stage of Capitalism, 1916.
The State and Revolution, 1917.
The Proletarian Revolution and the Renegade Kautsky, 1918.
'Left-Wing' Communism, an Infantile Disorder, 1920.
Lévi-Strauss, C., *The Savage Mind,* London, 1966.
Structural Anthropology, New York, 1967.
The Elementary Structures of Kinship, Boston, 1969.
Lichtheim, G., *The Concept of Ideology and Other Essays,* New York, 1967.
Lukács, London, 1970.
Lipset, S.M., *Political Man,* New York, 1960.
Locke, J., *Two Treatises of Civil Government,* 1690.
Project for the Reform of the Poor Law in England, 1695.
Lockwood, D., *The Black-Coated Worker. A Study in Class Consciousness,* London, 1958.
Lorca, F.G., 'La imagen poética en don Louis Góngora', *Obras Completas,* Madrid, 1957.
Löwy, M., *Pour une sociologie des intellectuels révolutionnaires,* Paris, 1976.
Lukács, G., *Der junge Hegel,* Vienna, 1948.
Die Zerstörung der Vernunft, Berlin, 1954.
Schriften zur Ideologie und Politik (ed. Peter Ludz), Neuwied. 1967.
Lenin, London, 1970.

History and Class Consciousness, London, 1971 (German edn., Berlin, 1923).
The Theory of the Novel, London, 1963.
Goethe and His Age, London, 1968.
The Ontology of Social Being: Hegel, London, 1978.
The Ontology of Social Being: Marx, London, 1978.
The Ontology of Social Being: Labour, London, 1980.
Record of a Life, London, 1984.
Lukes, S., 'On the Relativity of Power', in Brown, S.C. (ed.), *Philosophical Disputes in the Social Sciences,* Brighton, 1979.
Luxemburg, R., *The Accumulation of Capital,* London, 1951.
Social Reform and Revolution, London, 1968.
The Mass Strike, the Political Party and the Trade Unions, London, 1970.
The National Question, (ed. H.B., Davies), New York, 1976.

Macpherson, C.B., *The Political Theory of Possessive Individualism: Hobbes to Locke,* Oxford, 1962.
Democratic Theory: Essays in Retrieval, Oxford, 1973.
McCarney, J., *The Real World of Ideology,* Brighton, 1980.
Mallet, S., *La nouvelle classe ouvrière,* Paris, 1963.
Mandel, E., *Marxist Economic Theory,* London, 1968.
Europe versus America?, London, 1975.
Late Capitalism, London, 1975.
Mannheim, K., *Ideology and Utopia,* London, 1936.
Man and Society in an Age of Reconstruction, London, 1940.
Essays on the Sociology of Culture, London, 1956.
Mao Tse-tung, *Reports on an Investigation of the Peasant Movement in Hunan,* 1927.
On Contradiction, 1937.
On the Correct Handling of Contradiction among the People, 1957.
Marcuse, H., *Reason and Revolution,* London, 1941.
One-Dimensional Man, London, 1964.
An Essay on Liberation, London, 1969.
Die Permanenz der Kunst, München, 1977.
Marshall, T.H., *Citizenship and Social Class,* Cambridge, 1950.
Marx, K., *Difference between the Democritean and Epicurean Philosophy of Nature,* 1840–1.
Critique of the Hegelian Philosophy or Right, 1843.
Introduction to the Critique of the Hegelian Philosophy of Right, December 1843–January 1844.
Economic and Philosophical Manuscripts, 1844.

Draft Plan for a Work on the Modern State, 1845.
Theses on Feuerbach, 1845
The Holy Family, 1845.
The Poverty of Philosophy, 1847.
The Class Struggles in France, 1850.
The Eighteenth Brumaire of Louis Bonaparte, 1852.
A Contribution to the Critique of Political Economy, 1859.
Grundrisse der Kritik der Politischen Ökonomie, 1857–9,
Capital, 1867–83.
The Civil War in France, 1871.
Critique of the Gotha Programme, 1875.

Marx and Engels, *The German Ideology,* 1845–6.
Manifesto of the Communist Party, 1848.

Mattelart, A., *Multinational Corporations and the Control of Culture,* Brighton, 1979.
Mass Media, Ideologies and the Revolutionary Movement, Brighton, 1980.

Mattick, P., *Marx and Keynes,* London, 1969.
Critique of Marcuse, London, 1972.

Mayo, E., *The Social Problems of an Industrial Civilization,* London, 1949.

Meek, R.L., *Studies in the Labour Theory of Value,* London, 1956.

Merleau-Ponty, M., *Les aventures de la dialectique,* Paris, 1955.

Merton, R.K., *Social Theory and Social Structure,* New York, 1957.

Mészáros, I., *Satire and Reality,* Budapest, 1955.
La rivolta degli intellettuali in Ungheria, Turin, 1958.
Attila József e l'arte moderna, Milano, 1964.
Marx's Theory of Alienation, London, 1970.
Lukács's Concept of Dialectic, London, 1972.
The Work of Sartre: Search for Freedom, Brighton, 1979.
(ed.), *Aspects of History and Class Consciousness,* London, 1971.

Meyerhoff, H., (ed.), *The Philosophy of History in Our Time,* New York, 1959.

Michels, R., *Political Parties,* Glencoe, 1949.

Miliband, R., *Marxism and Politics,* Oxford, 1977.
Class Power and State Power, London, 1984.

Mills, C.W., *White Collar: the American Middle Classes,* New York, 1951.
The Power Elite, New York, 1956.
The Sociological Imagination, New York, 1959.

The Marxists, New York, 1962.
Mondolfo, R., *Umanismo di Marx: studi filosofici 1908–1966* (ed. N. Bobbio), Turin, 1968.
Montefiore, A., *A Modern Introduction to Moral Philosophy,* London, 1958.
Moore, B., Jr., *Political Power and Social Theory,* Cambridge, Mass., 1958.
Social Origins of Dictatorship and Democracy, Boston, 1966.
Moore, G.E., *Principia Ethica,* Cambridge, 1903.
Philosophical Studies, London, 1922.
Philosophical Papers London, 1959.
Mosca, G., *The Ruling Class,* New York, 1939.
Murdock, G.P., *Social Structure,* New York, 1949.
Myrdal, G., *Value in Social Theory,* London, 1958.

Nisbet, R.A., *The Quest for Community,* New York, 1953.
Nordlinger, E.A., *The Workingclass Tories,* London, 1967.
Norman, R., *Hegel's Phenomenology: A Philosophical Introduction,* London, 1978.
and Sayers, S., *Hegel, Marx and Dialectic: A Debate,* Brighton, 1980.

Offe, C., *Contradictions of the Welfare State,* London, 1984.
Olson, M., *The Logic of Collective Action: Public Goods and the Theory of Groups,* Cambridge, Mass., 1965.
Ossowski, S., *Class Structure in the Social Consciousness,* London, 1963.

Packard, V., *The Status Seekers: an Exploration of Class Behaviour in America* New York, 1959.
Pareto, V., *The Mind and Society,* London, 1935.
Parkinson, G.H.R. (ed.), *George Lukàcs: the Man, His Work and His Ideas,* London, 1970.
Parsons, T., *The Social System,* Glencoe, 1951.
Essays in Sociological Theory, New York, 1954.
and Smelser, N.J., *Economy and Society: A Study in the Integration of Economic and Social Theory,* London, 1956.
Pashukanis, E.B., *Law and Marxism: A General Theory,* (ed. and Introduction by C. Arthur), London, 1978.
Perlini, T., *Utopia e prospettiva in György Lukàcs,* Bari, 1968.
Autocritica della ragione illuministica, Rome, 1969.
Piaget, J., *Structuralism,* London, 1971.
The Principles of Genetic Epistemology, London, 1972.
Insights and Illusions of Philosophy, London, 1972.

Polányi, K., *The Great Transformation,* New York, 1944.
The Livelihood of Man, (ed. H.W. Pearson), New York, 1977.
Poulantzas, N., *Pouvoir politique et classes sociales,* Paris, 1968.
Procacci, G., (ed.), *La 'rivoluzione permanente' e il socialismo in un paese solo,* Rome, 1963.
Rée, J., Ayers, M., and Westoby, A. *Philosophy and Its Past,* Brighton, 1978.
Reissman, L., *Class in American Society,* Glencoe, 1959.
Révai, J., Review of G. Lukács's 'Geschichte und Klassenbewusstsein', *Archiv für die Geschichte des Sozialismus,* 1925.
Rex, J., *Key Problems of Sociological Theory,* London, 1961.
Riesman, D., *et al., The Lonely Crowd,* New Haven, 1950.
Roszak, T., (ed.), *The Dissenting Academy,* New York, 1967.
Rousseau, J.J., *A Discourse on the Origin of Inequality,* 1755.
A Discourse on Political Economy, 1758.
The Social Contract, 1762.
Rudas, L., 'Orthodoxer Marxismus?', *Arbeiterliteratur,* 1924, No. IX.
'Die Klassenbewusstseintheorie von Lukács', *Arbeiterliteratur,* 1924, Nos. X, XII.
Russell, B., *The Problems of Philosophy,* London, 1912.
Our Knowledge of the External World, London, 1914.
Inquiry into Meaning and Truth, London, 1940.
Human Knowledge: Its Scope and Limits, London, 1948.
Logic and Knowlege, London, 1948.
Power: a New Social Analysis, London, 1962.
and Whitehead, A.N., *Principia Mathematica,* 2nd edn., Cambridge, 1925–7.
Ryle, G., *The Concept of Mind,* London, 1949.
(ed. and Introduction), *The Revolution in Philosophy,* London, 1957.

Sánchez-Vázquez, A., *The Philosophy of Praxis,* London, 1977.
Ciencia y revolución, Madrid, 1978.
Sartre, J.P., *Being and Nothingness,* London, 1969.
Critique de la raison dialectique, Paris, 1960.
The problem of Method, London, 1963.
Between Existentialism and Marxism, London, 1974.
L'Idiot de la famille, I–III, Paris, 1971–2.
'Jean-Paul Sartre ou l'interview sans interview', article-interview by Pierre Lorquet, *Mondes Nouveaux,* 21 December 1944.

'Rencontre avec Jean-Paul Sartre', interview by Gabriel d'Aubarède, *Les Nouvelles littéraires,* 1 January 1951.
Sartre's Last Interview, *Le Nouvel Observateur,* 17 March–7 April 1980.
Sayer, D., *Marx's Method,* Brighton, 1979.
Schaff, A., *Marxismus und das menschliche Individuum,* Vienna, 1966.
Alienation as a Social Phenomenon, Oxford, 1980.
Schumpeter, J.A., *Imperialism and Social Classes,* Oxford, 1951.
Sebag, L., *Marxisme et structuralisme,* Paris, 1964.
Sinowjew, G., 'Gegen die Ultralinken', *Protokoll des V. Kongresses der Kommunistischen Internationale,* Moscow, 1925.
Skillen, A., *Ruling Illusions: Philosophy and the Social Order,* Brighton, 1977.
Smelser, N.J., *Theory of Collective Behaviour,* London, 1962.
Solomon, M., (ed.), *Marxism and Art: Essays Classic and Contemporary,* Brighton, 1979.
Sorel, G., *Réflexions sur la violence,* Paris, 1906.
Sorokin, P., *Social Mobility,* New York, 1927.
Society, Culture, and Personality, New York, 1947.
Sraffa, P., *Production of Commodities by Means of Commodities,* Cambridge, 1960.
Steiner, G., *Heidegger: the Influence and Dissemination of His Thought,* London, 1978.
Strachey, J., *Contemporary Capitalism,* London, 1956.
Strawson, P.F., *Individuals,* London, 1959.
Sweezy, P.M., *The Theory of Capitalist Development,* New York, 1942.

Taylor, C., Review of '*Cahiers de Royaumont, Philosophie No. IV: La Philosphie Analytique*', in *Philosophical Review,* LXXIII (1964).
Taylor, F.W., *The Principles of Scientific Management,* New York, 1947.
Tawney, R.H., *The Acquisitive Society,* London, 1921.
Equality, London, 1931.
Teale, A.E., 'Moral Assurance', *Proceedings of the Aristotelian Society,* Supplementary Volume, XXXI (1957).
Therborn, G., *What Does the Ruling Class Do When it Rules?* London, 1978.
Thompson, E.P., *The Making of the English Working Class,* London, 1963.
The Poverty of Theory, London, 1978.

Titmuss, R.M., *Income Distribution and Social Change*, London, 1962.

Tönnies, F., *Community and Association (Gemeinschaft und Gesellschaft)*, London, 1955.

Touraine, A., *La conscience ouvrière*, Paris, 1966.

Trentin, B., *Tendenze del capitalismo italiano*, Rome, 1962.

Trotsky, L., *The Permanent Revolution*, London, 1962.

Tumin, M.M., *Caste in a Peasant Society*, Princeton, 1952.

Vacca, G., *Lukàcs o Korsch?*, Bari, 1969.

Veblen, T., *The Theory of the Leisure Class*, New York, 1917.

Vranicki, P., *Mensch und Geschichte*, Frankfurt/M., 1969.

Warner, W.L., *(et al.)*, *Social Class in America*, Chicago, 1949.
and Low, J.O., *The Social System of the Modern Factory*, New Haven, 1947.

Warnock, H.M., *Ethics Since 1900*, Oxford, 1960.

Waxman, C.L., (ed.), *The End of Ideology Debate*, New York, 1968.

Weber, M., *The Protestant Ethic and the Spirit of Capitalism*, London, 1930.
The Methodology of the Social Sciences, Glencoe, 1947.
From Max Weber: Essays in Sociology (ed. H.H. Gerth and C. Wright Mills), London, 1947.
The Theory of Social and Economic Organization, New York, 1947.

Willner, A., *Images de la société et classes sociales*, Berne, 1947.

Williams B., and Montefiore, A., (eds.), *British Analytical Philosophy*, London, 1966.

Williams, R. *Culture and Society*, London, 1958.
Marxism and Literature, London, 1977.
Problems in Materialism and Culture, London, 1980.

Wittfogel, K.A., *Oriental Despotism*, New Haven, 1957.

Wittgenstein, L., *Tractatus Logico-Philosophicus*, London, 1922.
Philosophical Investigations, Oxford, 1953.

Wood, N., *The Politics of Locke's Philosophy*, Los Angeles, 1983.

Young, M. and Willmott, P., *Family and Class in a London Suburb*, London, 1960.

Zweig, F., *The Worker in an Affluent Society*, London, 1961.

Index